WOMEN AND GENDER IN ITALY (1500-1900) /
DONNE E *GENDER* IN ITALIA (1500-1900)
General Editor Helena Sanson
4

# Matilde Serao

This volume was published with the financial assistance
of the Alberto Italian Studies Institute, Seton Hall University,
and the Foundation for Italian Studies University College Dublin.

ALBERTO
Italian Studies Institute

UCD
DUBLIN

UCD Foundation
for Italian Studies

# Matilde Serao

## International Profile, Reception and Networks

Edited by Gabriella Romani, Ursula Fanning and Katharine Mitchell

PARIS
CLASSIQUES GARNIER
2022

Gabriella Romani is Professor of Italian and Director of the Alberto Italian Studies Institute at Seton Hall University. Her research focuses on gender and national identities in nineteenth-century Italy. Among her recent publications are *Postal Culture in Post-Unification Italy* (Toronto, 2013) and *The Formation of a National Audience: Readers and Spectators in Italy (1750-1890)* (Madison NJ, 2017).

Ursula Fanning is Professor in Italian Studies at the School of Languages, Cultures and Linguistics in University College Dublin. Among her publications are *Gender Meets Genre: Woman as Subject in the Fictional Universe of Matilde Serao* (Dublin, 2002) and *Italian Women's Autobiographical Writings in the Twentieth Century: Constructing Subjects* (Madison NJ, 2017).

Katharine Mitchell is Senior Lecturer in Italian Culture and Gender at the University of Strathclyde, Glasgow. Among her recent books are *Italian Women Writers: Gender and Everyday Life in Fiction Journalism, 1870-1910* (Toronto, 2014) and *Gender, Writing, Spectatorships: Evenings at the Theatre, Opera and Silent Screen in Late Nineteenth Century Italy and Beyond* (London, 2022).



ISBN 978-2-406-12851-9 (livre broché)
ISBN 978-2-406-12852-6 (livre relié)
ISSN 2551-3559

# INTRODUCTION

The idea for the present volume was conceived during a conference entitled "Cultural Encounters through Reading and Writing: New Approaches to the History of Literary Culture", held at the Glasgow Women's Library in June of 2016, which was part of the HERA project *Travelling Texts, 1790-1914: Transnational Reception of Women's Writing at the Fringes of Europe* led by Henriette Partzsch (University of Glasgow). One of the aims of the conference was to provide an initial mapping of nineteenth-century European women writers, and of the intersections and overlapping of their writings. Scholars presented their research, conducted in a variety of European countries, including Bulgaria, Finland, Italy, the Netherlands, Poland, Sweden, Spain and Turkey. We organized a panel on Matilde Serao (1856-1927) titled "Matilde Serao and her many audiences", which, without our knowing it at the time, was already directing us towards the production of this volume. During our conversations with scholars attending the conference, we came to realize that many of them were already familiar with the works of Serao, which had been translated for, and published in nineteenth- and early twentieth-century periodicals, literary anthologies, and volumes all over Europe. Such preliminary findings prompted us to conceive a volume meant to explore the idea that Serao enjoyed an international readership that went beyond France and England – the two countries which, traditionally, scholars have identified as the place where the Neapolitan writer could claim international literary fame.[1] Given the European focus of the initial conference, however, we decided to restrict our international enquiry to the countries represented at the Glasgow meeting, and invited scholars, who are specialists in different national literary traditions, to write an essay on the reception of Matilde Serao's

1 On Serao in France, see Pupino, 1978, then expanded in Pupino, 2004, and Mitchell, 2022, pp. 144-155.

work in their country of scholarly investigation.[2] This has resulted in the present collection of essays, which reveal new and unexpected details about the relationship between Serao and her European and American readership, as well as about the interconnections between late nineteenth-century Italian literature and the various literary traditions of Europe and beyond. Serao, along with Gabriele D'Annunzio, Edmondo De Amicis, Grazia Deledda, Antonio Fogazzaro, and Giovanni Verga were among the most popular Italian authors in Europe; it was through their writings that European readers fashioned their understanding and imaginative conceptions of modern Italy, and its national and regional identities.

Situating Serao within a predominantly European context suggests that the literary life of Italy (in all its ramifications through both major and minor writers) may, and indeed should, be viewed also within a web of European networks, which, as Alberto Asor Rosa suggested in his *Storia europea della letteratura* (2009), began more than eight centuries ago and has continued until the present time (Asor Rosa, 2009, p. x). From Romanticism to Positivism, Futurism and Symbolism, nineteenth-century Europe was a dynamic field of cultural exchanges and fruitful influences, and yet we still know very little about the influence that Italian authors may have had abroad when their work was presented in translation to international readers. Looking at Serao's European readership sheds light on the process of circulation, but also that of translation and the transnational consumption of her literary production: which of her works gained the most attention abroad? How was she viewed outside of Italy? Did her gender, national and regional identities influence the ways in which her work was perceived by foreign readers? Not surprisingly, the essays contained in this volume indicate a wide spectrum of interpretations of Serao's artistic voice, perceived as stemming from her Catholic, female, Italian and Neapolitan identities. In this sense, Serao presents a most interesting case study of how late nineteenth-century European readers perceived and consumed Italian

2 Each chapter includes at the end a bibliography of Serao's fictional works translated into the respective language and relevant to the period of time under discussion. These bibliographies do not, therefore, intend to be exhaustive. We decided to focus exclusively on Serao's fictional production, and not her journalistic writings or essays, because her international reputation was mainly based on her fiction translated into various European languages.

literature and the complexity of a transnational circulation of literary works, viewed in their own right, but also, inevitably, through the lens of the reader's cultural assumptions and, sometimes, the essentialized interpretation of the Italian character and national identities.

The present volume's main assertion is that Serao's fiction and, to a lesser extent, her journalistic writings, had a transnational appeal throughout Europe. These essays focus mainly on the timespan of the author's life, especially towards the latter part of the nineteenth century and beginning of the twentieth century, and the circulation in translation of her novels and short stories, reflecting both her so-called *verista* production, and her later production of fiction based thematically on women's travels, romantic escapades, and erotic desires. While in Italian literary manuals and anthologies Serao is often remembered as a regional author, and her *Il ventre di Napoli* (1884) remains still today her most praised piece of writing, her international reputation was not exclusively based on her 'naturalistic' writings and took into account both her early and later production of fictional works. Serao's *fin-de-siècle* international readership – made up of critics, translators, and of a general public of readers – tended to view her through a religious (Catholic), gender-based (as a woman writer), and national (Italian) understanding of her work, sometimes blurring her Neapolitan identity of origin into a more general Italian national identity.

Since Benedetto Croce's definition of Serao as "all realistic observation and sentiment", whereby sentiment means "intention: that great opponent of art",[3] critics in Italy have privileged Serao's production as a *verista* writer – a definition she defied throughout her life, but which has resulted in a traditional interpretation of her work as divided between a presumably better, early naturalistic production of fiction, thematically connected to Naples, and a second, more commercial and less artistically accomplished body of work (Croce, 1929, pp. 34, 71). As Pietro Pancrazi bluntly put it in 1944: "Serao's most felicitous period was from 1880 to 1905 [...]. From 1905 to 1927 – the year in which she died – instead, an inferior Serao came abundantly into the foreground: she was a fashionable writer" (Pancrazi, 1944, pp. VII-VIII).[4] Still today, critics abide by this view,

3 "tutta osservazione realistica e sentimento", "l'intenzionalità, la grande avversaria dell'arte".

4 "Il periodo felice della Serao va dal 1880 al 1905 [...]. Dal 1905 al 1927, che fu l'anno della sua morte, venne invece e abbondantemente in primo piano, quella Serao inferiore: ella fu scrittrice alla moda".

and Serao continues to be presented as an author worth reading mainly for her naturalistic Neapolitan production. Giulio Ferroni's *Storia e testi della letteratura italiana* (2002), for instance, positions Serao in a chapter entitled "La letteratura napoletana", while in Asor Rosa's aforementioned *Storia europea della letteratura italiana*, she appears in the chapter devoted to "Verismo: Le varietà regionali", where she is described as an expression of the "entangled Neapolitan social life" (Asor Rosa, 2009, p. 78). This narrow, regional focus on studying and reading Serao's work has, however, also been challenged by scholars who have interpreted her overall production more holistically. Already in 1995 in his *Introduzione a Serao*, Tommaso Scappaticci noted that Serao's narrative interest in both popular and aristocratic environments is clear from the very beginning of her literary career (Scappaticci, 1995, pp. 16-17), while Laura Salsini proposed a reading of Serao's work outside of "traditional dichotomies: language/dialect; invention-mimesis; participation-detachment, literature-popular fiction" (Salsini, 1999, p. 148). More recently, Romani has identified Serao's overall pessimism towards progress and modernity as the *fil rouge* of both her *verista* and sentimental fiction (Romani, 2013, p. 114), while Fanning's study of Serao's Gothic mode and Mitchell's investigation of Serao's overall implicit, moderate feminist message (in spite of the author's public position against feminism) have pointed to the need to move beyond traditional critical approaches to reading Serao (Fanning, 2007, pp. 119-138; Mitchell, 2014, p. 13).

With this volume of essays, we hope to further expand the critical discussion on Serao's overall literary production. The point of view of the international readership is valuable for it sheds light on the way in which international readers perceived Serao's overall œuvre, her narrative experimentations, thematic choices and writing style. The following essays seem to suggest that Serao's popularity abroad was not so different from the one she enjoyed in Italy, if not quantitatively at least in terms of readers' appreciation of her work. But readers abroad knew her more for her fiction than her journalistic writings and considered her, when compared to French naturalism, less cruel or pessimistic, and more compassionate. Serao was also seen as part of a cohort of Italian women writers, which included Neera, La Marchesa Colombi, Ada Negri, and Grazia Deledda (winner of the 1926 Nobel prize), whom she led as the most prominent and best known abroad.

Among Serao's works that were most commonly translated into European languages during the author's lifetime, we find *Fantasia* (1883a), *Fior di passione* (1888), *All'erta sentinella* (1889), *O Giovannino o la morte* (1889), *Il paese di Cuccagna* (1891) *Castigo* (1893), *La ballerina* (1899), *Dopo il perdono* (1906a), and *Evviva la vita!* (1909). Many of these fictional works were translated soon after their initial publication in Italy, although not all translations came directly from Italian. It was not uncommon, in fact, that French, German or Swedish translations mediated the translation of Serao's works into other languages, such as Russian, Finnish, or Bulgarian. Such transnational translations created a circulation of literary discourses and practices that reflected, on the one hand, the specific needs of the local literary system, and, on the other, the reality of an existing European network of literary exchanges whereby translators from different literary traditions, read, translated, and promoted the literary work of a foreign author as part of a shared and sharable space of cultural production and consumption. Such processes were not devoid of risks, however, as Serao's novels and short stories were adapted, and sometimes altered (if not censored) by the translators, especially when they viewed Serao's style as 'too passionate' or her tone unsuitable for northern readers' tastes. As scholars in translation studies have pointed out, "annexationist translations and hypertextual translations (pastiche, imitation, adaptation, free rewriting)" provide the space "where the play of deforming forces is freely exercised" (Berman, 2000, p. 242). Inevitably so, when texts travelled from distant lands, passing through the pens of different translators (from Italian to Russian and Swedish, for instance), and the author's copyright was not strictly enforced. Whether translated in its entirety or partially rendered, Serao's prose circulated widely across Europe, making Italian literature available to the burgeoning readership of the late nineteenth century, especially among women who used the book and periodical as an essential instrument of their domestic cultural education and entertainment.

Serao was aware of her international audience, as she jubilantly observed in an article titled "Alla celebrità internazionale", published in her "Api, Vespe, Mosconi" column in 1900:

> As a subscriber to that excellent institution that is the *Courrier de la Press*, I am sent cuttings from all the newspapers of the world in which my books and I are written about, and I see that my small column has been reported

> by eighteen foreign newspapers: in Germany, Belgium, Holland, the United States. Oh, Heaven! Oh, Heaven which makes all things possible, including that my small column has reached international acclaim! (cited in Sarcina, 1995, p. 300).[5]

While Serao was known internationally for her journalistic writings and activities, it was her fiction, widely translated into French, English, German, Dutch, Spanish, Finnish, Swedish, Russian, and Bulgarian, that determined her international fame – a popularity enhanced by the wide publicity given to her books by foreign periodicals. In September 1925, the British *Daily Mail* reported the publication of *The Severed Hand* [*La mano tagliata*, 1912], tapping into her reputation as an author in great vogue:

> English readers, who like to read the works of great contemporary writers of other countries, will be interested in the forthcoming novel by that famous Italian woman, Matilde Serao. Ten of her books have already been translated into English, and have a big vogue in this country, the title of the new book is "The Severed Hand" ("Severed Hand", 1925).

The present volume is structured in alphabetical order of author in a gesture that steers the reader away from assumptions or suggestions as to Serao's apparent predominance in a given country. In the opening chapter, Ulla Åkerström revisits the widely held view that Serao "lost" the Nobel Prize for Literature in 1926 to Grazia Deledda based on Serao's anti-war stance expressed in her novel *Mors tua* (1926) to refute any suggestion that Mussolini had an influence on the Nobel Prize Committee's decision as implausible. Arguing that there is a general unawareness regarding the historical mechanisms of the Nobel Prize, Åkerström sets out the regulations of the Swedish Academy in order to examine in detail the proposals that saw Serao being nominated (by two individuals) as a Nobel Prize candidate for the first time in 1922, after which she was proposed four times and in subsequent consecutive years. Comparing her to Grazia Deledda who was first nominated in

5 "Dal *Courrier de la Presse*, eccellente istituzione francese, che mi manda, come abbonata, tagli di tutti i giornali del mondo, ove si parla dei miei libri e di me, veggo che questo articoletto è stato riportato da diciotto giornali stranieri, di Germania, del Belgio, dell'Olanda, degli Stati Uniti. O Numi! O Numi che tutto permettete, anche questo doveva accadere che la piccola posta passasse alla celebrità internazionale".

1913, and again in successive years, until she received the prize in 1926, Åkerström examines the four Seraian proposals from 1922, 1923, 1924 and 1925 to argue that Serao really did not have a chance of obtaining the Nobel Prize, because she was never considered seriously as a potential laureate. Serao was in any case disadvantaged due to Deledda having been proposed for the prize nine years previously. Finally, Åkerström suggests that Serao was regarded by the Swedish Academy as "too Neapolitan".

Nadezhda Alexandrova and Boyka Ilieva provide an overview of Serao's transnational influence and reception in Bulgaria between the 1890s and the 1920s. They discuss the seventeen literary works by Serao that appeared in Bulgarian, five of which were translated more than once, making a total of twenty-six translations in sixteen different periodicals, and four of which were in women's periodicals. Identifying the names and/or initials of sixteen translators – fourteen men and three women (there are four anonymous translations) – Alexandrova and Ilieva discuss the various periodicals in which Serao's fiction tended to be published, arguing that whether a given story was selected for publication and consumption in Bulgaria was done on the basis of their function as moral *exempla* that reveal the psychological motives behind certain types of behaviour. The authors then explore the influence of Serao on Bulgarian female authors whose writings reveal similar plots and characters, as well as on her male translators, before turning to Serao's critical reception, which, in concert with the findings of other essays in this volume (Fanning; Parente-Čapková; Åkerström; Romani) is shown to be essentializing in its focus on Serao as a woman writer and as a Southern Italian.

The third chapter by Maria Belova focuses on the circulation and critical reception of Serao's works in Russia from 1885 onwards and on the various translations of *All'erta, sentinella!* which circulated between 1890 and 1911 in publications aimed at different readerships, but also offers a detailed overview of other works in translation by Serao. Belova, like other scholars here in their different contexts (Fanning; Alexandrova and Ilieva), suggests that there was a strongly gendered response to the reception of Serao's work in Russia, and she illustrates this through a comparison of the critical views expressed by Vladimir Frice and the critical focus of the (female) journalist E.V. Fuks, who interviewed Serao in 1900 in Paris, illustrating the complex transnational links referenced earlier in the Introduction.

Ursula Fanning examines the allocation and transmission of Serao's literary status by critics in Italy, Britain, Ireland and North America at the *fin-de siècle*. Drawing explicitly on Said's seminal work on 'othering' in his *Orientalism* ([1978] 1991), Fanning focuses her discussion on contemporary important voices in English-language criticism, namely: Paul Sylvester (a pseudonym of the English writer of German origin, Pauline Schletter), in the British and Irish contexts, and Henry James in America. Beginning with the Italian context, Fanning discusses Benedetto Croce's aforementioned 1903 essay on Italian literature in the second half of the nineteenth century published in *La Critica*, to show how his reading of Serao reveals a two-pronged othering based on her gender and her Southernness; these are aspects which reoccur in her reading of Henry James's critique of Serao, as well as in Paul Sylvester's (with the exception that *her* 'othering' is exclusively in relation to Serao's 'Southernness'). Fanning finds the to-ing and fro-ings between these stereotypes in transnational critical readings of Serao's work fascinating in what they reveal about cultural transmission and reception in particular contexts at the turn of the twentieth century.

Rossana Melis and Maria-Luisa Wandruszka turn their attention to Germany and Austria, specifically to Vienna, and to the young Leo Spitzer's analysis of Serao and her work as elaborated in his inaugural address of 1912 to the University of Vienna, in which his primary focus was on *Evviva la Guerra!*, published in that same year. Their analysis allows us to note again the transnational elements of Serao's reception, in Spitzer's reading of Serao against the French naturalists, in his awareness of the nature of Serao's reception in France and in his engagement with Croce's criticism on Serao dating from 1903. Notable, too, in this essay, is the authors' recognition of the way in which Spitzer was primarily struck by what he saw as the 'Neapolitanness' of Serao, as well as the political significance of Spitzer's essay at that time in the Viennese context.

Viola Parente-Čapková explores Serao's rich reception in Finland from the 1890s to the 1910s through a reading of translations cited in articles and advertisements in the periodical press of the late nineteenth century and listed in Finland's major libraries. Parente-Čapková presents a survey of Serao's multilingual presence in the *Fennica* national database and Finnish libraries, including the National Library of Finland, the

Turku City Library, and the libraries of Åbo Akademi and the University of Turku. She then discusses Serao's translations published in Finland and their Finnish translators. Similarly to Fanning's observations on male critics' 'othering' and stereotyping, Parente-Čapková demonstrates how some Finnish critics also drew attention to Serao's essentializing features – her Italianness, Neapolitanness, and gender.

Gabriella Romani focuses on Serao's *Nel paese di Gesù* (1898), which was translated into various foreign languages, including English. Romani argues that this book marks a crucial moment in the career of Matilde Serao who was seeking renewal in her artistic inspirations and affirmation, not only domestically, but abroad as well. Although critics have traditionally neglected this work, considered excessively verbose and moralistic, Romani demonstrates that Serao's travelogue provides useful insights into the author's break from her early-career writing style and into her interconnection with an international network of authors, translators, and readers.

Amelia Sanz and Laura Iasci present an overview of Serao's fortune and reception in the Spanish press between 1884 and 1939. Their research benefits from an ongoing digitisation project over the past ten years, and they choose to focus on the language used by reviewers and journalists in the presentation of Serao's work to the Spanish public, searching for word clusters which appear in sequence and identifying peaks and troughs in frequency of mention. Their word cloud gives a clear graphic, also in terms of relative importance, of terms linked to Serao, which are mostly centred on her origins and draw attention primarily to her fiction. Their collocation graph further refines this search, highlighting the absence of references to her journalism and a notable stress on her role as a woman writer.

The final chapter by Igor Tchehoff on Serao in Sweden considers how Serao's work was received in the Swedish press between 1885 and the early years of the twentieth century. He shows that the Swedish reception of Serao was more rounded and comprehensive than was the case in many of the other countries considered in this volume, since she received attention there for both her journalism and her fiction. The fact that she was a woman writer was also regularly referenced in the various presentations of Serao to the Swedish public, and discussions around gender were significant in her reception. Fascinatingly, Serao was perceived as the most representative author of contemporary Italy during that period in Sweden – a voice of the new Italy, as Tchehoff puts it. Notwithstanding this, her Neapolitanness is regularly noted (often with a mixture of dismay and admiration) by contemporary Swedish reviewers and critics.

Widely translated across Europe, Serao reached a notoriety during her lifetime that reflected her ambition to become an Italian writer who was also known internationally, to the chagrin of those critics who have pigeonholed her as an author with mere regional resonance and limited artistic impact. The simple fact that international critics (sometimes the same people as the translators), publishers, and readers considered Serao one of the main literary voices of modern Italy only confirms the important role she played in the circulation of Italian literature outside of Italy at the end of the nineteenth century and at the beginning of the twentieth, and in reaching – as a forerunner perhaps, of another woman writer today, Elena Ferrante – a level of international popularity that few of her fellow Italian writers could boast abroad.

Though there is undoubtedly more work to be done on unravelling the web of exchanges and influences of Serao's works on her European and international readerships, it is the editors' hope that this volume will inaugurate further research of this kind in the future. The present study represents a first step in the quest to map Serao's global readerships, and hopefully future contributions to Serao studies will facilitate new directions for, and new discoveries of this remarkable Italian writer.

Gabriella ROMANI
Seton Hall University

Ursula FANNING
University College Dublin

Katharine MITCHELL
University of Strathclyde

# MATILDE SERAO AND HER 'LOST' NOBEL PRIZE

A rumour can shift from an assumption or a hypothesis to become an accepted fact. In some ways, this describes what happened with the story of Matilde Serao's 'lost' Nobel Prize. It is a widespread belief that the novel *Mors tua*, published in 1926 – just one year before the Neapolitan writer's death in 1927 – prevented her from being awarded the famous Swedish Prize because of the book's anti-war and anti-fascist stance. It has been suggested that her candidacy was blocked by Mussolini. This belief, often presented as fact, was reported in several reviews of the novel when it was republished in 2016 by Garamond. An example is the article by Roberto Coaloa, which appeared in the newspaper *Libero* on 12 August 2016 with the intriguing headline: "The Nobel Lost due to Two Enquiries".[1] In his article, Coaloa claims that Serao was close to being awarded the Nobel Prize for literature in 1926, but that she lost it because she was "blocked by the bourgeois world of *salons*, war industries and the Italian government, who all conspired to urge the Stockholm Academy to desist from supporting her victory" (Coaloa, 2016).[2] Coaloa also suggests that the novel *Vita e avventure di Riccardo Joanna*, published in 1887, "definitively ruined any possibility" of Serao winning the Nobel Prize (*ibid.*).[3]

1 "Il Nobel perso per due inchieste".

2 "bloccata dal mondo borghese dei salotti, dalle industrie belliche e dal governo italiano. Tutti concordi nello spingere l'Accademia di Stoccolma nel desistere dal sostenerne la vittoria".

3 "tagliò le gambe, definitivamente". Other reviewers of the new edition of *Mors tua* make the same remarks, for example, Razzano (2016, p. 19), who wrote that "It was the political descent, the fresco of the storms of History that devastates the bourgeois stillness" and that "Donna Matilde should have been awarded the Nobel, but instead it went to Grazia Deledda" ("Fu l'affondo politico, l'affresco delle bufere della Storia che devasta la quiete borghese e avrebbe dovuto consegnare a Donna Matilde il Nobel, e invece andò a Grazia Deledda") and Oliva (2016, p. 25) who wrote: "After a long career characterized

The story of Serao's 'lost' Nobel Prize is, in fact, an old story, which has been repeated in books and encyclopedias over many years. Carlo Buzzi, for instance, wrote in 1981: "Perhaps her non-alignment with the regime together with her opposition to the Duce cost Serao the Nobel Prize in 1926, which was awarded instead to Deledda. Matilde is very upset about this" (Buzzi, 1981, p. 63).[4] Buzzi was followed by several critics (Fanning, 1994; Scappaticci, 1995; Wood, 1995; Amoia, 1996; Romani, 2007), some of them more cautious regarding the question, some less. It is difficult to establish who first voiced this speculation, but certainly Anna Banti, in her biography of Serao published in 1965, played a major role in its dissemination. Banti claims that Serao had to pay for her "bad novel" *Mors tua* and suffer to see the "mediocre" Deledda be awarded the Prize (Banti, 1965, p. 284).[5] In her book, Banti attempts to understand the Academy's decision, by guessing that the Swedish "experts" were, for linguistic reasons, not entirely capable of perceiving the supremacy of Serao's work over that of Deledda. And then she presents the following view, with no reference to a single source:

> But it seems that the fascist government and, indeed, Mussolini himself, opposed Serao's nomination: and the pretext was precisely that unfortunate *Mors tua*, a polemic against the war in 1914-1918 and against every war; hence, anti-militaristic and anti-fascist. It is understood that the novel also paid for the anti-fascist sins of *Il Giorno* newspaper (Banti, 1965, p. 284).[6]

Such examples reveal a possible lack of awareness regarding the mechanisms of the Nobel Prize and how literary Nobel laureates were and are chosen. Therefore, before we proceed with the main aim of this chapter, which is to examine the Swedish Academy's thinking behind

---

by many battles, Donna Matilde died in the hope of obtaining the Nobel Prize, which, were it not for her last novel, *Mors tua*, would have been hers" ("Dopo una lunga carriera caratterizzata da tante battaglie, Donna Matilde si spegneva nel desiderio di ottenere il Premio Nobel, che le sarebbe spettato se non fosse stato per l'ultimo romanzo, *Mors tua* [...]").

4 "Forse il non allineamento con il regime, e l'opposizione del Duce, costano nel 1926 alla Serao il Premio Nobel, assegnato alla Deledda. Matilde ne soffre molto".

5 "cattivo romanzo".

6 "Ma pare che il governo fascista e anzi Mussolini stesso opponessero un non gradimento al nome della Serao: e il pretesto fu proprio quel disgraziato *Mors tua*, polemico contro la guerra '14-18 e contro ogni guerra, quindi antimilitarista e antifascista. S'intende che il romanzo scontava anche i peccati antifascisti del *Giorno*".

Serao and the other Italian candidates during the 1920s, let us first consider the criteria for the award of the Nobel Prize for Literature.[7]

## SCOPE THE REGULATIONS OF THE SWEDISH ACADEMY

The Swedish Academy was founded in 1786 by King Gustaf III as a Swedish equivalent to the French Academy. According to Alfred Nobel's will, dated 27 November 1895, the Academy was appointed as responsible for the literary Nobel Prize from the inception of the prize in 1901. In the original regulations, which were established on 29 June 1900, among other things it was stated that the concept of 'literature' meant not only fiction, but also other forms of texts with literary value. It was also mentioned that the awarding institution must appoint a Nobel Committee consisting of three to five members. To be awarded the Prize, a writer must have been proposed by a person entitled to make the proposal, which then must be submitted by January each year. It was, and it is not possible to put oneself forward, and one cannot apply for the Prize. The regulations also outline who has the right to nominate candidates for the Prize. These include: members of the Swedish Academy; members of similar institutions, such as the French and Spanish Academies, as well as members of similar humanities institutions and societies; and teachers in aesthetics, literature, and history at universities (Svensén, 2001a, p. XI).

The regulations were partially altered in 1949. They are available on the Academy's website, where it states who may nominate candidates today:

> the members of the Academy, members of academies and societies similar to it in membership and aims, professors of literature and language, former

7 Although the Swedish Academy in recent years has gone through a considerable crisis, it must be noted that this crisis did not centre on the awarding of the Nobel Prize. However, the Prize was not awarded in 2018 as a result of controversy, but in 2019 two laureates were awarded the Prize: Olga Tokarczuk for 2018, and Peter Handke for 2019.

> Nobel laureates in literature, and the presidents of writers' organisations which are representative of their country's literary production.[8]

The process has essentially remained the same ever since. Proposals, preferably "accompanied by supporting reasons" as stated on the website, must be sent to the Nobel Committee by January each year. The Nobel Committee – supported by experts – examines the nominations and compiles a list of possible candidates with approximately twenty names, which before the summer is reduced to a shortlist of around five. In October, based on the Committee's preparatory work, the Academy decides the name of the new Laureate. The Academy styles itself as an independent institution with no ties to the Swedish or any foreign government. The suggestion that Mussolini could have had any responsibility in influencing the decision of the Nobel Prize is therefore simply not plausible. The Swedish Academy would never have accepted such a claim, since it has always taken great pride in its independence. Kjell Espmark, a member of the Academy and for many years president of the Nobel Committee, states in one of his studies of the Nobel Prize that the often-heated discussions about its integrity could be explained by the fact that it has not been generally understood that the Academy holds an autonomous position regarding states and governments. He also notes that it is unthinkable that the Academy should act on diplomatic levels to seek the support of any government (Espmark, 2001, pp. 173-174). The story about what really happened to Serao's candidacy, who proposed her and how the Nobel Committee evaluated her literary works, is quite different, something which will be discussed in more detail below.

## THE PROPOSALS OF 1922

In 1922, the same year Serao was proposed for the Nobel Prize for the first time, a new president of the Nobel Committee was elected, the writer Per Hallström. He would remain in office for twenty-four years,

8 http://www.svenskaakademien.se/en/the-nobel-prize-in-literature (last accessed 28 November 2020).

making a considerable contribution to the Academy, for better or for worse. Enrico Tiozzo highlights in his detailed study of Italian literature and the Nobel Prize that it is surprising how Hallström could act as president and at the same time as his own special "expert" on writers from all over the world, despite his background as an engineer and chemist (Tiozzo, 2009, pp. 323-324). The other members of the Committee were Erik Axel Karlfeldt, Henrik Schück and Anders Österling, all of them well-known authors. While Grazia Deledda had been a candidate for the Nobel prize as early as in 1913, and in several subsequent years, Serao had to wait until 1922 for her first candidacy. She was then proposed in four consecutive years: 1922, 1923, 1924 and 1925. As shown in the list (Fig. 1), from Deledda's first candidacy in 1913 until 1927 when she received the Nobel Prize of 1926, the Sardinian writer was favourite among the Italian candidates.[9] Deledda was proposed for twelve years, while Serao and the playwright Roberto Bracco were only proposed for four years each, and the historian Guglielmo Ferrero for five years (the last time in 1933). We can assume, therefore, that Deledda's position in the Academy was much stronger than those of her Italian competitors and had been long before Mussolini came to power.[10]

In 1922 Serao was put forward in two separate proposals to the Academy. One was handed in by Francesco Torraca, Professor in Comparative Literature at the University Federico II in Naples.[11] Two other prominent representatives of Italian cultural life also signed the

9 Regarding a more detailed description of Deledda's achievement of the Nobel Prize, see Schwartz, 2020.

10 The names of all nominated writers between 1901 and 1950 are listed in Svensén, 2001a and 2001b, as well as in the Nomination Database on the Official Web Site of the Nobel Prize, http://www.nobelprize.org/nomination/archive/ (last accessed 28 November 2020).

11 The proposal is held in the Archive of the Swedish Academy in Stockholm. It is transcribed and published in Tiozzo, 2009, pp. 154-156. The Archive of the Swedish Academy and the Nobel Archive are private. A fifty-year confidentiality policy applies to documents in the Nobel Archive, which contains the statements that the Nobel Committee submits to the Academy in the previous year, including, letters of proposal, candidate lists and expert opinions. There exists no public catalogue with precise collocations of the material that the archive holds. Researchers who wish to make use of documents within it must make a written request to obtain permissions, specifying which documents are of interest. Permission to consult the material is granted after an individual assessment. The archive has initiated a digitalization project and is in the process of publishing documents from the archive online. See https://www.svenskaakademien.se/svenska-akademien/akademiens-arkiv (last accessed 1 December 2020).

nomination, though they were not entitled to propose: the famous philosopher Benedetto Croce, former Minister of Public Education (1920-1921) and Leonardo Bianchi, Senator and also former Minister of Public Education (1905). Torraca would repeat his nomination in 1923 and 1924. The Torraca-Croce-Bianchi nomination was written in December 1921 and submitted to the Swedish envoy in Rome, Carl Bildt, a member of the Swedish Academy from 1901; on 23 December 1921, Bildt forwarded the nomination to his fellow Academy members in Stockholm. In the nomination letter, written by hand, Serao's long career as a writer was described alongside her literary development over the years, from her early writings that showed "the temperament of a youthful, energetic and prolific artist"[12] to her later descriptions of Neapolitan people, "an abundant and diverse representation of people, events and incidents, extremely effective in the truthfulness of its brush-strokes and colours" (*ibid.*).[13] To reinforce the proposal, the nominators cited Paul Bourget's judgement of Serao's abilities as a writer, taken from his *preface* to the French translation (1898) of *Il paese di Cuccagna* (1891) (Tiozzo, 2009, p. 155).

The other proposal in favour of Serao in 1922 was sent by Roberto De Ruggiero, General Secretary of the *Accademia Pontaniana*, and it was also signed by other prominent figures (who were, however, not entitled to do so): the Senator Pasquale Grippo, and the Archaeologist Vittorio Spinazzola.[14] This proposal, written in Italian, was based on the notion that Serao was not only a "great writer", "an illustrious woman", a "powerful talent", with a "vast and powerful body of work", but also because "the best of her output corresponds perfectly to the will and testament of Alfred Bernard Nobel".[15] Her books, which are listed in the text,

---

12 "un temperamento di artista giovanilmente vigoroso, ardito e fecondo", Archive of the Swedish Academy. All material about Serao from the Archive of the Swedish Academy, unless specified, remains unpublished and uncatalogued.

13 "rappresentazione abbondante e varia, di persone, di casi, d'incidenti, efficacissima per verità di tocchi e di tinte".

14 Roberto De Ruggiero's proposal from 1922 is unpublished and can be found in the Archive of the Swedish Academy. Literal formulations from this proposal are repeated in subsequent published proposals (Tiozzo, 2009, pp. 162-163).

15 "grande scrittrice", "illustre donna", "possente talento", "vasta e possente opera di arte", "ciò che ella ha prodotto di meglio corrisponde perfettamente alla volontà testamentaria di Alfredo Bernardo Nobel", Archive of the Swedish Academy.

> are tales of the private and social lives of the Neapolitan people. In these works, we see a deep and tender understanding of the soul of the common people of Naples: there is a sense and a representation of the virtues, the sorrows and sufferings of these good people: we have the city of Naples, itself described in its everlasting beauty: we see the filial and brotherly love of the writer for Naples and the Neapolitans. No one has understood Neapolitan life better, nor created and brought it more fully to life for hundreds of thousands of readers.[16]

One of the Swedish Academy's special experts from the Nobel Institution, Karl August Hagberg, compiled a written report on Serao's literary production later in 1922.[17] It was the first review that the Committee commissioned on Serao, and therefore was longer and more detailed than subsequent ones about her. In his report, Hagberg cites the proposals of Torraca and De Ruggiero and then goes through the author's life and works. He talks about her "hectic working life"[18] and quotes Ugo Ojetti's interview with Serao published in *Alla scoperta dei letterati* (Ojetti, 1899); he bases his description of Serao's novel *Il paese di Cuccagna* on Bourget's previously mentioned introduction. Inevitably, Hagberg also compares Serao's style to that of Grazia Deledda, to the Neapolitan writer's disadvantage: "Serao doesn't possess, as she herself admits, this sober, artistic style, which, for example, her sister Deledda has managed to obtain; rather, she has a southern verbosity which in a way intoxicates itself with its own eloquence".[19] What most strikes Hagberg is Serao's ability to depict Naples:

> However, first and foremost Matilde Serao is the describer of her hometown Naples, for better and for worse. One nominator, Benedetto Croce, has (in *La Critica* 1903) dedicated an essay to her authorship. There, he gives the following

16 "rappresentano la storia della vita intima, e della vita sociale del popolo napoletano. È in queste opere la comprensione profonda e tenera dell'anima popolare napoletana: è la intuizione e la rappresentazione delle virtù, delle tristezze, dei dolori di questo buon popolo: è la città istessa di Napoli descritta nella sua eterna bellezza: è l'amore filiale, è l'amore fraterno della scrittrice per Napoli e per la gente napoletana. Niuno meglio intese, creò, fece palpitare innanzi a centinaia di migliaia di lettori la vita napoletana", Archive of the Swedish Academy.

17 This evaluation is unpublished and can be found in the Archive of the Swedish Academy.

18 "jäktade arbetsfyllda liv", Archive of the Swedish Academy. All translations from Swedish are my own.

19 "Serao äger icke, såsom hon också själv erkänner, denna sobra, konstnärliga stil, till vilken exempelvis hennes medsyster Deledda kämpat sig fram, utan en sydländsk ordrikedom som liksom berusar sig av sig egen vältalighet", Archive of the Swedish Academy.

> summary review about Serao's storytelling: "characteristic surroundings, tenderness of feelings, passionate struggles". The characteristic description of the surroundings that C[roce] talks about appears of course, naturally, mostly in her Neapolitan descriptions, while "the passionate struggles" play a greater part in her later works. But the "tenerezza di sentimenti" or this "warmth of life", of which she herself speaks, flows through all of Matilde Serao's works and represents one of the most appealing features of her rich production.[20]

Hagberg's report was, on the whole, positive, but it appears quite clear that Serao was at a disadvantage in relation to Deledda, who had been proposed some years prior to Serao. Furthermore, Deledda had a great admirer in Henrik Schück, who offered her the kind of support that Serao lacked in the Academy. Comments on Schück's admiration for Deledda recur in the reports and, according to Tiozzo, there would have been no Nobel Prize for Deledda without his efforts (Tiozzo, 2013, p. 99).

In 1922 the Swedish Academy counted twenty-two names proposed for the Prize. Among these, three were Italian: Grazia Deledda, who appeared for the eighth time, and the two newcomers Roberto Bracco and Matilde Serao. In his summary report of the twenty-two nominated writers, the president of the Nobel Committee, Per Hallström, dismissed Serao's candidacy in a few words:

> Number 6. *Matilde Serao* is, as the expert's report claims, an exuberant and powerful descriptor of society, stylistically characterized by descriptive naturalism, admired more some decades ago than now. Partly this training, partly her strong journalistic disposition, with corresponding limitations in her gifts as a writer, seem to have prevented her from achieving a significant purely artistic effect. In this respect, the committee has considered letting her stand aside for her contemporaneously proposed fellow countrywoman, Grazia Deledda, along with the members'

---

20 The quotations from Benedetto Croce are in Italian. "Först och sist är emellertid Matilde Serao hemstaden Neapels skildrarinna så i gott som ont. En av dem, som med sitt namn understött hennes kandidatur till Nobelpriset, Benedetto Croce, har (i *La Critica* 1903) ägnat hennes författarskap en uppsats. Han lämnar där följande sammanfattande omdöme om Seraos berättarkonst: 'ambienti caratteristici, tenerezza di sentimenti, lotte passionali'. Den karaktäristiska miljöteckning C. här talar om framträder ju naturligt nog mest i hennes neapolitanska skildringar, under det att 'le lotte passionali' spelar en större roll i hennes senare verk. Men 'la tenerezza di sentimenti' eller denna 'livets värme', som hon själv talar om, strömmar genom alla Matilde Seraos verk och utgör ett av de mest tilltalande dragen i henne ymniga alstring", Archive of the Swedish Academy.

> particular attitude towards the latter, which will be treated in its place (Svensén, 2001b, p. 25).[21]

Grazia Deledda had already been discussed several times by the Nobel Committee, as is obvious from Hallström's words. It is also clear that the Committee did not agree on Deledda's suitability as a possible Nobel Prize laureate. While Henrik Schück was her greatest supporter, Per Hallström had quite a different opinion of her:

> Number 4. *Grazia Deledda* has, as she had some years ago, the support of Mr. Schück. In previous debates about her, different opinions have become well known; in a few words, they amount to the view that her considerable stylistic art does not correspond to a sufficient substance in the depiction of life and delineation of character, above all not by sufficient richness. There is a kind of monotony and narrowness in this narrative art, which really boils down to lyrical impressions, and these are somewhat tiresomely persistent and emphasized impressions. The proposal has received considerable support (and at length) from her native country, but it does not seem that they have had Deledda in mind as the most suitable representative in the world for modern Italian literary production (Svensén, 2001b, p. 29).[22]

Hallström dedicates double the space to Bracco compared with Serao. He states that Bracco is "not only in his own country, but also elsewhere, subject to a most vivid appreciation" (Svensén, 2001b, p. 27),[23] that the "renewal of the possibilities of expression of drama" (*ibid.*)[24] which his admirers have highlighted, seems to the Committee

21 "N:o 6. *Matilde Serao* är, såsom sakkunnigutlåtandet hävdar, en frodig och kraftig samhällsskildrare, i formen präglad av den för några decennier sedan högre än nu beundrade beskrivande naturalismen. Dels denna skolning, dels hennes starkt journalistiska läggning, med en motsvarande inskränkning i hennes diktargåvor, tyckas ha hindrat henne att nå en betydande rent konstnärlig verkan. I detta avseende ansåg kommittén henne stå tillbaka för den ävenledes föreslagna landsmaninnan, Grazia Deledda, frånsett ledamöternas särskilda hållning mot denna senare, varom på sin plats mera."

22 "No 4. *Grazia Deledda* har, liksom under flera år förut, herr Schücks stöd. Vid föregående debatter om henne, ha motsatta meningar redan blivit nog kända; de gå i korthet ut på, att hennes ansenliga stilistiska konst icke motsvaras av tillräcklig halt i livsskildring och karaktärsteckning, framför allt icke av tillräcklig rikedom. Det ligger något enformigt och trångt i denna epik, som egentligen går ut på lyriska intryck, och något tröttsamt vidhållna och betonade intryck. Förslaget har omsider fått beaktansvärd anslutning från hemlandet, men av sig själv och omedelbart tycks man där ej ha fått tanken på Deledda som den lämpligaste representanten inför världen för modern italiensk diktning".

23 "icke blott i sitt hemland utan även på andra håll föremål för en ytterst livlig uppskattning".

24 "Den förnyelse av dramats uttrycksmöjligheter".

to have been already accomplished much more strongly and accurately by Ibsen and his successors, also with regard to the content of ideas and their formulation. Hallström then compares Bracco to the Spanish playwright Jacinto Benavente, who seems to "possess practically all Bracco's merits in a more gracious and tasteful form, and with an immediacy and simplicity that surpasses Bracco's in his best moments, which also has its foundation in a more poetic and humanly richer nature" (*ibid.*).[25]

Further on, when Hallström in the Committee's report evaluates Benavente, the Spanish playwright is treated together with William Butler Yeats in a long discussion of their plays and poems. It does not seem strange, therefore that Benavente in fact was awarded the Nobel Prize in 1922. Apparently, the Swedish Academy had no intention of awarding it to an Italian writer that year.

## THE PROPOSALS OF 1923

The following year, a new proposal regarding Serao was submitted by two Neapolitan professors, Giuseppe De Lorenzo and Francesco Torraca, as well as by Benedetto Croce. It was dated 1 January 1923 and consisted of two typewritten pages, very similar to the first proposal.[26] In 1923 the Nobel Committee discussed a total of twenty proposed writers, of which five were Italian. Deledda, Bracco and Serao were accompanied by Ferrero, proposed for the first time, and by Dora Melegari. The Italian-French writer Melegari, who wrote in both French and Italian, had already been proposed once before, in 1914, by Louis Dechesne, a member of the French Academy. In 1923 she was proposed by Professor Luigi Luzzatti. In the summary report, Melegari is dismissed directly in the following way:

> The expert's report does not attach to this writer any particularly high literary rank; and you don't have to read much to agree. The Committee has

25 "tyckes denne äga så gott som alla Braccos förtjänster i graciösare och smakfullare form och därtill en omedelbarhet och enkelhet som övergår Braccos i hans bästa stunder, och som har sin grund i en poetiskt och mänskligt rikare natur".

26 The proposal from 1923 is transcribed and published in Tiozzo, 2009, pp. 162-163.

found – now as well as some years ago – that this proposal is not worthy of attention (Svensén, 2001b, p. 41).[27]

Ferrero was proposed by several different professors and members of Academies within and outside Italy: Gaetano Mosca, A. di Viti de Marco, Gaetano Salvemini, Niccolò Rodolico, E. P. Cheyney (Philadelphia), four professors in Geneva, Paul Bourget, G. Hanotaux, Anatole France, H. Pirenne (Gand), a number of members from the academy in Rio de Janeiro, and, furthermore, by one of the Swedish Academy members, Nathan Söderblom (Svensén, 2001b, p. 35). Ferrero's expert report was written by Henrik Schück, and Hallström dedicated more space to Ferrero than to Serao and Deledda in his summary report, probably because it was the first time that the historian was proposed. Hallström writes that Schück's report does not give him "an importance that is decisive enough to assure him of the prominent place in his discipline that is required for a Nobel Prize" (Svensén, 2001b, p. 41).[28] Ferrero would be proposed for the Nobel Prize four more times: in 1924, 1925, 1927 and for the last time in 1933. Hallström dedicates approximately the same space to Bracco but dismisses his possibilities of receiving the Nobel Prize and comments that he still needs to develop his writing before he could be considered. Regarding Deledda, Hallström is quite laconic, mentioning only that Henrik Schück had once more expressed his great admiration for the Sardinian writer during the Committee's meeting, and that he wished to assign the Prize to her (Svensén, 2001b, p. 39). Even more laconic is Hallström's statement about Serao, who had received a new review by Hagberg: "[Serao] was not subject to any discussion. Last year she was not considered important enough to be eligible for the Prize" (Svensén, 2001b, p. 39).[29] Thus, even if Italy had five candidates out of twenty (that is, 25%), not one of them had any real chance of receiving the Prize. Tiozzo describes the situation in the following way:

27 "Sakkunnigutlåtandet tillmäter icke denna författarinna någon vidare hög litterär rang; och man behöver icke läsa mycket av hennes romaner för att instämma. Kommittén fann – nu liksom för några år sedan – detta förslag icke beaktansvärt".

28 "tillmäter honom icke en betydelse, avgörande nog att försäkra honom om en så förnämlig plats inom sin vetenskap, som för ett Nobel-pris kräves".

29 "Blev icke föremål för någon diskussion. Hon ansågs förra året icke betydande nog för att kunna ifrågakomma till pris".

> This is further demonstration of the mediocre standard of the Italian candidates in the 1923 competition, which is further underlined in the very succinct and almost offensive statement with which Hallström dismisses Serao. The writer had been proposed again on 1 January 1923 in an impassioned declamation, full of love for the Parthenopean city but, in fact, this left the Nobel Committee unmoved, if not actually irritated; after all, it was made up of Swedes and not of Neapolitans (Tiozzo, 2009, p. 162).[30]

What the proposers regarded as a great qualification and positive argument in favour of Serao, became instead a negative for her. It is certainly here that one could search for the explanations as to why Serao was never awarded the Nobel Prize: she was seen as "too Neapolitan" by the Swedish Academy and was never seriously considered for the famous award. This was the situation before the publication of *Mors tua* and before Mussolini's dictatorship.

## THE PROPOSALS OF 1924

In its 1922 report, the Nobel Committee had paid great attention to Jacinto Benavente and William Butler Yeats. Subsequently, as noted earlier, the Spanish writer received the Prize in 1922, and Yeats received it in 1923. In 1924, four Italian candidates were discussed: Bracco, Deledda, Ferrero and Serao. In this year, Serao was proposed by Francesco Torraca "and others" (Svensén, 2001b, p. 48). The "others" were Croce and De Ruggiero (Tiozzo, 2009, p. 165). In all, the names of eighteen writers were discussed, and the Committee discussed Ferrero in a more serious manner. Per Hallström wrote in his summary report that two members, himself and Anders Österling, had spoken in favour of Ferrero, while Henrik Schück and Erik Axel Karlfeldt were against. A discussion seems to have taken place, and Hallström stated that

30 "È un'ulteriore dimostrazione della scarsa competitività, nella tornata del 1923, dei candidati italiani, ribadita anche dal comunicato estremamente succinto e quasi offensivo con cui Hallström si sbarazza della Serao. La scrittrice era stata nuovamente candidata da Napoli il 1° gennaio del 1923 con un'appassionata perorazione, vibrante di amore per la città partenopea ma, in realtà, tale da lasciare indifferente se non addirittura da irritare la commissione Nobel, composta innegabilmente da svedesi anziché da napoletani".

Ferrero and Deledda were among the candidates who were considered seriously that year. Regarding Deledda, Schück had again expressed his great admiration for her, and Karlfeldt was on his side. Hallström and Österling were against. Concerning Bracco and Serao, the Committee had nothing new to add about them. On the latter, Hallström noted the following in his report on the Committee's discussions:

> No new work by her has been added. The great appreciation that this writer has been met with, – above all by her compatriots in a narrower sense, the Neapolitans, – is not something the committee members have been able to support. Now, as before, the purely literary value of her production, has been seen as insufficient for a Nobel Prize (Svensén, 2001b, p. 50).[31]

We can here note evidence of the Committee's diffidence towards Serao's depiction of the Neapolitan people. It is quite clear that the Committee was not impressed. At the same time, as Tiozzo affirms, one cannot but notice the "ambivalence at the heart of the Swedish Academy and its committees throughout the 1920s, at least in relation to Italian literature and its candidates for the Prize" (Tiozzo, 2009, p. 171).[32]

## THE PROPOSALS OF 1925

In 1925, Serao was proposed for the final time "by four professors and academy members from Naples" (Svensén, 2001b, p. 61).[33] These were: Giovanni Miranda, Pasquale del Pezzo, Enrico Corchia and Pasquale Grippo. The text of the proposal was the same as the one presented the preceding year, then signed by Croce, Torraca and De Ruggiero (Tiozzo, 2009, p. 177). Bracco, Ferrero and Deledda were also proposed

31 "Något nytt verk av henne har icke tillkommit. Den höga uppskattning, denna författarinna rönt av sina landsmän, – framför allt landsmännen i trängre mening, Neapolitanarna, – ha Kommitterade icke kunnat biträda. Nu, liksom förut, har det rent litterära värdet av hennes alstring tyckts otillräckligt för ett Nobelpris".

32 "approssimazione, che regnava in seno all'Accademia di Svezia e alla sua commissione degli anni '20, almeno nei confronti della letteratura italiana e dei suoi candidati al premio".

33 "föreslagen af 4 professorer och akademiledamöter i Neapel".

again, as well as the Italian newcomer Giovanni Schembari, who was suggested by Achille Loria, a member of the *Accademia dei Lincei* in Rome. Altogether there were twenty-one writers proposed. Hagberg wrote a joint report about Bracco, Deledda and Serao. The report consisted of four typewritten pages, of which about three were dedicated to Deledda, and only a few lines to Bracco and Serao:

> Neither Roberto Bracco, nor Matilde Serao, have, during the last two years, published any new work. Bracco is this year proposed by H. Shetelig (of the Norwegian Society of Science) and Serao by some professors and academy members in Naples. They repeat almost the same arguments as the two last years, holding out the mighty production of the nearly seventy-year old writer and, in particular, her significance in describing Neapolitan everyday life – an authorship which culminated in her masterpiece *Il paese di Cuccagna* (1891).[34]

These few words explain that although Serao was still popular, she had reached her high point as a writer many years previously, which was not regarded as positive. While she was considered as mostly a Neapolitan writer, Deledda appears to have been upgraded, from initially having been seen as a Sardinian author, to become "all-Italian", as Hagberg writes at the end of his report. He also mentions some complaints from the Italian press that the nation had not been awarded the Nobel Prize for Literature since 1906, when Carducci had received it:

> The Italian press complains often about the fact that their literature, which is not lacking in distinguished representatives, has been neglected in Sweden. And they point most often and with the greatest consensus at Grazia Deledda as a candidate. And, surely, a Nobel Prize for the former Sardinian, now all-Italian, authoress who, despite her rich production lives in modest circumstances, would be greeted with approval and understanding not only in Italy, but in the whole educated world.[35]

---

34 "Varken Roberto Bracco eller Matilde Serao ha under de två senaste åren publicerat något nytt arbete. Bracco är detta år föreslagen av H. Shetelig (Norsk Videnskapsselskab) och Serao av några professorer och akademiledamöter i Neapel. Dessa upprepa i det närmaste samma motivering som de två föregående åren, framhållande den populära, nu snart sjuttioåriga författarinnans mäktiga produktion och särskilt hennes betydelse såsom skildrarinna av Neapels liv – ett författarskap, som kulminerade i hennes mästerverk *Il paese di Cuccagna* (1891)", Archive of the Swedish Academy.

35 "Den italienska pressen klagar ofta över att deras litteratur, som ju icke saknar framstående representanter, blivit förbisedd i Sverige. Och man pekar då oftast och med största samstämmighet på Grazia Deledda såsom kandidat. Och helt säkert skulle ett Nobelpris till den forna

Hallström's summary report of the Nobel Committee was positive about Ferrero, while his attitude towards Serao and Bracco was unaltered. Schembari was dismissed as unthinkable. Regarding Deledda, even Schück, her greatest admirer, declared that he hesitated about her that year. Consequently, the Academy decided to suspend the Nobel Prize for literature in 1925. As Tiozzo suggests, it was probably because of this that the Italian proposers felt disorientated the following year, which could explain why neither Bracco, Deledda, Ferrero nor Serao were proposed in 1926 (Tiozzo, 2009, p. 178). Instead, a new Italian name came up, namely that of Ada Negri.

In 1926, in all twenty-nine writers were proposed. The Nobel Committee was not completely convinced by Ada Negri's authorship, but all the same wrote in its report that her candidacy could be considered in a subsequent year (Svensén, 2001b, pp. 80-81). On 11 November 1926, the Academy decided that the Nobel Prize of 1925 was to be awarded to George Bernard Shaw and that the Prize of 1926 would be decided the following year (Svensén, 2001b, p. 87). On 10 November 1927 the Academy finally chose Grazia Deledda, proposed by Henrik Schück, to be the Nobel Prize Laureate of 1926 (Svensén, 2001b, p. 105). By that time, it was too late for Serao. She had passed away at her writing desk on 25 July 1927.

## CONCLUSIONS

What conclusions can be drawn from this? It appears that Matilde Serao's prospects of obtaining the Nobel Prize were limited. Even though she was proposed on four consecutive years, the documents of the Swedish Academy nonetheless reveal that she was never considered a viable candidate. Grazia Deledda, on the other hand, was in a much stronger position and was lucky to have a great admirer in the Academy member Henrik Schück, who fought for her Prize for many years.

sardiska, nu riks-italienska författarinnan, vilken trots sin rika produktion lever i blygsamma omständigheter, mötas med gillande och förstående icke blott i Italien utan hela den bildade världen", Archive of the Swedish Academy.

Serao was regarded as "too Neapolitan" and lacked the support in the Academy that Deledda possessed. The idea that Mussolini should have intervened in some way is not supported by the documentation in the Academy's archive. Such an intervention would, in any case, most likely never have been permitted by the Academy, which was, and is, proud of its independence; it would never have accepted political interventions, nor interventions of any other kind. Moreover, there is no evidence that Mussolini was engaged in any way regarding the decision not to award Serao the Nobel prize.

Ulla ÅKERSTRÖM
University of Gothenburg

| | |
|---|---|
| 1913 | Grazia Deledda |
| 1914 | Grazia Deledda<br>Salvatore Farina<br>Dora Melegari |
| 1915 | Grazia Deledda |
| 1916 | --- |
| 1917 | Grazia Deledda |
| 1918 | Grazia Deledda |
| 1919 | --- |
| 1920 | Grazia Deledda |
| 1921 | Grazia Deledda |
| 1922 | Roberto Bracco<br>Grazia Deledda<br>Matilde Serao |
| 1923 | Roberto Bracco<br>Grazia Deledda<br>Guglielmo Ferrero<br>Dora Melegari<br>Matilde Serao |
| 1924 | Roberto Bracco<br>Grazia Deledda<br>Guglielmo Ferrero<br>Matilde Serao |
| 1925 | Roberto Bracco<br>Grazia Deledda<br>Guglielmo Ferrero<br>Giovanni Schembari<br>Matilde Serao |
| 1926 | Ada Negri |
| 1927 | Grazia Deledda<br>Guglielmo Ferrero<br>Ada Negri<br>Cesare Pascarella |

FIG. 1 – Italian writers nominated for the Nobel Prize 1913-1927.

# THE RECEPTION OF MATILDE SERAO IN BULGARIA, 1890s-1920s

The following essay explores Matilde Serao's abundant literary presence in the Bulgarian literary landscape at the turn of the twentieth century. The most intensive reception of Serao's works in Bulgaria happened over the course of three decades: from the 1890s to the beginning of the 1920s, and on the pages of various periodicals. Firstly, we will provide an overview of the number of her titles found in Bulgaria, the places of their publication, and the identity of their translators. We will then discuss the themes of her writing that most attracted Bulgarian readers, before indicating the nature of the possible impact of Serao's fiction on Bulgarian (women) writers and on literary critics.

## SCOPE OF RECEPTION

The proliferation of the creative work of Matilde Serao on the Italian literary scene at the turn of the nineteenth century corresponds to the aftermath of the Russo-Turkish war of 1877-1878 when Bulgaria gained independence from Ottoman rule. Until the 1870s the literary life of the Bulgarian intelligentsia took place mostly in the big cultural centres of Central, Southern and Eastern Europe, but the establishment of the Bulgarian kingdom after 1878 led to a substantial enhancement of the literary production within the country. In parallel with the process of building a national canon there was a growth in literary translations, and Italian literature was no exception to this trend. Although the acquaintance of the Bulgarian readership with Italian writers started earlier in the nineteenth century,[1] its true flowering can be observed towards the end of the century. Both classical authors such as Dante, Petrarch, Boccaccio and Ariosto, and modern poets and novelists, such as Giacomo Leopardi, Giosuè Carducci and Edmondo De Amicis, were being translated for the first time. Similarly, Bulgarians' first encounter with Italian women's writing was through a translation of a short story by Serao. Her piece "Salvazione" from the volume *Piccole anime* (Serao, 1883b) was published in 1891 with the title "Na samin" ["In Private"] in the newspaper *Iskra*. Serao's popularity grew in the following years together with that of her Italian 'sisters' Ada Negri, Neera and Grazia Deledda.[2] The latter three writers gained visibility on the Bulgarian literary scene later than Serao. Taken together, their reception reveals a very rich corpus of Italian women's writing in Bulgaria during the first half of the twentieth century, though Serao was undoubtedly its forerunner.

The quantitative data survey included here reveals the wide scope of Serao's reception (see Fig. 1). For the period in question, twenty literary works appeared in Bulgarian, of which four were translated more than once, making a total of twenty-nine translations. These publications can be found in two collections and in fifteen different periodicals, four of which are considered periodicals for women. A very significant fact about Serao's reception is that it is not limited to the capital city of Sofia, but rather is spread throughout the country. Her works appeared in journals published also in Tarnovo, Shumen, Plovdiv, Tchirpan, Vratsa, and even in Thessaloniki, which at that time was still within the Ottoman Empire and had a considerable number of Bulgarian residents. Overall, Serao received a positive response from Bulgarian literary critics. A few of her translators added footnotes to the main text in which they explained the role she played in European literature of

1 The beginning of the reception of Italian literature in Bulgarian started in 1854 with the translation of the play *La Pamela maritata* by Carlo Goldoni. It was translated through Greek by one of the first Bulgarian women writers – Irina Popgeorgieva Exarch, who signed her translation under the initials I.P.G.E. Until the 1880s, Bulgarian readers were also able to read translations of three more Italian authors – Giulio Cesare Croce, Francesco Domenico Guerrazzi and Silvio Pellico (Ilieva, 2012).

2 The first publication by Ada Negri consisted of three poems which appeared in 1895-1896 in the newspaper *Den*. Grazia Deledda's first Bulgarian translation was the novel *L'ombra del passato*, published in 1913. In both cases the translator was the same: Konstantin Mutafov.

the time. Serao was also mentioned in one translated critical review in an encyclopaedia entry, and she was granted a lengthy literary portrait on the pages of the newspaper *Mir* in 1911.

The process of reconstructing a translated work typically involves identifying its original, discovering its translator, and distinguishing channels of transfer to the receiving culture. When collecting our data, we used a methodological framework derived from the fields of translation theory and comparativism, but in the case of Serao's prose in Bulgarian it was very difficult to retrace all stages of this reception process. From the 1840s onwards, Bulgarians were translating foreign literature according to the Schleiermacherian principle of "moving the author to the reader", thus allowing for adaptations of the original work for the sake of intelligibility.[3] Even though in the late nineteenth- and early twentieth centuries the attitude to translation changed in favour of a stricter and more faithful literary translation, Bulgarian translators still adapted foreign works to the receiving context. The most frequent adaptation strategy for Serao's works was to change the original title of a short story, for example, without giving information about the collection from which it derived. Up to now we have discovered original titles for sixteen translations, but one further translation has yet to be identified. The translators usually kept the original story line. They did not make changes in the composition; neither did they replace names or observations about the characters. Subtle differences can be detected in cases where certain short stories had several Bulgarian translations, but the nature of these changes can be explained by the translators' stylistic preferences rather than by any deliberate intention to edit the original.

Regarding the language of translation, Serao's case reveals two phenomena typical of this time in Bulgaria's history of translation. The first is that most of the works (twenty) do not indicate the language from which they were translated; there are only nine works out of twenty-nine

3 In his renowned study "On the Different Methods of Translating" Friedrich Schleiermacher (2003) writes about the two roads open to the translator who "either leaves the author at peace and moves the reader towards him or leaves the reader at peace and moves the author toward him" (Schleiermacher, cited in Lefevere, 1992, p. 149). The latter method is usually practiced in cases when the translator cannot convey the exact meaning of a notion from the original text to the translation; or where s/he is inclined to sacrifice the original meaning for the sake of readers' better understanding of another language and culture.

that mention this information. The second is that only five of these works are direct translations from Italian; the others indicate the presence of a mediating language that stands between the original and that of the receiving context. Translators have used Russian (in two works), French (in two works), and Serbian (in one work) to present Serao's prose in Bulgaria, and when the transfer of meaning has passed through such mediations there are inevitable diversions from the original. Since the translators did not mention the titles of the collections of short stories or journal they used, it is impossible to reconstruct the channels of transfer for each of those works. A better strategy is to expand the list of the possible languages of translations on the basis of the translators' biographies, or their usual writing practice. As a result of these efforts, we were able to identify four further translations from French, and one from Polish.

The process of identifying the translators themselves did not go smoothly either. We have identified the names and/or initials of nineteen translators – sixteen men and three women. There are six anonymous translations. It was easier when the translators declared their original source and wrote an autograph of their name. For instance, three Bulgarian translators indicated that they made direct translations from Italian. These are Kiril Hristov, translator of three works: "Apparenze", "Scuola normale femminile", and another one, which is not identified yet, "Negoden!" ["Incapable!"]; Konstantin Mutafov, translator of one work, "O Giovannino o la morte"; and Ivan Dokumov, translator of one work, "L'abbandonata". Several translators mentioned both their name and the language from which they translated: V.K. Vladev (French), Georgi Tsanev (Russian) and St. D-va (Serbian). Three other translators, namely, K. Dyankov, St. Georgiev, and Stoyan Koledarov left their signatures, but did not indicate the language of translation. Through a consideration of their other translated works, we deduced that they translated indirectly from French.

The most difficult task was to identify the texts signed only by initials. This is the case with the translators of the short stories "Iz uchilishtnite tipove" ["Alla scuola"]; "Nasame" ["Salvazione"]; "Raznoglasie" ["Dissidio"]; "Silueti" ["Profili"]; "Tri pisma" ["Falso in scrittura"]; "Pokayala se" ["Salvazione"]; "Parva lybov" ["Viottole"], translated respectively by A.P.N., D-ev, A., M.V, T.D.N., V. Kirova, St. D-va and

G.T.Ch. Sometimes a grammatical suffix can help identify at least the gender of the translators. The feminine gender is marked with the suffix "a" at the end of the verb or the family name. Such are the cases with "T.D.N." (where the verb preceding the initials bears the suffix for the feminine gender); and with "St. D-va" (where the family name "D-va" indicates that the translator is a woman). Similarly, the translation of "Falso in scrittura" was done by a woman. Her autograph "V. Kirova" indicates that the translator is female. In this case, we could go further in discovering the identity of the translator since a number of translations by Venda Kirova already existed. Her biography reveals that in the course of twenty years, from 1907 to 1927, she translated four books from Polish to Bulgarian. All of them were related to motherhood, women's health, and hygiene. Thus, we added Venda Kirova to the list of women translators; her translation is a rare example of Serao's works reaching Bulgaria from a Polish source. Another difficult case of identification was that of of St. D-va. In the abbreviation of her surname, we recognized a woman translator. Furthermore, her translation appeared in the first feminist journal *Zhenski glas* in 1900. After a short investigation of the archival collection of this journal we were able to determine that the signature belonged to St. P. Dragneva, who had family ties in Serbia and was an active member of the Bulgarian feminist movement at the turn of the twentieth century.

Women's initiatives in translating, publishing, and promoting fictional works by other women writers were part of a new emancipatory trend of advocacy for women's place in the public sphere (Daskalova, 2012). At the turn of the twentieth century Bulgarian society was still very much inclined to urge women to maintain their traditional roles as caretakers and to judge severely those who demanded suffrage, equal pay and a position in the workplace. The first step towards emancipation was the rise of literacy due to the spread of educational institutions for women. Data reveals that between 1880 and 1926, women's literacy grew significantly from 1.5% to 37.2% (Nazarska, 2003, p. 60). In 1901, the Bulgarian Women's Union was established to support women's efforts to claim their rights. At its outset as an organization, it comprised twenty-seven women's associations, and it united women with diverse political opinions. Its goal from the beginning was to further enhance women's education in high schools and universities, and after that to propose enfranchisement and equal pay for women. Although it often experienced internal conflicts and political mockery, the Bulgarian Women's Union survived until 1945.[4] Throughout this time, it also published an official feminist newspaper called *Zhenski glas*. Its pages often included fiction or other translated materials that offered examples of women's hardships and their struggles for social acknowledgement. From its very beginnings, *Zhenski glas* sought to engage larger audiences and followed trends fashionable in modern fiction. Despite Serao's declarations that she was not a feminist herself, her prose was appreciated by the editors of *Zhenski glas* because it presented a women's voice which spoke openly about women's hardships and personal choices.

Psychological portraits of women and of their perspectives on life and love are very common in Serao's prose. It is no wonder that not only *Zhenski glas* in its early years, but also other women's journals, such as *Savremenna domakinya* (and its supplement *Chetivo za svobodnoto vreme: spisanie za zhenata*), *Moda i domakinstvo* and *Balgarka* privileged her prose on their pages.[5] All of them targeted a female readership, but emphasized different kinds of materials. *Zhenski glas* introduced an activist feminist approach, but it also published works by women writers as illustrations of women's growing sense of self and artistic presence. *Moda i domakinstvo* had a science and literature section where it published contemporary fiction (Vacheva, 2014, p. 99). It also provided space for discussions on housework, fashion, cooking, and childcare. Similarly, the magazine *Balgarka* included biographies of exemplary women and

---

4 In 1903 the Bulgarian women's union experienced internal conflicts between those feminists who believed that education had greater priority than political and social rights for women (Yulia Malinova and Ekaterina Karavelova, for example) and those who demanded urgent measures to secure political rights for women from all social milieus (including Anna Karima and Vela Blagoeva). The latter, the "socialist feminists", were convinced that full gender equality could be achieved only *after* a change in the political order by means of a revolution, whereas the so-called "liberal feminists" wanted to take gradual steps to enfranchisement by means of lobbying and gaining international acknowledgment. In 1937, after numerous efforts on the part of the liberal feminists, and with the consent of the government, Bulgarian women gained partial rights to vote. After 1944, however, the Socialist feminists took over, closed the "bourgeois" women's union, and established the "Peoples' women's union of Bulgaria" (see on this Daskalova, 2012).

5 During the period in question, more than ten Bulgarian women's journals strove to contribute to women's moral and physical accomplishments, to improve their knowledge on pedagogy, health, hygiene, housework, and, last but not least, their skills in reading and interpreting contemporary literature (see Konstantinova, 2012).

many translations from foreign literature. In addition, it emphasized pedagogy, ethics, and patriotism, as may be deduced from the title of the magazine. Among the four journals, *Moda i domakinstvo* had the greatest affinity with Serao's style. In the course of eight years (1898-1906), there were six publications of her works there: "Sebeotrichanie" ["Salvazione"], "Tri pisma" ["Falso in scrittura"], "Raznoglasie" ["Dissidio"], "V teatara" ["Apparenze"], "Samoubietsat" ["Un suicidio"], and the *novella* "Pred praga na zhivota" ["Scuola normale femminile"]. In 1898, two short stories appeared in *Balgarka*: "Nesaglasie" ["Dissidio"] and "Chest" ["Novella d'amore"]; *Zhenski glas* published only one of her short stories on its page in the first years of its existence: "Pokayala se" ["Salvazione"] in 1900.

Serao was much appreciated also on the pages of polythematic journals, which were published in various cities throughout Bulgaria. For instance, the magazine *Iskra* published three stories by the Italian writer between 1891 and 1893. The journals *Trud*, from the town of Tarnovo, published the short story "Izkuplenie" ["Salvazione"], and *Razvitie* from Vratsa published the short story "Chuden san" ["Sogno di una notte d'estate"]. A major success on the Bulgarian cultural scene was indicated by the appearance of a translation of one of Serao's stories on the pages of a very prestigious modernist magazine entitled *Misal*. Its editors were known for their desire to break with old literary traditions and to establish high standards of writing and translation. Their publications always underwent a strict and highly-scrutinized process of selection, in line with their aesthetic programme. They insisted on the adaptation of the norms of European modernist writing to the stylistic features of authors from the Bulgarian literary realm. The publication of the short story "Negoden!" in 1890, whose original we have not yet been able to identify, speaks of the high esteem in which Serao was held in Bulgarian modernist literary circles.

## THEMATIC CHOICES

Judging by the thematic scope of the works translated from Serao, it is clear that the guiding principle for selection was their function as moral *exempla* that reveal the psychological motives behind certain types of behaviour. The translated short stories and excerpts from larger works typically deal with the topics of love, poverty, and school life. The topic of love varies from adultery ("Sebeotrichanie" / "Salvazione", "Tri pisma" / "Falso in scrittura"), to disappointment ("Ili Giovanino ili smart" / "O Giovannino o la morte", "Chuden san" / "Sogno di una notte d'estate", "Napusnata" / "L'abbandonata", "Parva luybov" / "Viottole") or impossibility ("Raznoglasie" / "Dissidio", "Chest" / "Novella d'amore", "V teatara" / "Apparenze", "Tayna" / "Il segreto (Cariclea)"). The story "Edna tsvetarka" / "Una fioraia" touches upon the subject of social inequalities. It was translated twice, perhaps because of its realistic representation of poverty and urban alienation. Excerpts from novellas which deal with the question of education occupy a special place among all the translated works. They focus on the experience of women teachers and their interactions with female pupils ("Pred praga na zhivota" / "Scuola normale femminile", "Uchilishtni tipove" / "Alla scuola"). The case studies dealing with difficult childhoods and inappropriate norms for the educational treatment of girls suggest a possible resolution for issues that might be encountered by Bulgarian teachers in pedagogical practice.

The appreciation of family values, faithfulness, and honour in Serao's fiction makes her short stories didactic. Sometimes moral instruction through literary examples did not occur directly, but rather came through adaptation of certain elements from the original text during their translation. In the case of the Bulgarian translations, the most common feature involves a change in the title of the Bulgarian version. The utilization of new titles for Serao's short stories in periodicals created the potential to attract a larger audience and to disseminate moral exempla among a wider readership. This may be the reason why several works appeared under changed titles in different journals during the period in question: Bulgarian readers enjoyed reading about virtue. For instance, the most translated short story by Serao is "Salvazione". It was published five times over a period of twelve years from 1891 to 1902-1903, in different journals under different titles. It is the story of an adulterous couple in which Flavia, the female lover, takes the drastic decision to give up her love for Cesare for the sake of preserving his family. The turning point in her moral transformation is a private meeting with her lover's son, Paolo. The pure and innocent child's confession of the loneliness he and his mother felt during his father's absence touches Flavia's sensitive heart. Their conversation ends with her determination to restore the balance in the broken family by sacrificing her own love. The Bulgarian translators experimented with the title of the story. In three of the titles, "Sebeotrichanie" ["Self-Denial"], "Pokayala se" ["Repented"], and "Izkuplenie" ["Redemption"], the Christian notion of guilt and salvation of the soul is present. The translators emphasize Flavia's moral transformation: she sacrifices her love out of compassion, and believes she is restoring order by abandoning her lover so that he can return to his family. The other two titles, however, are based on the culmination of the storyline: "Nasame", "Na samin" ["In Private"]. They privilege the moment of privacy between Flavia and Paolo, their sincere exchange that unlocked Flavia's remorse and her final decision to separate from her lover.

The end of the story fits well with the traditional esteem in which Bulgarian readers held family and marriage. They approved of Flavia's feelings of remorse about adultery and, as in many other cases, the story normalizes the self-sacrificial gesture of the female character. Bulgarian literature of the nineteenth century contains many examples of such characters, who renounce their personal feelings for the good of society, or for the betterment of the whole nation (Alexandrova, 2012, pp. 151-168). Usually, society tends to approve of male promiscuity, whereas it often sanctions women for their "sinful affairs" (Vacheva, 2014).

Adultery is the prevailing theme of another very popular short story by Serao: "Falso in scrittura" has been translated four times in Bulgarian, in three different magazines and in one collection. Instead of offering a literal translation of the title, the three different translators all preferred to entitle the story "Tri pisma" ["Three Letters"]. Indeed, the short story is written in an epistolary form, presenting the relationships between the characters as three stages of the development of an adulterous relationship. In fact, all the letters have the same female sender, Adriana, whose attitude to her object of desire changes over time. The first letter resembles very well-known formulaic letters of rejection of a man's attention to a woman because of its impropriety. Adriana follows this standard model of epistolary conversation to declare her chastity and faithfulness in marriage. The second letter presents a new stage of the secret relationship when the two lovers passionately consume their love. Here, Adriana informs her lover that her husband is absent and confesses her desire for her lover. This second letter is the shortest one. The reason for this may be that no one is interested in "happy relationships", to paraphrase Tolstoy's epigraph for *Anna Karenina*. Yet another reason for this could be Serao's presumption that the emphasis of the short story should be on the virtuous behaviour of the woman (Romani, 2013, p. 137). Adriana's expression of grief and remorse for her adultery in the third letter supports this statement. Adriana declares that future meetings between the lovers are impossible. Her decision is based on her feelings of guilt towards her benevolent and trusting husband.

"Three letters" is an experiment with the readers' expectations of the relationship between the narrator and the protagonist. In the epilogue of the short story, the narrator confronts the readers with the challenge of distinguishing "which of the three letters is a lie". The narrator reflects on the question of sincerity in the intimate relationship. Adriana might have lied either about her desire, or about her true feelings, or about her capacity to feel remorse for adultery. In all cases the uncertainty around her sincerity questions her repentance and provokes the reader of the short story to reflect on the concept of faithfulness. As in the case of "Salvazione", the translation of "Falso in scrittura" into Bulgarian shifts the emphasis of the original piece from the "falso" to the dynamics of the love discourse in the three pseudo-epistolary fragments. The motivation for the Bulgarian translation remains unknown. The persistent preservation of the title, "Three letters", in four different publications over the course of seventeen years (1892 to 1908) could be explained by the usage of one and the same source for indirect translation, a source in which the original title had already been changed. Despite all efforts, we could not discover information about the process of translation of this short story. Thus far, we can only observe its large popularity at the end of the nineteenth century.

Serao's story "Dissidio" was also among the most popular ones for the Bulgarian readers. It was translated twice: in 1898 in *Balgarka*, and in 1898-1899 in *Moda i domakinstvo*. Both publications are women's journals, and in both cases the translator remains unknown. Despite these difficulties in deciphering the source of the translation process, we can see that the way in which the story deals with the entrapments of love appears to strike a chord with Bulgarians. The story is a dialogue between two lovers whose feelings fluctuate between the excitement of being together and the distress caused by their inevitable separation. The Bulgarian translators have managed to retain all nuances of eroticism in the conversation between the two protagonists, who finally come to terms with their separation.

The dynamics of the conversation in "Dissidio" display the female lover as braver in confessing her feelings than her beloved. Similar dynamics can be traced in stories, such as "Avgustovska nosht" ["Notte di agosto"] and "Nepozhatiya" ["Sconosciuto"]. In the first one the two lovers, Giorgio and Kleliya, hide their feelings from one another while listening to a musical tune. Although their dialogue reveals their different attitude to life – his is realistic, and hers is romantic – the characters demonstrate a hopeful mutual understanding of the secret of love without yet being able to confess this feeling to the other. In "Nepoznatiya" three girlfriends confess to one another about a man they desire. In the end it turns out to be the same man who has managed to steal the heart of each of those three girls.

The moment of renouncing dignity is typical of female protagonists in Serao's stories translated into Bulgarian. The *novella* "Chuden san" ["Sogno di una notte d'estate"] presents the story of the disappointed Luisa, who falls in love with the older and more experienced Massimo. For him, the young girl is just a momentary amusement, whereas Luisa's feelings for Massimo become deeper and deeper. Although she is ashamed to confess her deep affection, she opens up to Massimo in an attempt to make him change his mind about leaving for St. Petersburg with his lover. His rejection brings disappointment to the innocent Luisa and leaves her in distress.

Typically, the main character of a given story becomes incapable of handling her loneliness, and the ending of such short stories reveals a tragic outcome. Female protagonists are either left in distress or are depicted in the moment of dying. For instance, in the story "Tayna" ["Il segreto. Cariclea"], readers are party to the tragic last days and hours in the life of a mother whose only son, in his utter desperation, questions her about his father's name. Even in the face of death, the mother keeps her secret from her child. This time it is the son who is left in utter loneliness when he loses the only relative he has ever had.

In Serao's stories, suicide is one step beyond desperation. A good example is the short story "O Giovannino o la morte", translated into

Bulgarian in 1906-1907 with the same title. The main character is poor Chiarina, who loves her fiancé Giovannino but disagrees with his efforts to earn money from pawnbroking. Disregarding her opinion, Giovannino becomes an assistant to Chiarina's greedy stepmother, Donna Gabriella. Soon Chiarina realizes that Giovannino has become Donna Gabriella's lover. Giovannino's act of rejection and abandonment is the cause of Chiarina's decision to commit suicide.

Later on, this state of melancholy and grief was to become a staple of the identity of the female character in modernist prose. Irene Zanini-Cordi (2008) critically regards the feelings of incapability, grief and stagnation as part of a rigid stereotype of the representation of the female nature in androcentric patriarchal writing. This stereotype works equally well for both Italian and Bulgarian modernist literature and may be found in the works of both male and female writers. In her prose, Serao frequently explores the question of the capacity of female characters to act according to their subjective drives instead of subordinating themselves to patriarchal tradition. The psychological portraits of her female characters display a willingness to actively search for love and to declare their choice of beloved. Yet the collision between their expressed will and the harsh response of patriarchal society leads to a tragic resolution. The female character is doomed to social exclusion, moral decline, or physical (self)-punishment.

## BULGARIAN WRITERS INFLUENCED BY MATILDE SERAO

Although it is difficult to find proof of direct influence of Serao's stories on the writings of Bulgarian writers, sometimes the similarities in terms of plot and character types are striking. In addition, we discovered that several of her translators into Bulgarian became very prominent writers during the modernist period. One such example is Evgenia Mars (1877-1945). She was one of the first Bulgarian women writers to publish collections of short stories, travelogues, plays and memoirs. Her career as a writer began in 1906 when she published her first collection of short stories, *Iz zhivota* ["Driven from Life"]. The characters in her prose are often caught in a psychological state of distress: they suffer from abandonment or socially-unacceptable love. The short story "Ugasna" ["Fading out"] tells a story of a lethally ill woman who rejects her lover when she becomes aware that death is near. The short stories "Chestita nova godina" ["Happy New Year"] and "Koznodejstvo" ["Betrayal"] also describe male characters' disappointments in love. After a long period of absence, the men return to Bulgaria to find their beloved has forgotten them and/or married someone else. The internal monologues at the beginning of the short stories express hope and aspiration and then those feelings turn into despair with the apprehension that the purity of first love was just an illusion. It was not a surprise to us to find proof that Evgenia Mars had read Serao's prose, and that she even intended to translate some of her works. The clue was hidden in an exchange of letters between her literary mentor – the Bulgarian poet Ivan Vazov – and the editor of the literary journal *Balgarska sbirka*, Stefan Bobchev (Vazov, 1979, p. 9). A letter from September 1909 contains an enquiry as to whether the editor of *Balgarska sbirka* would publish a short story by Serao, translated by Evgenia Mars. Though in the issues of subsequent months (1909-1910) we were not able to find any such translation, we suspect that the Bulgarian woman writer knew Serao's prose well and was partially influenced by it.

A very interesting parallel can be drawn between Serao's prose and that of the Bulgarian writer and feminist Ana Karima (1871-1949). As mentioned above, the latter was a founder and the first editor of the Bulgarian feminist journal *Zhenski glas*, in which a short story by Serao was published in 1900. A year later, Ana Karima published a *novella* titled "Pod natiska na zhivota" ["Under the Pressure of Life"]. This original *novella* by Karima very much resembles Serao's "Scuola normale femminile", which was translated just the previous year in *Moda i domakinstvo*. The type of the woman teacher who faces the challenges of the profession together with personal setbacks is common to both women writers. In both *novellas* there are tragic events at the end, although the final lines of "Scuola normale femminile" contain an air of a hope. In Karima's *novella*, there is a tragic melodramatic ending with the death of the protagonist. Her trauma comes from the fact that no one in that small town could fully understand the conflict between her intimate love and her social standing. Serao's *novella* contains reference to many of the former college girls' tragic stories and life trajectories. When they later became teachers, some of those women died of exhaustion, poverty, illness, or desperation. Yet, towards the end of "Scuola normale femminile", we also learn that one of the characters, Isabella Diaz, has managed to improve her pedagogical standing through initiating campaigns for new kindergartens and orphanages, and becoming a headteacher herself. Even if we cannot trace a direct influence from Serao's prose to that of the aforementioned Bulgarian women writers, we can infer a dominant trend of describing tragic love stories that are not simply a product of sentimentalism, but are always related to deepening concerns with issues of women's physical and moral "health", of social injustice, and class consciousness.

In several cases, Serao exerted an influence over her male translators who also had their own place in the Bulgarian literary landscape. Among them are Kiril Hristov (1875-1944) and Konstantin Mutafov (1879-1946). Both translated the Italian writer directly from Italian. They had extensive experience as translators and often influenced the literary taste of Bulgarian readers through their critical essays, pamphlets, and reviews. Kiril Hristov's own writing encompasses several volumes of poetry and prose. When he was nineteen, he went to study in the Marine academy in Trieste (1895-1896). His stay was decisive for his enduring interest in Italian literature and culture. While he was there, he became a contributor to *Misal* magazine, in which he published translations of Matilde Serao, Giacomo Leopardi, Lorenzo Stecchetti, and Ugo Foscolo. His attraction to Italy continued, and in 1897 he travelled to Naples. The journey to this city provided the inspiration for Kiril Hristov to write his second poetry book called *Trepeti* [*Excitements*] in 1897. He also translated part of Dante's *Divine Comedy* (1935),[6] as well as Ada Negri's works in a collection entitled *Liricheski stihotvorenia ot Ada Negri* [*Lyrical Poems by Ada Negri*] (Negri, 1896).

While investigating his personal archive, we came upon an unfinished fictional text whose plot very much resembles that of Serao's "Scuola

6 Kiril Hristov translated *Inferno* – the first part of the *Divine Comedy*. Instead of "Hell" ("Ad" in Bulgarian) he used the word "Preizpodnya". It is a more archaic word from Old Church Slavonic language.

normale femminile".[7] The topic of both works is the same: the everyday life of the students at a girls' college where religion and strict rules are at the core of the educational process. Another similarity between the two works is in the narration's double perspective. In the forefront there is the everyday life of the pupils, their exams, interactions, and playful chatting. But in the background, there is a deeper and more sober perspective. This reveals the girls' suppressed emotions, rooted in their traumatic childhood, or in present loves and aspirations. In both cases, the authors present life at the college through the eyes of several pupils. However, in Kiril Hristov's text the story gradually comes to focus on just two girlfriends, Kornelia and Maria, whereas in Serao's earlier *novella*, there is a whole gallery of portraits of *little women*.

Another distinguished Bulgarian writer who acted as a translator of Serao's stories is Konstantin Mutafov (1879-1946). The peak of his career was during the interwar period when he was also a theatre critic, traveller, and journalist. He studied drama in Florence and was a great promoter of Italian culture in Bulgaria. Among the authors translated by Mutafov are Edmondo De Amicis, Giovanni Verga, Antonio Fogazzaro, Vittorio Alfieri, Luigi Pirandello, and Grazia Deledda. In 1899, he translated Serao's story "O Giovannino o la morte". There is a notable resemblance between the title of his collection of short stories *Prosti dushi* [*Simple Minds*], published in 1938 and Serao's collections of prose *Piccole anime* (1883) and *L'anima semplice: Suor Giovanna della Croce* (1901). This similarity can be interpreted as an indicator of Serao's possible influence on her Bulgarian translator. In terms of the stories themselves, however, one finds hardly any similarities due to the strong ethnographic and decorative style of Konstantin Mutafov's prose.

Bulgarian translators are attracted to the themes of poverty and deprivation in Serao's prose. The work "Tsvetarkata" ["Una fioraia"] has been translated twice.[8] It depicts the unhappy fate of an orphan girl, who is astonished by the clean and wide streets of the upper-class neighbourhoods of Naples which are so different from the slums where she lives.

7 CSA (Central State Archives), Fund 131K, List 2, Unit 75.

8 The first translation (as "Tsvetarka") is from 1918, and the second (as "Edna tsvetarka") is from 1934. The latter is a comparatively late translation of Serao's stories and falls outside of the time period of this study. However, we decided to include it in the list in order to illustrate that the image of the poor florist had a longer and steady tradition of reception in the Bulgarian cultural context.

Through the gaze of this innocent child, readers are presented with class difference and the social exclusion of the poor, whose vulnerability predetermines their misfortune. After the cheerful culmination of the story when a florist suddenly gives a big bunch of flowers to the girl and then a soldier buys the flowers in a gesture of compassion, the happy orphan girl is hit by a passing carriage and dies on the street. The topic of poverty and destitution is explored very frequently by certain leftist Bulgarian writers and poets, including Hristo Smirnenski (1898-1923). In his work from 1923 *Zimni vecheri* [*Winter Evenings*], he includes several poems on the subject, as well as one with the exact same name, "Tsvetarka" ["The Florist"]. In the scarce biographical sources on this Bulgarian poet, there is no evidence that he was familiar with Serao's works. Moreover, at that time Bulgarians could have also read another short story by an Italian woman writer, which deals with similar themes. We have found that Neera's short story "La falena" from the volume *Voci della notte* (1893) was published in 1895 under the title "Noshtnata peperudka" ["The Night Butterfly"]. Its main character is also a poor young woman who is about to offer up her own fragile body for sex to strangers who pass through the streets of the city. Despite the lack of evidence of any direct influence, we believe that the publication of work by Italian women writers, and by Serao in particular, has added strength to a general engagement with social issues on the part of Bulgarian writers.[9]

## MATILDE SERAO FROM THE PERSPECTIVE OF BULGARIAN CRITICS

In what follows, we summarize the critical reception of Serao on the pages of Bulgarian periodicals by suggesting from the start that this is positive, essentialist insofar as it pronounces on women's writing, and is perhaps not entirely the work of Bulgarian critics but a translation of views from abroad. Certainly, many features can be explained by the

9 In fact, the short story "Noshtnata peperudka" was falsely attributed to Serao in a translation which appeared in *Balgarska sbirka* in 1895. After consulting with the editors of this volume, we concluded that the original short story belongs to Neera.

dominant way in which women's writing was perceived in Bulgaria at the time: it was seen as intrinsically related to the emotions, and as thematically rooted in love, marriage, and upbringing. It is important to note, however, that when it comes to foreign women writers, critics readily acknowledged the skilfulness of their writing, whereas Bulgarian women writers still suffered a great deal from accusations of epigonism.

The article "Contemporary Italian literature according to Ugo Odetti [*sic*]"[10] was published in the rubric "News from Foreign Journals" in the journal *Iskra* (Ojetti, 1896-1897). The text is a translation from the French literary journal *Revue de Paris*, which was a benchmark for critical reviews on European literature. The author enumerates the five most distinguished Italian writers and includes Serao in the company of Carducci, D'Annunzio, Fogazzaro, and Verga. The review claims that Serao is much more skilled stylistically than many other Italian women writers, but that there are weaknesses in her work too. She is accused of stylistic inaccuracy and lack of precision which she herself admits and attributes to the speedy pace at which she works (Danchev, 1911). The critic is ironic about Serao's marriage to one of her former literary rivals, but he praises her for her ability to combine writing with family duties. Finally, Ojetti suggests that the spontaneity of her expression and her eye for peculiarities are what makes Serao's prose so popular.

The opinions of Ojetti and Ivan G. Danchev tend to converge. The latter was a specialist in lexicography and French literature. His article "Matilde Serao" was published in a supplement to the newspaper *Mir* in 1911. The review includes a few biographical facts about Serao, and pays attention to her writing. Danchev considers Serao's ability to accurately transform real social problems into fictional narratives to be the outstanding characteristic of her literary works. Speaking of Serao's early years in Naples, Danchev admires her assiduousness and creativity as a journalist and political commentator. He emphasizes her "Southern identity", and stereotypically associates it with sensuality and spontaneity.[11] The Bulgarian critic presents Serao as an emancipated woman who can cope successfully with all of life's challenges.

10 The Bulgarian translator of the article misspelled the original name of the Italian critic Ugo Ojetti to "Ugo Odetti".

11 Already in the first half of the nineteenth century with the first printed textbooks on geography, Bulgarians inherit the stereotypes about northern and southern Italian identity:

The conclusion of Danchev's article marks just one of the similarities between his review and that of Ugo Ojetti. At times, Danchev's text includes direct quotations from Ojetti. Clearly, the Bulgarian critic had read and compiled previous foreign reviews of Serao's works and had barely researched her local reception. Danchev mentions several volumes of Serao's original works in a footnote, without pointing out that some of them had already been translated into Bulgarian. In addition, he does not mention any parallels with Bulgarian literature, nor does he include any references to Bulgarian women writers. Certainly, he was unlikely to have been aware of the breadth of Serao's reception up to that moment since it was dispersed in many journals across the country. Yet, he would have been aware of the difficulty in delineating a text's full reception and distinguishing its level of adaptation and motivation in every case, from the twenty-nine translations of Serao's works into Bulgarian. An even more difficult task would be to trace the appreciation of the writer's works on the part of women readers and the various members of the Bulgarian literary scene in the long nineteenth century. Despite all the uncertainties that entanglements of literary histories might suggest, we can claim with certainty that in the period from 1890 to 1918 Serao *did* enjoy a significant presence in Bulgarian periodicals; her prose was part of a whole stream of inspiration for local writers to explore their female characters' subjectivities, and the origins of social inequalities, in their own prose works.

Nadezhda ALEXANDROVA
Sofia University 'St. Kliment Ohridski'

Boyka ILIEVA
South-Western University 'Neofit Rilski', Blagoevgrad

northern Italians are polite and mild in temper, whereas southerners are passionate. In a similar vein, Bulgarians learn at school that Naples is the most beautiful city in Italy, perfectly situated, but having many poor people and beggars (see Radulov, 1843; Petkov, 1868; Andreev, 1851).

## MATILDE SERAO'S FICTION TRANSLATED INTO BULGARIAN

Serao Matilde, 1891, "Na samin" ["Salvazione"], *Iskra*, 3, trans. Vasil Varbev, pp. 155, 158-160.
Serao Matilde, 1892, "Chuden san" ["Sogno di una notte d'estate], *Trud*, 1, trans. Georgi Tzanev, pp. 3-36.
Serao Matilde, 1892-1893, "Iz uchilishtnite tipove" ["Alla scuola"], *Iskra*, 2, trans. A.P.N., pp. 63-67.
Serao Matilde, 1892-1893, "Tri pisma" ["Falso in scrittura"], *Iskra*, 3, trans. T.D.N., pp. 133-135.
Serao Matilde, 1893-1895, "Nasame" ["Salvazione], *Knizhitsi za prochit*, 3, trans. D-ev, pp. 23-26.
Serao Matilde, 1895 (attributed to Serao but authored by Neera), "Noshtnata peperudka" ["La falena"], *Balgarska sbirka*, trans. Iliya Bobchev, pp. 84-86.
Serao Matilde, 1896, "Negoden!" [original not identified], *Misal*, 2, trans. Kiril Hristov, pp. 126-130.
Serao Matilde, 1898, "Nesaglasie" ["Dissidio"], *Balgarka*, 4-6, trans. unknown, pp. 71-77.
Serao Matilde, 1898, "Chest" ["Novella d'amore"], *Balgarka*, 7-9, trans. V.K. Vladev, pp. 118-127.
Serao Matilde, 1898-1899, "V teatara" ["Apparenze"], *Moda i domakinstvo*, 6, trans. Kiril Hristov, pp. 5-6.
Serao Matilde, 1898-1899, "Pred praga na zhivota" ["Scuola normale femminile"], *Moda i domakinstvo*, 8-9, trans. Kiril Hristov, pp. 7-9; 10-11, pp. 9-12; 12, pp. 6-7; 13, pp. 6-7.
Serao Matilde, 1898-1899, "Sebeotrichanie" ["Salvazione"], *Moda i domakinstvo*, 17-18, trans. unknown, pp. 12-13.
Serao Matilde, 1898-1899, "Raznoglasie" ["Dissidio"], *Moda i domakinstvo*, 24, trans. A., p. 6-7.
Serao Matilde, 1900, "Pokayala se" ["Salvazione"], *Zhenski glas,* 23-24, trans. St. D-va, pp. 13-16.
Serao Matilde, 1902-1903, "Izkuplenie" ["Salvazione"], *Razvitie*, 2, trans. Stoyan Koledarov, pp. 23-25.
Serao Matilde, 1904-1906, "Tri pisma" ["Falso in scrittura"], *Moda i domakinstvo*, 18, trans. V. Kirova, pp. 1-2.
Serao Matilde, 1904-1906, "Samoubietsat" ["Un suicidio"], *Moda i domakinstvo*, 19, trans. K. Dyankov, pp. 1-2.

Serao Matilde, 1905, "Chakane" ["L'attesa"], *Biseri iz chuzhdite literaturi*, 2 vols, trans. St. Koledarov, ed. Stoyan Atanasov, vol. 1, pp. 286-299.
Serao Matilde, 1905, "Tri pisma" ["Falso in scrittura"], *Malak dnevnik*, 4, trans. St. Georgiev, December, pp. 3-4.
Serao Matilde, 1906, "Tayna" ["Il segreto (Cariclea)"], *Ilyustratsia svetlina*, 6, trans. N.D. Stoilov, pp. 18-19.
Serao Matilde, 1906-1907, "Ili Dzhovanino ili smart" ["O Giovannino o la morte!"], *Biblioteka*, 7-8, trans. Konstantin Mutafov, pp. 1-40.
Serao Matilde, 1907, "Nepoznatiya" ["Sconosciuto"], *Biseri iz chuzhdite literaturi*, 2 vols, trans. unknown, ed. Stoyan Atanasov, vol. 2, pp. 35-39.
Serao Matilde, 1908, "Tri pisma" ["Falso in scrittura"], *Izbrani razkazi*, trans. unknown, no page.
Serao Matilde, 1909, "Parva lyubov" ["Viottole"], *Ilyustratsia svetlina*, 6, trans. G.T. CH., pp. 21-23.
Serao Matilde, 1911, "Avgustovska nosht" ["Notte di agosto"], *Mir*, 25, trans. N.D. Yordanov, pp. 3-4.
Serao Matilde, 1912, "Uchilishtni tipove" ["Alla scuola"], *Chetivo za svobodnoto vreme*, 9, trans. Stoyan Koledarov, pp. 8-12.
Serao Matilde, 1913-1914, "Napusnata" ["L'abbandonata"], *Listopad*, 29, trans. Ivan Dokumov, pp. 212-213.
Serao Matilde, 1917-1918, "Tsvetarkata" ["Una fioraia"], *Literaturno eho*, 4, trans. unknown, pp. 13-14; 5, pp. 14-16.
Serao Matilde, 1917-1918, "Silueti" ["Profili"], *Literaturno eho*, 19, trans. M.V., pp. 11-13.
Serao Matilde, 1924-1926, "Gradat na lyubovta" ["La città dell'amore"], *Listopad*, 5-6, trans. Hristo Brazitzov, pp. 141-145.

| ORIGINAL TITLE / COLLECTION / YEAR OF PUBLICATION | TITLE IN BULGARIAN – TRANSLITERATED TITLE/ YEAR OF PUBLICATION | LANGUAGE FROM WHICH THE WORK IS TRANSLATED | TRANSLATOR | JOURNAL / NEWSPAPER / COLLECTION | CITY OF PUBLICATION / CHIEF EDITOR |
|---|---|---|---|---|---|
| "Salvazione"/ Piccole anime/ 1883 | На самин – "Na samin"/ 1891 | Not mentioned | Varbev | Сп. Искра, Iskra | Shumen, ed. V. Yordanov |
| | Насаме – "Nasame"/ 1893-1895 | Not mentioned | D-ev | Сп. Книжици за прочит, Knizhitsi za prochit | Thessaloniki, ed. K.G. Samardjiev |
| | Себеотричание – "Sebeotrichanie"/ 1898-1899 | Not mentioned | Unknown | Сп. Мода и домакинство, Moda i domakinstvo | Sofia, ed. Elena Usheva |
| | Покаяла се – "Pokayala se"/ 1900 | From Serbian | St.D-va | Сп. Женски глас Zhenski glas | Sofia, ed. Yulia Malinova |
| | Изкупление – "Izkuplenie"/ 1902-03 | Not mentioned (perhaps French) | Stoyan N. Koledarov | Сп. Развитие Razvitie | Vratza, ed. Georgitza Georgieva |
| "Falso in scrittura"/ Fior di passione/ 1888 | Три писма – "Tri pisma"/ 1892 | Not mentioned | T.D.N. | Сп. Искра Iskra | Shumen, ed. V. Yordanov |
| | Три писма – "Tri pisma"/ 1905-06 | Not mentioned (perhaps French) | St. Georgriev | В. Малък дневник Malak dnevnik | Sofia, ed. Georgi Nikolov |
| | Три писма – "Tri pisma"/ 1904/06 | Not mentioned (perhaps Polish) | V.Kirova | Сп. Мода и домакинство Moda i domakinstvo | Sofia, ed. Elena Usheva |
| | Три писма – "Tri pisma"/ 1908 | Not mentioned | Unknown | Сб. "Избрани разкази" Izbrani razkazi | Sofia |

| | | | | | |
|---|---|---|---|---|---|
| "Alla scuola"/ Piccole anime/ 1883 | Из училищните типове – "Iz uchilishtnite tipove" /1892-1893 | Not mentioned | A.P.N. | Сп. Искра, Iskra | Shumen, ed. V. Yordanov |
| | Училищни типове – "Uchilistni tipove" /1912 | Not mentioned (perhaps French) | Stoyan N. Koledarov | Сп. **Четиво за свободното време** Chetivo za svobodnoto vreme supplement to Savremenno domakinstvo | Sofia, eds. Ruska knizharnitza et al |
| "Dissidio"/ L`infedele/ 1897 | Несъгласие – "Nesaglasie"/ 1898 | From French | Unknown | Сп. Българка, Balgarka | Tchirpan, eds Panayot and Alice Karshovski |
| | Разногласие – "Raznoglasie"/ 1898-1899 | Not mentioned | A. | Сп. Мода и домакинство Moda i domakinstvo | Sofia, ed. Elena Usheva |
| "Novella d`amore"/ Fior di passione, 1888 | Чест – "Chest"/ 1898 | From French | V.K. Vladev | Сп. Българка, Balgarka | Tchirpan, Panayot and Alice Karshovski |
| "Apparenze"/ Dal vero/ 1879 | В театъра – "V teatara"/ 1898-1899 | From Italian | K. (Kiril Hristov) | Сп. Мода и домакинство Moda i domakinstvo | Sofia, ed. Elena Usheva |
| "Scuola normale femminile"/ Il romanzo della fanciulla/ 1886 | **Пред прага на живота** – "Pred praga na zhivota"/1898-1899 | From Italian | K. (Kiril Hristov) | Сп. Мода и домакинство Moda i domakinstvo | Sofia, ed. Elena Usheva |
| "Un suicidio"/ Gli amanti/ 1894 | Самоубиецът – "Samoubietzat"/ 1904-1906 | Not mentioned (perhaps French) | K. Dyankov | Сп. Мода и домакинство Moda i domakinstvo | Sofia, ed. Elena Usheva |

| | | | | | |
|---|---|---|---|---|---|
| "L'attesa"/<br>L'infedele/ 1897 | Чакане – "Chakane"/<br>1905 | Not mentioned<br>(perhaps French) | Stoyan<br>Koledarov | Сб. "Бисери из чуждите литератури", кн.1<br>Collection "Biseri iz chuzhdite literaturi", vol.1 | Sofia, ed. St.<br>Atanasov |
| "Il segreto<br>(Cariclea)" /<br>Gli amanti/ 1894 | Тайна – "Tayna"/<br>1906 | Not mentioned | N. D. Stoilov | Сп. Илюстрация Светлина<br>Ilyustratsia Svetlina | Sofia, ed. Yordan<br>Mihaylov |
| O Giovannino, o<br>la morte/ 1889 | Или Джованино, или смърт – "Ili Giovanino, ili smart"/1906-1907 | From Italian | Konstantin<br>Mutafov | Сп. Библиотека<br>Biblioteka | Plovdiv, ed. Pavel<br>Genadiev |
| "Sconosciuto" /<br>Fior di passione/<br>1888 | Непознатия –<br>"Nepoznatiya"/<br>1907 | Not mentioned | Unknown | Сб. "Бисери из чуждите литератури", кн.2<br>Collection "Biseri iz chuzhdite literaturi", vol.2 | Sofia, ed. St.<br>Atanasov |
| "Viottole" /<br>Pagina azzurra/<br>1883 | Първа любов – "Parva lyubov"/<br>1909 | Not mentioned | G. T. CH. | Сп. Илюстрация Светлина<br>Ilyustratsia Svetlina | Sofia, ed. Yordan<br>Mihaylov |
| "Notte di<br>agosto"/<br>Dal vero/ 1879 | Августовска нощ –<br>"Avgustovska nosht"/<br>1911 | Not mentioned | N. D. Yordanov | В. "Мир"<br>Mir | Sofia, ed. M.<br>Madzharov |
| "L'Abbandonata"/<br>Il Pellegrino<br>appassionato/<br>1911 | Напуснатата –<br>"Napusnatata"/<br>1913-1914 | From Italian | Ivan Dokumov | Сп. Листопад<br>Listopad | Sofia, ed. Dimitar<br>Babev |
| "Una fioraia"/<br>Piccole anime/<br>1883 | Цветарката – "Tzvetarkata"/<br>1917-1918 | Not mentioned | Not mentioned | Сп. Литературно ехо<br>Literaturno eho | Sofia, ed. Vladimir<br>Necev Samin et al |

| | | | | | |
|---|---|---|---|---|---|
| "Profili"/ Piccole anime/ 1883 | Силуети – "Silueti"/ 1917-18 | Not mentioned | M.V. | Сп. Литературно ехо Literaturno eho | Sofia, ed. Vladimir Nedev Samin et al |
| "La città dell'amore"/ Leggende Napoletane/ 1891 | Градът на любовта – "Gradat na lubovta"/ 1924-1925 | Not mentioned (perhaps French) | Hr.B. (Hristo Brazitzov) | Сп. Листопад Listopad | Sofia, ed. Dimitar Babev |
| "Sogno di una notte d'estate"/ Le amanti/ 1890 | Чуден сън – "Chuden san"/ 1892 | From Russian | G.Tz.G. (Georgi Tzanev) | Сп. Труд Trud | Veliko Tarnovo, ed. Tzani Ginchev et al |
| Not identified | Негоден! – "Negoden!"/ 1896 | From Italian | Kiril Hristov | Сп. Мисъл Misal | Sofia, ed. Krastyo Krastev |

FIG. 1 – Serao's works translated into Bulgarian.

# THE CIRCULATION AND CRITICAL RECEPTION OF MATILDE SERAO'S WRITINGS IN RUSSIA

The end of the nineteenth century and the beginning of the twentieth century evidenced Russia's continued interest in Italy, a country that for many Russian poets and artists represented the *beau idéal* and a place of inspiration.[1] As a result of the positive relationship between the Russian intelligentsia and Italian intellectuals at this time, many magazines focussed on Italy: one of the leading literary-political journals, *Severny Vestnik* (1885-1898), had a special section "Pisma iz Italii" ["Letters from Italy"]. Some Italian reviewers even wrote for Russian periodicals. For example, in the periodical *Vesy* (1904-1909), there are reviews by Giovanni Papini, who between 1904 and 1906 contributed pieces on Giovanni Pascoli, Giosuè Carducci, Gabriele D'Annunzio, Filippo Tommaso Marinetti, Ada Negri, and Francesco Chiesa, in a section which was also entitled "Pisma iz Italii". In one of Papini's "letters", dated 1904, Serao is also mentioned alongside D'Annunzio and Fogazzaro (Papini, 1904, p. 23).

One of the aims of this chapter is to explore Serao's popularity in Russia and the reception of her works, which in 1885 began to appear in Russian translation. Matilde Serao was published in journals, newspapers, separate volumes, and anthologies which also featured other authors. This article traces the circulation of the Russian translations of her work, identifying some of the key decisions made by publishers when selecting which works to translate from her considerable output. My focus will be on those translated works and on the period 1900 to

1 Much research explores the Russian-Italian relationship of that time analysing Italian motifs in works by Alexander Blok, Nikolay Gumilev, Anna Akhmatova, Osip Mandelshtam, Marina Zvetaeva, Vyacheslav Ivanov, Maksim Gorkiy, Mikhail Vrubel, Konstantin Bogaevsky, and Mstislav Dobuzhinsky, to mention just a few. See Lo Gatto, 1971; Strada, 1995.

1911, the most prolific timeframe for her Russian publications. Secondly, I will discuss Serao's critical reception, including an interview with E.V. Fuks,[2] conducted in Paris in 1900 and published in 1907, and one critical review written by Vladimir Frice in 1911. The former sheds new light on Serao's views on feminism; the latter offers insights on the reduced number of translations of Serao's works after 1911 as a result of the publishers' increased interest in texts about children rather than the salon and aristocratic women's lives.

## TRANSLATIONS AND READER-RECEPTION

The first Russian translation of a text by Serao dates back to 1885 with the publication of her short story "V zhenskoy shkole" ["Scuola normale femminile"][3] in one of the most popular journals of the time, *Russkaya Mysl*.[4] A brief introduction by an unknown author precedes this first publication by the Neapolitan writer in Russia. Here, Serao is placed alongside other Italian writers such as Anton Giulio Barrili, Giovanni Verga, Salvatore Farina and Vittorio Bersezio. According to this article, Serao takes the portrayal of women in the novel to a new level, at a time when they are frequently not represented in sufficient detail by male writers. The author notes Serao's ability to provide multifaceted portrayals of women – whether they are from high society or

2 No information is available about E.V. Fuks. I was unable to identify the full name of this female journalist.

3 For each Russian translation I provide the transliterated title from Cyrillic, since several translations under different titles are available. All translations into English are my own unless otherwise indicated.

4 The political and literary journal *Russkaya Mysl* was published in Russia between 1880 and 1918, when it was closed due to problems with censorship. With a focus on a wide range of social, religious, and cultural topics and because of its eclectic nature, *Russkaya Mysl* had an extensive section on literature and literary criticism and published texts by Nikolay Leskov, Maksim Gorky, Anton Chekhov, and Ivan Bunin, to mention just a few. The number of subscribers in some years reached 14,000 and it increased drastically in 1885, as another leading democratic journal *Otechestvennye Zapiski* was shut and its members joined *Russkaya Mysl*. From 1918, the journal was published abroad, and the last issue came out in 1927 in Paris. Interestingly, it has been revived in the twenty-first century and is now published in London.

the working-classes – as well as her focus on the different roles of women in society, in family life and in marriage. Additionally, the author states that: "Matilde Serao is not one-dimensional, specializing only in female issues, but she also depicts male characters with equal truth and competence" (Serao, 1885, p. 161).[5] Regarding her style, the author remarks that Serao is able, with two or three pen-strokes, to convey a detailed picture "without false sensibility", "obdurate naturalistic patterns", or "intricate composition" (*ibid.*).[6]

After this first publication of Serao's work, two novels appeared in Russian translation, not in periodicals, but as separate volumes: *Roman devushki* [*Il romanzo della fanciulla*], published in 1887 (very close to its Italian publication date of 1886), and *Zhizn i priklyucheniya Rikorda Ioanna* [*Vita e avventure di Riccardo Joanna*], published in 1888, and again differing by only one year from the original Italian publication date. We know from the reviews written in 1886 by Semyon Nadson[7] that Serao's 1883 novel *Fantazia* [*Fantasia*] was published in several issues of another widely read journal, *Severnyi Vestnik* during the same period. Reviewing the selection of translated works published in one of the issues of the journal, Nadson observes that the choice could not be better because it includes the beginning of the novel *Fantasia*. He does not write much about the translation of this novel but promises to return to the topic later. He goes on to describe Serao as "a young writer to whom it is worth paying attention [whose novel *Fantasia*] is considered her best work" (Nadson, 1887, p. 141).[8] Nadson writes that Serao is not well known to Russian readers due to the availability of only two previous translations of her work, in *Russkaya Mysl* and in the

5 "Матильде Серао не односторонняя специалистка по женскому вопросу, и с одинаковой правдивостью и умением рисует она и мужские характеры".

6 "Но она столько же чужда ложной чувствительности, как и чёрствых натуралистических приёмов; не ищет она также хитросплетениях замыслов."

7 Semyon Nadson (1862-1887) was a poet and literary critic. In 1882, he published "Three Poems" in *Otechestvennye Zapiski*. After his debut, influential journals and newspapers, such as *Delo*, *Ustoi*, and *Russkaya Mysl*, started to publish his writings. He collaborated with *Otechestvennye Zapiski* (1883-1884), and the newspaper *Zarya* (1886). From 1883, he was confined to his bed with tuberculosis and died in Yalta in 1887. Between 1885 and 1917, his poetry collection was reprinted twenty-nine times. While in Yalta, he received an important literary award, the Pushkin Prize, from the Russian Academy of Science.

8 "Между тем молодая писательница очень стоит внимания. Роман Фантазия считается лучшим её произведением".

liberal Russian daily newspaper *Russkiye Vedomosti*. Thus, to facilitate a better introduction for Russian readers to such a "talented and refined" writer (*ibid.*),[9] he provides his own translation of one of her short stories, "V avgustovskuyu noch" ["Notte di agosto"], taking the original version from *Pagina azzurra,* a Milanese literary journal where it had first been published in 1883.

The year 1890 was quite a prolific one for Russian translations of Serao's works, as it saw at least four publications, mostly in periodicals. First, two novellas, "Szena" ["Scena"] and "Ideal" ["Ideale"], were published in *Russkiye Vedomosti* in March 1890, followed by the novella *Slu-u-shay!* [*All'erta, sentinella!*] in August, in five issues of the same newspaper. November and December of the same year saw the publication in *Severnyi Vestnik* of another of Serao's novels, *Proschay lyubov* [*Addio, amore!*], while a further short story, "Chydnyi son" ["Sogno di una notte d'estate"], was included in the anthology *Inostrannye Belletristy* [*Foreign Fiction Writers*], published in Moscow. However, the most interesting example concerns the short story "Naedine" ["Salvazione"],[10] which was also published in December 1890 by *Russkaya Mysl*.

There is evidence that Leo Tolstoy saw and read the Russian translation of "Salvazione". On 31 December 1890, Vladimir Chertkov, head of the publishing house Posrednik, sent Tolstoy two short stories, one of which was the translation of Serao's "Salvazione", and asked him for his opinion on these. On 8 January 1891, Maria Tolstaya, Tolstoy's daughter, answered on his behalf saying that he found the text "too refined" (Tolstoy, 1937, pp. 66-67).[11]

However, "Salvazione" was published by Chertkov in 1893,[12] after he had left the publishing house owing to a disagreement over censorship; the collection in which it appeared was one of the last projects he undertook before leaving. The collection, which has the homonymous title *Naedine* for the Russian translation of Serao's novella "Salvazione" also includes works by Alphonse Daudet, Bjørnstjerne Bjørnson, Frank

9 "Симпатичное и изящное дарование".

10 Its Russian title Наедине literally means "tête-a-tête".

11 "Об этих рассказах М.Л. Толстая писала Черткову 8 января 1891 года: «Папа поручил мне написать вам, что он прочел оба рассказа, которые вы прислали, и ни тот, ни другой ему не нравятся. «Наедине» слишком утонченно, а «Жаворонковы» грубо".

12 The cover states 1894.

Harris, Henry Longfellow, Guy de Maupassant, Oscar Wilde, Paul Margueritte, François Cappée, Jean Richepin, Enrico Castelnuovo, and Paul Bourget. Interestingly, whereas for all the above authors the editor included only one work, for Serao, the editor chose two, "Scena" and "Duetto di passione". In addition, Serao is the only female writer in this collection.

Subsequently, the novel *Salvazione* was published in 1893 as a book; three years after its publication in periodicals, Serao's novel *Addio, amore!* was published as a separate volume in Moscow in 1894, following its publication in a Russian newspaper in 1890. *Il paese di Cuccagna* was published in Saint Petersburg in 1897, while another novel, *Cuore infermo* [*Bolnoye serdze*], was published in 1899. The same year also marked the publication of *Beregis chasovoy* [*All'erta, sentinella!*], this time in Moscow, as well as the short stories "Dzhovannino ili smert" ["O Giovannino o la morte"] and "Kanituchchya" ["Canituccia"], all previously published in 1890. These three works enjoyed a vast circulation in Russia and were published repeatedly. I will discuss this further below in the case study of multiple translations of *All'erta, sentinella!*.

In 1900, at least four publications of Serao's works had circulated, including the short story "Bankovskiy krah" ["Trenta per cento"] as a supplement to the journal *Zhenskoe Delo* and, in the anthology entitled *Italianskye rasskazy* [*Russian Short Stories*], which also contained works by Luigi Capuana, we find, the short stories "Ozhidanie" ["Aspettando"], "Razlad" ["Dissidio"], and "Zigzagi" ["Zig-zag"]. However, it was the two volumes of Serao's short stories entitled *Stories* [*Rasskazy*], which ten years later became the third volume of a five-volume collection, that had the widest circulation. The two volumes of *Rasskazy* include Serao's texts from various collections. For example, the first volume contains "Ili Dzhovannino ili smert" ["O Giovannino o la morte"] and "Lotereynyi bilet" ["Terno secco"] from her *Racconti napoletani*, and "Na kazyonnom telegrafe" ["Telegrafi dello stato"] from *Il romanzo della fanciulla*. The second volume opens with "V zhenskoy uchitelskoy seminarii" ["Scuola normale femminile"] from the same *Romanzo*, but also includes novellas from *Fior di passione,* such as "Povest lyubvi" ["Novella d'amore"], as well as "Szena" ["Scena"] and "Ideal" ["Ideale"], which had both appeared previously in the press in 1890. "O Giovannino o la morte" was published again in 1902, 1903 and 1904 together with the novel *Blondinochka* [*La biondina*] by Marco Praga. It was then not republished until 1960, in a collected volume of Italian novellas. This noticeable gap in the dates of publication was due to the fact that after the revolution and her success in the early twentieth century, Serao's texts almost completely disappeared from circulation.

The sheer volume of translations of Serao's works circulating in Russia at this time was significant, and it is impossible to cover it within the constraints of one essay. Therefore, I will focus on a few interesting aspects identified from my research conducted in the Russian archives.

## A CASE STUDY: THE RUSSIAN TRANSLATIONS OF *ALL'ERTA, SENTINELLA!*

One interesting example of Serao's publication in Russia, owing to its numerous translations between 1890 and 1911, is offered by *All'erta, sentinella!*. The different translations reflected a desire to adapt this story for different readerships. The first translation appeared in 1890 in the newspaper *Russkie Vedomosti*, one year after its publication in Italy. The translator, Ernest Karlovich Vatson, shortened the title to one word, *Slu-u-shai!*, but retained the original imperative and exclamation mark: *Slu-u-shai!* ["Li-i-sten!"], through creative use of onomatopoeia and syllable-splitting, gives the impression of a military command.

The same work was published nine years later in 1899, as a book by an unidentified publisher in Moscow and by Slepzova in Saint Petersburg. Both versions have a two-word title: *Beregis' chasovoy* and *Vozle rebyonka*. The former, closer to Serao's original, literally means "Beware sentinel", while the latter could be translated from Russian as "Near to a child". Slepzova's *Near to a Child* was widely circulated in Russia, in the children's literature series "Knizhka za knizhkoy" ["Book by Book"] and was re-printed in 1901, 1904 and 1912. The significance of this children's series in Russia possibly explains the popularity of *Near to a Child* at this time. To promote circulation, each volume in the series provided on the inside flyleaf the full list of other titles in the series and this influenced two later publications of this text. For example, on the inside flyleaves of writings by Gogol' in 1902 and Vladimir Nemirovich-Danchenko in 1901, 1910 and 1912, we find the complete list of books in the series, with Serao's *Near to a Child* appearing as number 88. Thus, translations of Serao's works benefitted from further circulation in Russia through being advertised on the flyleaves of volumes by other authors in this series.

The title *Vozle rebyonka* [*Near to a Child*] of course shifts the focus of this story to the child. A simple explanation for this is that this series primarily targeted young readers and, furthermore, *Near to a Child* appeared in multiple recommended reading lists for children. For example, in the reading list recommended for children aged between seven and sixteen, we read a synopsis of the text that also includes the reason for suggesting this book to children: "The story is written in a very warm and appealing manner and will inspire children to be compassionate towards poor convicts" (Annenskaya *et al.*, 1908, p. 225).[13]

Almost at the same time that this popular version of *Near to a Child* was published, two other publishers decided to translate *All'erta, sentinella!*, the story of a "poor prisoner" (*ibid.*). First, the story with yet another title, *Ljubov' ubijcy* [*Love of a Murderer*], had at least two publications: in 1901 and again in 1904. Second, *All'erta, sentinella!* may have been published in 1900 under the title *Ryzhak* [*The Red-Haired One*]. Both publications acknowledge the circulation of other translations. In *Ljubov' ubijcy* we read on the cover of the book that "the text has been already translated as *Near to a Child*" (Serao, 1901b),[14] while *The Red-Haired One* acknowledges both translations. Since the version entitled *The Red-Haired One* published in 1900 references the translations of both *Near to a Child* and *Love of a Murderer*, it follows that *The Red-Haired One* was published after the other two translations. *Love of a Murderer* may therefore have appeared in 1900, rather than in 1901, as stated on the cover.

The publisher Posrednik produced works by Serao that were advertised on the cover of the book as material "for intelligent readers" (*ibid.*)[15] and the text's title *Love of a Murderer* included elements geared towards

13 "Рассказ написан очень тепло, производит впечатление и заронит в детях гуманное чувство к несчастным каторжникам".

14 "Пер. также под загл.: Возле ребенка".

15 "для умных читателей".

attracting the target market, namely the psychological element of love and the element of crime. The book did not address a young readership, but rather was geared towards an adult public, and would immediately attract their attention rather than suggesting any educational purpose, unlike the case of the children's series.

It is interesting that the third version in circulation at the time (*The Red-Haired One*) was published neither in Saint Petersburg nor in Moscow, but in Kharkiv, Ukraine, where the aim of publishers was to spread literacy to the masses. Thus, the text is also considered to be formative and educational. Indeed, the children's version, *Near to a Child*, includes a foreword providing historical context about the unification of Italy.

In 1899, the same year as the publication of *Near to a Child*, another Serao short story entitled "Canituccia" appeared.[16] "Canituccia", popular in Russia even after the revolution, attests to the targeting of a young readership for Serao's work, in a manner similar to *Near to a Child*. "Canituccia" was also published after the revolution in 1923 in another anthology, edited by Vladimir A. Popov and entitled *Svinopaska Kanituchchiya*, which included stories about young girls as part of the series "Young working girls from different countries and nations".[17] Consequently, "Canituccia" would no longer have been an appropriate title, because the focus of the anthology had shifted to the activities of the girls in the stories. The anthology title *Svinopaska Kanituchchiya* made specific reference to the job title of the girls: its literal translation is *Swineherd Canituccia*.

Finally, another translation of *All'erta, sentinella!* was included in the five-volume collection of Serao's writings produced in 1911. As mentioned earlier, Alexandra Veselovskaya translated several of Serao's short stories in two books. Her translation of *All'erta, sentinella!* also appeared in volume three in 1911, with the title *Slushay chasovoy!* [*Listen Sentinel!*].

16 This story is about a little orphan girl who had a close relationship with a piglet, considering him a friend, was published with other similar texts featuring animals, translated from French, English and Italian. One author only represented English and French literature respectively, while both Serao and Verga represented Italian literature.

17 The volume has the subtitle "Маленькие труженицы разных стран и народов" ["Young Female Workers from Different Countries and People"] and was published in the homonymous series.

## CRITICAL RECEPTION: SERAO AND DELEDDA

In 1911, the well-known critic and Soviet Academy fellow Vladimir Frice (1870-1929), who worked in the world literature department of Moscow University at that time,[18] wrote an article about Serao and Grazia Deledda (Frice, 1911). The article was published in the journal *Novyj Zhurnal Dlya Vseh*, whose title suggested a wide potential readership. Summarizing and critiquing the novels *Addio, amore!* and *Dopo il perdono* by Serao and *L'ombra del passato* and *Cenere* by Deledda, Frice compares the literary styles and characterisation employed by both authors, analysing their differences and similarities. He states that only one of Deledda's novels, *L'ombra del passato*, was available in Russia at the time of his review. This is noteworthy with regard to the circulation of Italian literature in Russia, because Serao was by then already an acclaimed author there and, indeed, 1910-1911 may be considered the peak period for Russian translations of her work. Her novel *Dopo il perdono,* published in Moscow by Mamontov, was translated in 1910 by A. M-va,[19] and 1910-1911, as we saw earlier, saw a five-volume edition and the two-volume collection of short stories from *Fior di passione* and *Addio, amore!*, both published by Moscow's Athenaeum.

The story of the Russian publication of the novel *Addio, amore!* is also interesting because the date of its appearance in the journal *Severny Vestnik* with a translation by Ekaterina P. Letkova, that is, 1890, almost coincides with its publication in Italy. In 1894, it was published in book form and in 1911 it became the second of the five-volume edition of Serao's writings, translated by Varvara A. Koshevich and published again

18 Vladimir Maksimovich Frice (1870-1929) was a Soviet Academy fellow who had a Marxist approach to literature. His public talks on literature and arts gathered large audiences. Among his books were the publications: *Ocherki po istorii zapadnoevropejskoj literatury* [*Essays on Western European Literature*, 1908]; *Zapadno-evropejskaja literatura XX veka* [*Western European Literature of the 20th Century*, 1926]; *Sociologija iskusstva* [*Sociology of the Art*, 1927]; *Zametki o sovremennoj literature* [*Notes about Modern Literature*, 1928].

19 Female translators often remained anonymous or used initials instead of their names. However, surnames ending in -va in Russian clearly indicate the feminine gender.

by Moscow's Athenaeum.[20] The last available print of the novel *Addio, amore!* was published twenty-nine years ago, in 1992, along with the novel *Castigo*, by the Moscow publisher Zeus in the series "Lyubovnyi roman: Bestseller bylyh vremyon" ["Romantic Novels: Bestsellers of Times Past"].[21]

In his review, Frice compares the environments depicted by Serao and Deledda in their novels. He states that both writers are known outside Italy and are deeply rooted in their respective regional traditions. However, although this adherence to regional tradition is common to both, he argues that Serao's work has a more "cosmopolitan" feel (Frice, 1911, p. 95).[22] It is clear that Frice prefers the "primitive" characters and environment of Deledda's novels to the opulent interiors seen in Serao's work. He contrasts the "huts of *muzhiki* and shepherds; blocks of houses inhabited by people of a 'former' time, logging where the axe of the lumberjack resounds and the black figures of coalminers dart back and forth" (*ibid.*, pp. 96-97)[23] with "the world exclusively for nobles" found in Serao's work, and lists the various *milieux* she describes: "ancient palazzos, refurbished with ducal splendour, in glorious villas, in a stadium for horse racing, overcrowded with fashionable carriages, in a theatre, during the premiere of an opera, where diamonds sparkle and ladies' bare shoulders glisten, in first-class hotels affordable only to the rich" (*ibid.*, p. 96).[24]

---

20 Varvara Aleksandrovna Koshevich was a noblewoman who translated texts mainly from English and German, but also from Italian, French and Spanish. She collaborated with many journals. In addition, an interesting link to Vladimir Frice is that she translated the novel *La barraca* (*Prokljatyj hutor*) by Vicente Blasco Ibáñez in 1926 for his collected works, while Frice wrote the introduction for this volume.

21 Regarding recent publications, it is worth mentioning that the Società Dante Alighieri, in order to mark the 150th anniversary of Serao's birth in 2006, published two novels, namely *La ballerina* and her most renowned novel, *Fantasia*. This *Fantasia* is a collective translation by several different translators.

22 "В романах Гр. Деледда, впрочем, более местного колорита, тогда как Серао более космополитична, как космополитичнее описываемая ею среда".

23 "Перед нами хаты мужиков и пастухов-скотоводов; кварталы, населённые ‹бывшими› людьми, рубка леса, где раздается топор дровосека и мелькают чёрные фигуры угольщиков; площади маленьких городов, где движется почти первобытная толпа, объятая разнузданным весельем карнавала".

24 "Матильда Серао знает и воспроизводит исключительно великосветский мир (и близкое к родовой знати часть крупной римской буржуазии). В её романах действие происходит, обыкновенно, в старинных палаццо, обставленных с княжеской роскошью, в восхитительных виллах, на ипподроме, запруженном модными колясками, в театре, в день первого представления оперы, где сверкают

Turning his attention to the characters depicted by the two writers, Frice notes that both novelists are pessimists who describe "catastrophes rather than victories" with their "negative point of view, full of sadness, perplexity and melancholy" (*ibid.*, pp. 97-98).[25] One controversial criticism made by Frice concerns the gender of the novelists' heroes. He reproaches Serao for inadequate development of her male characters, and also references a complete absence of children in her works. Frice attributes this supposed lack of child characters to his belief that in aristocratic families, of the type depicted by Serao, a child is seen only as a means of continuing the family line, and that to have many children is *mauvais ton* (*ibid.*, p. 97). However, it is notable that Serao was popular in Russia not only for her stories about high society, but also because in *All'erta, sentinella!,* she wrote about a man and about his feelings for a child. Given the popularity of *All'erta, sentinella!*, it is strange that Frice was either unaware of or chose to ignore this work, especially since it featured in many anthologies for children.

Frice continues to point to the depiction of the opulent world of high society in Serao's writing, stating that the role of men in a society where women are objects of pleasure and luxury is merely to provide the perfect ground for the cult of love:

> Genteel men in tailcoats, with a flower in their buttonhole and beautiful women with svelte bodies in lavish gowns appear in Serao's novels – a world of indolent parasites, passing the time between flirting and gossip, infidelities and reconciliations, children of the Cockaigne, the land of dalliance and pleasure, and *paese di cuccagna* is the title of one of Serao's novels. Women, perceived to be the most precious objects of luxury and pleasure, play a major role in high society as well as in the novels of the Neapolitan writer; by contrast, men, who are supposed to envelop women with luxury, serve only as a trigger for the female psyche (*ibid.*).[26]

---

бриллианты и обнаженные женские плечи, в первоклассных отелях, доступных только богачам".

25 "Как ни разнятся обе писательницы по своим симпатиям и кругозору, в одном они сходится. Обе они – пессимистки. [...] В обоих этих царствах, как ни мало похожи они друг на друга, может сложиться лишь отрицательный взгляд, полной печали, растерянности и уныния. Обе писательницы предпочитают рисовать не победы, а катастрофы".

26 "В романах Серао выступают элегантные мужчины с корректными манерами, во фраках и с цветком в петлице, красавицы-дамы с холеным телом и в роскошных туалетах – мир праздных паразитов, разделяющих время между флиртом и

In Deledda's works, however, Frice notes that men are given prominence, appearing as protagonists. He also welcomes Deledda's inclusion of child characters: "Those bright, energetic and sad children make the Sardinian writer's work distinctly soulful and attractive" (*ibid.*).[27]

It is odd that Frice appears not to notice the presence of children in Serao's work, and that he ignores the circulation in Russia of such previously mentioned works as "Salvazione", "Scuola normale femminile" and *Piccole anime*. He appears not to want to acknowledge the existence of children in Serao's narratives, and stresses instead their total absence: "children are valuable only in terms of being bearers of the family name and title in this aristocratic society, where having many children is considered tasteless" (*ibid.*).[28] According to Frice, Serao depicted characters from an aristocratic society that was already historically obsolete.

At the end of the article, Frice highlights one further differentiating feature between Serao and Deledda, namely their treatment of religion in their writings. The Catholic "aristocratic" Serao is contrasted with the "democratic" Deledda. Again, high society demands from Serao that she be a good Catholic: "Impiety here is considered to be bad manners, akin to those of the 'petty bourgeoisie'" (*ibid.*, p. 101).[29] However, Frice admits that Serao's faith goes deeper than mere ritual piety and refers to her article *I cavalieri dello Spirito* about Antonio Fogazzaro and Paul Bourget in *Il Mattino*, dated 8 July 1894 (Serao, [1894] 1992). Frice ends his detailed analysis of both authors with a harsh criticism: "No matter how finely these talented writers depict a life, it still does not constitute a whole life, only a small part of it. And I must confess, the most interesting parts remain out of sight for both of them" (*ibid.*, p. 102).[30]

---

сплетнями, изменами и примирениями, дети блаженной страны безделья и утех, paese di cuccagna, как озаглавлен один из романов Серао. В светской среде главную роль играют женщины – наиболее ценимый предмет роскоши и наслаждения – и главную роль играют они и в романах неаполитанской писательницы; напротив, мужчина, в жизни обязанный обставлять роскошью даму, в романах Серао является лишь возбудителем и двигателем женской психики".

27 "Эти то светлые, бойкие и грустные, детские головки придают творчеству сардинской писательницы особую задушевную прелесть".

28 "Так как дети в светской среде ценны лишь как продолжатель рода и титула, так как многодетность здесь считается признаком дурного тона, так и в романах Серао дети совершенно отсутствуют".

29 "Иррелигиозность здесь считается признаком дурного вкуса, 'мещанством'".

30 "Как ни талантливо изображена она [жизнь] обеими писательницами, это далеко не вся жизнь, а только небольшой её кусочек. И надо признаться, её наиболее

In this critical review of Deledda and Serao, it is clear that Frice prefers the former. While highlighting the talent of both writers, he points out some elements common to their works, such as pessimism, and concludes by drawing attention to what he sees as their misplaced focus. If, according to Frice, Serao focuses only on women in an aristocratic society that is part of the "historical past",[31] Deledda illustrates instead a bourgeoisie on the verge of economic crisis able to surmount these barriers and move up in society, but whose attempts are ultimately doomed to failure due to their tormented souls and to "shadows from the past".[32] Both authors are pessimists and choose themes that are limited, according to Frice, leaving out crucial areas.

Frice's article offers a subjective view, possibly reflecting the political mood of the time, rather than a balanced picture of Serao's work. His review helps us to understand the prevailing atmosphere of the time and how political views were changing, for to be a Catholic and to write about an aristocratic lifestyle was already considered out of date and no longer appropriate. Serao focussed primarily on Naples, helped the poor by raising money for charity through her connections, and actually described their lives in some detail in her writings; moreover, children do appear in her texts, as in *Piccole anime.* The fact that Frice comments on a lack of male and child characters and focuses on her representations of the aristocracy suggests that he was not, in fact, very well acquainted with her work. Although his 1911 article is referenced in all the entries for Serao in Russian encyclopaedias, it fails to give a truly comprehensive portrayal of the author.

---

интересные сферы остались вне поля зрения обеих писательниц".

31 "Мир, изображенный Серао, – исторический пережиток, историческая ненужность".

32 "Так отражается в судьбе героев Гр. Деледда, стремящихся стать выше своей среды и терпящих крушение, трагедия значительной части того класса, к которому они принадлежат. То и дело фатальное стечение обстоятельств ('тени прошлого') низвергает выходцев этого класса обратно из мира, где все преисполнено 'света: радости и поэзии', в мир, где жизнь течет 'меланхолической' чредой".

## CRITICAL RECEPTION: AN INTERVIEW WITH MATILDE SERAO

The second article-interview analysed in this essay adds to the portrayal of Serao in Russia and further clarifies the importance of women as mothers and educators in Serao's writings. The interview was published in one of the leading feminist journals, *Zhensky Vestnik*. This monthly periodical published in Saint Petersburg between 1904 and 1917 was committed to promoting women's equality and social advancement.[33] The article I focus on here presents an interview conducted by the Russian journalist E.V. Fuks with Serao. It has an interesting publication history, since this meeting took place in Paris during the World Exhibition in Autumn 1900, but the interview was published only in April 1907 in *Zhensky Vestnik*. One reason for its delayed publication is that the journal did not exist at the time of the interview, and therefore in the title of the article, "Matilde Serao (From Personal Memories)", we can already see a reference to recollections from the past (Fuks, 1907).

The introduction to the interview reads like a diary entry and explains the connections between feminist newspapers in Moscow, London and Paris. Fuks begins the article by describing how she came to meet Serao. From 1899, Fuks worked in London as a correspondent, where she met another journalist from the French feminist newspaper *La Fronde*, and through networking she began to communicate with both the editor of *La Fronde*, Marguerite Durand, and other colleagues. When Fuks later went to Paris to meet these colleagues in the editorial office, she learned that two of the journalists planned to visit Serao, who happened to be in Paris at that time. The two French journalists agreed with Serao by phone that a Russian journalist would also be present at the meeting;

33 In contrast with traditional journals or magazines for women, the editor of *Zhensky Vestnik*, who called herself "editor-doctor" Maria Ivanovna Pokrovskaya, refused to use images, pictures, or advertisements in her journal. Financing the publication herself and trying to find funding from other influential women, she often struggled to keep the journal in print. Therefore, the first issue was delayed and published only in September 1904, although she had had the licence for it since 1902 (Kradetskaya, 2013).

according to Fuks, she "was very pleased to see a Russian woman the next day" (Fuks, 1907, p. 117).[34]

The meeting took place the following day in the Hotel Continental. Initially, Serao paid tribute to the professionalism of the women working for *La Fronde* and acknowledged the impact that this had on the status of women:

> Your editor and publisher is a real warrior and advocate of women's rights. If only a small number of women shared her energy and knowledge it would be wonderful. Then, feminism, which in recent years has made such great breakthroughs, thanks to your newspaper, would be further strengthened (*ibid.*, pp. 117-118).[35]

The conversation with Fuks began with Serao noting that she had visited both Saint Petersburg and Moscow. Fuks's first question concerned the status of women in Italy, and Serao acknowledged what she called the "hamstrung upbringing"[36] (*ibid.*, p. 118) of Italian girls:

> In Italy, one can say that the woman question does not exist. Women are content with their destiny there. Brought up exclusively for marriage, they start to prepare for a life of domesticity from a tender age. And, in general, happy to be spouses, they devote themselves body and soul to their husband and children. This is the result of a centuries-long atavism. There would be no need to criticise such an upbringing if it did not deprive them of any kind of initiative, any desire for learning outside of the home and kitchen. This system produces excellent mothers, loving and docile, but boring wives with little culture (*ibid.*).[37]

---

34 "Она скоро вернулась и сказала мне, что М. Серао очень рада видеть у себя на завтра русскую женщину".

35 "Ваша редактор-издательница настоящая воительница и поборница женских прав. Хорошо, если бы хотя у небольшой части женщин были её энергия и знания. Тогда феминизм, сделавший в последние годы, благодаря вашей газете, такие огромные успехи, совершенно бы окреп".

36 "искалеченное воспитание".

37 "В Италии, можно сказать, не существует женского вопроса. Женщины там довольствуются своей участью. Воспитанные исключительно для выхода замуж, они с раннего возраста приготовляются к семейной жизни и, вообще довольно счастливые в супружестве, они душой и телом отдаются мужу и детям. Это результат многовекового атавизма. Нечего было бы и критиковать в подобном воспитании, если бы оно не лишало всякой инициативы, всякого желания научиться чему-нибудь, выходящему из круга хозяйства и кухни. Эта система дает прекрасных матерей, любвеобильных и покорных, но мало развитых и скучных жён".

The conversation continued, exploring the topic of the education system in Italy. Serao highlighted the problem of female teachers, who were forbidden to work in boys' schools, even though "Italian women are marvellous educators, and matchless teachers" (*ibid.*).[38] It was rivalry with male teachers that prevented female teachers from working in boys' schools, yet male teachers could work in girls' schools. Serao bucked this trend to some extent by hiring a governess from Piedmont to home-school her four sons, until they went to high school. Another issue tackled during the interview was the role of women in society and the impossibility of their having access to any career other than teaching. According to Fuks, Serao agreed that women were not allowed to work as cashiers in larger stores, in communications or in the post-office (*ibid.*).[39] However, it is well known that Serao, like other young women, also worked in telecommunication. This contradicts what Fuks's report of what Serao says in the interview and may be a result of Fuks having conducted the interview several years before publishing it and relying on her 'recollections' to construct it.

The discussion then turned to the city of Naples. Serao bemoaned the plight of its incredibly impoverished and disadvantaged citizens who wrote to her asking for help in her capacity as a journalist, newspaper editor, and in the context of her status as an influential woman in Naples. She also commented that she appreciated the financial help received from other affluent friends who donated to the poor and helped her in this matter:

> But I am not alone. Kind sisters, merciful souls open their wallets for me. My old friend, Baroness Rothschild, visits me often in Naples and always leaves me an eye-watering sum of money for my paupers. But there are so many of them that it is always insufficient (*ibid.*, p. 119).[40]

It is interesting to see how differently these two texts by Russian critics that were written only four years apart represent Serao. Fuks's interview

---

38 "Итальянки идеальные воспитательницы и несравненные учительницы".

39 "Их [девушек] не принимают ни кассиршами в большие магазины, ни на телеграф, ни на почту, ни в какие правления, мотивируя это тем, что наши молодые люди, занимающие там должности, слишком галантны".

40 "Но я всё-таки не одна. Добрые сестры, сострадательные души, открывают мне свои кошельки. Моя старая приятельница, баронесса Ротшильд часто навещает меня в Неаполе и всегда оставляет мне значительную сумму для моих бедняков. Но их столько, что мне никогда не хватает".

with Serao further highlights the importance of children and children's education, thereby refuting Frice's criticisms. The brief but very precise introduction of Serao in 1885 in *Russkaya Mysl* that precedes the text of "Scuola normale femminile" seems more thorough and more objective, in fact, than does Frice's piece, in the end.

## CONCLUSIONS

This chapter has illustrated the extent to which Serao's work was translated and published in Russia at the end of the nineteenth- and the beginning of the twentieth centuries. Her works began to be published in Russian in 1885 in the leading journals and newspapers of the day, such as *Russkaya Mysl*, *Russkie Vedomosti*, and *Severny Vestnik,* and were followed by the publication of individual books and anthologies, especially around 1900.

The analysis of the sources illustrates that Serao's translations reached Russia via two routes. In some cases, they came directly from Italy and from Italian periodicals (some Russian critics mention *Nuova antologia*, *Il Mattino*, and *Pagina azzurra*). Yet, we have seen that there was also a second route by which her texts arrived in Russia: there was a French connection, as demonstrated by the interview between Fuks and Serao when they met in Paris, and by the fact that the Russian translation of *Il paese di Cuccagna* was published with an introduction written by the French novelist and critic Paul Bourget.

Serao's popularity and the demand for her work in Russia led to the publication of a five-volume edition of her collected works in 1910-1911. After that, her popularity in Russia began to decline. In 1911, Frice criticized Serao's description of high society life that seemed out of date in the changing reality of pre-revolutionary Russia.

Furthermore, because many of her works embraced a variety of subjects, the Neapolitan writer was published not only in well-known, popular journals and newspapers, but also in specialized periodicals targeting a different audience, which focused on such matters as religion (*Mir Bozhiy*, *Vestnik Teosofii*, theatre *Teatr i Iskusstvo*, women's rights and feminism (*Zhenskoe Delo*, *Zhensky Vestnik*).

It would be interesting to study Serao's translation and reception in the historical context of the pre- and post-Russian revolution. Her work's circulation in Russia during those years illustrates both the breadth of her subject matter and the changing political views and censorship at that time. In Russia, after 1911, translations of Serao's children's books replaced those of her romantic novels and short stories. There also seems to have been a notable shift in the works chosen for publication from adult to children's literature, as illustrated through the case study of *All'erta, sentinella!* There is certainly more work to be done in this field.

Maria Belova
University of Warwick

## MATILDE SERAO'S FICTION TRANSLATED INTO RUSSIAN

Serao Matilde, 1885, "V Zhenskoy shkole" ["Scuola normale femminile"], trans. A.V., *Russkaya Mysl*, 7, pp. 161-193.

Serao Matilde, 1886, *Fantazia* [*Fantasia*], trans. A.V., *Severny Vestnik*, 6, pp. 85-118; 7, pp. 103-139; 8, pp. 87-126; 9, pp. 99-142.

Serao Matilde, 1886, "V avgustovskuju noch'" ["Notte di agosto"], trans. S. Ya. Nadson, Semyon Nadson, 1887, *Literaturnye ocherki (1883-1886) S.ya. Nadsona* [*Critical Essays by S.ya. Nadson (1883-1886)*], St Petersburg, Skorokhodov, pp. 141-149.

Serao Matilde, 1887, *Roman devushki* [*Il romanzo della fanciulla*], trans. unknown, n. p., n. pub.

Serao Matilde, 1888, *Zhizn i priklyucheniya Rikorda Ioanna* [*Vita e avventure di Riccardo Joanna*], trans. unknown, St Petersburg, n. pub.

Serao Matilde, 1890, "Chydnyi son" ["Sogno di una notte d'estate"], trans. unknown, *Inostrannye Belletristy* [*Foreign Fiction Writers*], Moscow, n. pub., pp. 171-222.

Serao Matilde, 1890, "Naedine" ["Salvazione"], trans. unknown, *Russkaya Mysl*, 12, pp. 62-67.

Serao Matilde, 1890, *Proschay lyubov* [*Addio, amore!*], trans. Ek. Letkova, *Severnyi Vestnik*, 11, November, pp. 255-290; 12, December, pp. 271-331.

Serao Matilde, 1890, *Slu-u-shay!* [*All'erta, sentinella!*], trans. E.K. Vatson, *Russkiye Vedomosti*, 2 August, pp. 2-3; 8 August, pp. 2-3; 13 August, pp. 2-3; 17 August, pp. 2-3; 20 August, pp. 2-3.

Serao Matilde, 1890, "Szena", "Ideal" ["Scena", "Ideale"], trans. A. Ves-ya, *Russkiye Vedomosti*, 15 March, pp. 2-3.

Serao Matilde, 1893, "Naedine" ["Salvazione"], *Naedine,* trans. unknown, Moscow, Posrednik, pp. 3-9.

Serao Matilde, 1894, *Proshhaj ljubov'* [*Addio, amore!*], trans. V. Mosolova, Moscow, n. pub.

Serao Matilde, 1897, *Zemlja obetovannaja* [*Il paese di Cuccagna*], trans. unknown, St. Petersburg, n. pub.

Serao Matilde, 1898, "Cenoju zhizni" ["Per il prezzo della vita"], trans. K. Pellegrini, April, supplement to *Svet,* St. Petersburg.

Serao Matilde, 1899, *Beregis chasovoy* [*All'erta sentinella!*], trans. unknown, Moscow, n. pub.

Serao Matilde, 1899, *Bolnoye serdze* [*Cuore infermo*], trans. unknown, Moscow, n. pub.

Serao Matilde, 1899, *Dzhovannino ili smert* [*O Giovannino o la morte*], trans. unknown, Moscow, n. pub.

Serao Matilde, 1899, "Kanituchchya" ["Canituccia"], *Gore starogo katorzhnika,* trans. unknown, ed. Pierre Loti, Moscow, Posrednik.

Serao Matilde, 1899, *Vozle rebyonka* [*All'erta, sentinella!*], trans. unknown, series Knizhka za knizhkoy 88, St Petersburg, M.N. Slepzova.

Serao Matilde, 1900, "Bankovskiy krah" ["Trenta per cento"], trans. A. Nikiforova, supplement to *Zhenskoe Delo,* 6/7-8/9.

Serao Matilde, 1900, "Ozhidanie", "Razlad", "Zigzagi" ["Aspettando", "Dissidio", "Zig-zag"], Serao Matilde – Capuana Luigi, *Ital'janskie rasskazy* [*Italian Novellas*], trans. unknown, St Petersburg, Zvonarev.

Serao Matilde, 1900, *Rasskazy* [*Novellas*] 2 vols, trans. A.Veselovskaya, Moscow, n. pub.; vol. 1 includes: "Ili Dzhovannino ili smert", "Loterejnyj bilet", "Na kazennom telegrafe" ["O Giovannino o la morte", "Terno secco", "Telegrafi dello stato"]; vol. 2 includes: "V zhenskoj uchitel'skoj seminarii", "Chem konchajutsja devich'i sljozy", "Szena", "Ideal", "Povest' lyubvi" ["Scuola normale femminile", "Il romanzo della fanciulla", "Scena", "Ideale", "Novella d'amore"].

Serao Matilde, 1900, *Ryzhak* [*All'erta, sentinella!*], trans. unknown, ed. L.B. Khavkina, Kharkov, Obshhestvo rasprostranenija gramotnosti v narode.

Serao Matilde, 1901, *Ljubov' ubijcy* [*All'erta, sentinella!*], trans. unknown, Moscow, Posrednik.

Serao Matilde, 1901, *Vozle rebyonka* [*All'erta, sentinella!*], trans. unknown, 2nd edn, series Knizhka za knizhkoy 88, St Petersburg, M.N. Slepzova.

Serao Matilde, 1902, *Dzhovannino ili smert* [*O Giovannino o la morte*], trans. M.N. Nikolaeva, St Petersburg, M.O. Volf.
Serao Matilde, 1902, *Sestra Dzhiovanna* [*L'anima semplice: Suor Giovanna della Croce*], trans. E.V. Lazarevskaya, St Petersburg, Obshhestvennaja pol'za.
Serao Matilde, 1902, *Tridcat' na sto* [*Trenta per cento*], trans. M.N. Nikolaeva, St Petersburg, M.O. Volf.
Serao Matilde, 1903, *Ili Dzhovannino ili smert* [*O Giovannino o la morte*], trans. unknown, Moscow, Pravda
Serao Matilde, 1904, *Ljubov' ubijcy* [*All'erta, sentinella!*], trans. unknown, 2nd edn, Moscow, Posrednik.
Serao Matilde, 1910, *Posle proschenija* [*Dopo il perdono*], trans. A.M-voy, Moscow, A.I. Mamontov.
Serao Matilde, 1910-1911, *Cvety strasti* [*Flowers of Passion*], trans. unknown, 2 vols, Moscow, Athenaem; vol. 1 includes: "Povest' ljubvi"; "Paulo Spada"; "Na mogile"; "Dezertir"; "Farforovoe serdce"; "Zhenshhina v chernom", "s korallovym ozherel'em na shee"; "Szena"; "Ideal"; "Pas'jans"; "V ozhidanii"; "Salonnyj dujet"; "Maskarad"; "Lozh'"; "Pervyj den'"; "Grecheskaja povest'" ["Novella d'amore"; "Paolo Spada"; "Sulla tomba"; "La settimana delle novelle"; "Cuore di porcellana"; "La donna dall'abito nero e dal ramo di corallo rosso"; "Scena"; "Ideale"; "Giuoco di pazienza"; "Aspettando"; "Duetto di salone"; "Al veglione"; "Falso in scrittura"; "Primo giorno"; "Novella greca"]; vol. 2 includes: *Proshhaj ljubov'* [*Addio, amore!*].
Serao Matilde, 1910-1911, *Sobranie sochinenij v 5 tomah* [*Complete Works in 5 volumes*], 5 vols., Moscow, Athenaem; vol. 1 includes: *Volosy Samsona* [*I capelli di Sansone*], trans. I.A. Mevsky; vol. 2 includes: *Proshhaj ljubov'* [*Addio, amore!*] trans. V.A. Koshevic; vol. 3 includes: "Slushaj chasovoj!" ["All'erta, erta, sentinella!"]; "Loterejnyj bilet" ["Terno secco"]; "Na kazennom telegrafe" ["Telegrafi dello stato"]; "V zhenskoj uchitel'skoj seminarii" ["Scuola normale femminile"]; "Chem konchajutsja devich'i grjozy" ["Il romanzo della fanciulla"]; "Povest' ljubvi" ["Novella d'amore"], trans. A. Veselovskaya – N. Piastro; vol. 4 includes: *Posle proshhenija* [*Dopo il perdono*], trans. Valentin Dol; vol. 5 includes: *Vozmezdie* [*Castigo*], trans. Valentin Dol.
Serao Matilde, 1912, *Vozle rebyonka* [*All'erta, sentinella!*], 3rd edn, series Knizhka za knizhkoy 88, trans. unknown, St Petersburg, M.N. Slepzova.
Serao Matilde, 1914, *Malen'kie dushi* [*Piccole anime*], trans. L. Semyonova, Moscow, Polza.
Serao Matilde, 1916, *Malen'kie dushi* [*Piccole anime*], trans. L. Semyonova, 2nd edn, Moscow, Polza.
Serao Matilde, 1923, *Svinopaska Kanituchchiya*, ed. Vladimir A. Popov, trans. unknown, Moscow, Zemlya i fabrika.

# RE-READING SERAO THROUGH ANGLOCENTRIC EYES

This essay will discuss critical evaluations of the writings of Matilde Serao from her own time, looking briefly at the Italian context of her immediate reception, but focussing mainly on the English-language context (American, English and Irish) in which her work was received and analysed. I suggest here, based on my readings of particular critical responses to her, that there are two outstanding factors worth bearing in mind in considering Serao's reception in these contexts: one is the issue of gender (her reception as a woman writer and the nature of that gendered reception, but also the kind of reading that is offered taking into consideration the sex of the critic); the other is the question of Serao's Neapolitan-ness, Southernness and/or Italian-ness based on the positionality of the critic him or herself. These factors arise repeatedly as significant in readings of Serao's work, and are often as revealing of her critics (and, sometimes, of the views of their societies) as they are of the author and her work (Henry James turns out to be a case in point), and become ever more revealing as Serao is shoehorned into a pre-fashioned critical space into which she is obliged to fit.

## AT HOME – ITALIAN VIEWS

In the Italian context, Serao's influence and status in the early 1890s can be read through Gabriele D'Annunzio's dedication of his second novel, *Giovanni Episcopo*, to her. At the time of publication of his novel, D'Annunzio was a relatively inexperienced writer, keen to garner good reviews for his work and hopeful that Serao would comment favourably on the novel; he was also strongly influenced by her, as Maryse Jeuland-Meynaud noted in her 1986 study of Serao: "With regard to D'Annunzio's debt to Serao, there is a sizeable chapter yet to be written" (Jeuland-Meynaud, 1986, p. 26).[1] D'Annunzio's dedication, indeed, is better defined as a preface, some six pages long, in which he figures Serao as an "eminent lady" while he appears as an "anxious craftsman" (D'Annunzio, [1891] 1988, p. 337).[2] Most of the preface focuses on the inspiration for the novel and on its process of composition, but Serao is depicted here more than once as an exceptionally hard-working writer and, at the close of the preface/dedication, appears in a light which would become familiar to later critics and readers of her work, although it is commented on relatively rarely – that is, she is seen here in resolutely masculine terms "you who [...] are the Italian example of virile [...] workmanship" (*ibid.*, p. 342).[3] A gendered reading comes into play here through the association of hard work and masculinity, and in the attribution of that quality to Serao.[4] This masculine quality implicitly elevates Serao's production in the context in which it is claimed, and makes of her a worthy mentor for the younger writer.

More important than this indication of Serao's status in the eyes of D'Annunzio in the late nineteenth century, though, are the views articulated by Benedetto Croce in the early twentieth century that were to shape the reception of Serao in the Italian context for the foreseeable future. In his 1903 essay on Italian literature in the second half of the nineteenth century, Croce said much that was positive on Serao's output, but he also made some decidedly negative comments. He is late to engage with Serao, not only in the Italian context but – more significantly for this volume – in the international frame, but he makes up for this with the length of his essay, and in the amount of space and serious consideration he gives to her writings here, including lengthy citations from several of her works. Both the positive and the negative

1 "Circa i debiti del pescarese nei confronti della Serao, ci sarebbe un grosso capitolo da aprire" (all translations from Italian are my own). See the recent work by Alessandra Trevisan (2019), which goes some considerable way towards this.

2 "illustre signora", "artefice inquieto".

3 "voi che [...] date in Italia l'esempio di un'operosità [...] virile".

4 Indeed, Serao often chose to define herself as a "scrittore" in order to link herself more closely with her (canonical) male counterparts. See her interview with Ugo Ojetti (1895, p. 233).

features individuated by Croce recur in later critical analyses of Serao *ad nauseam*. The very first sentence of Croce's article highlights that first issue that I want to focus on here for Serao – her Neapolitan-ness. Here Croce notes that Serao is familiar with "the petit bourgeois environment in Naples" as well as with "many aspects of the life of the Neapolitan working class" (Croce, 1903, p. 321).[5] There is no value judgment made here initially, but a few lines later, he comments on the limited nature of Serao's Neapolitan world: "narrow and rather naïve [...] between 1870 and 1880" (*ibid.*).[6] This restrictiveness and lack of sophistication appears not to be associated specifically with Serao's portrayal of that world, but is rather presented here as an intrinsic quality of Naples itself. At any rate, it is the Neapolitan setting of Serao's work that first strikes Croce as worthy of mention (although he does admit, a little later, that her work ranges beyond that setting). It is perhaps to Croce, then, that we need to look, in the Italian context, for that primary association of Serao and Naples.

Hot on the heels of the references to Naples come the considerations of gender, my other concern here. Croce is astute in his naming of Serao's focus on the emotional lives of her female characters and on the female erotic, and he individuates this focus as particular to her as a woman writer; she has, he says, "an insight into the erotic passions of women [...] the knowledge that only a woman's heart can have of women's hearts" (*ibid.*, p. 322).[7] He goes on to implicitly link Serao's femaleness to her capacity for observation – on which he frequently looks favourably, but which he sees here as contaminated by that sentiment associated by him with femininity: "She is all realistic observation and sentiment: or rather, observation guided by sentiment" (*ibid.*).[8] Croce's focus on Serao's capacity for observation contributed in no small way to the labelling of Serao's "good" work as predominantly realist (at least in terms of her earlier output), and to the positive critical evaluations of those of her works that were defined as realist in her own time (which included the collection of articles *Il ventre di Napoli* (Serao, 1884a), her short stories

5 "l'ambiente della piccola borghesia napoletana", "molti aspetti della vita della plebe napoletana".

6 "ristretto e alquanto ingenuo [...] tra il 1870 e il 1880".

7 "una penetrazione della passionalità erotica femminile [...] la conoscenza che solo un cuore di donna può avere dei cuori delle donne".

8 "È tutta osservazione realistica e sentimento; o meglio, osservazione guidata dal sentimento".

"La virtù di Checchina" (Serao, 1884b) and "Terno secco" (Serao, 1889) along with *Il paese di Cuccagna* (Serao, 1891) which remains, arguably, her most enduring work – and all of these receive some attention from Croce. This realist definition was, of course, one that Serao herself sought to encourage, since it allowed her to claim a place alongside writers such as Verga, De Roberto, Capuana and, importantly, Zola (Ojetti, 1895, p. 233), and thus to bolster her literary reputation. It is interesting, too, that Croce devotes a good deal of space (three pages in all) in this article to a discussion of *Fantasia* (1883), which is a text central to analyses of Serao's work abroad as well as at home. Croce is extraordinarily positive about this novel, given his previously-voiced concerns about the subject of passion in Serao's writing: "The novel", he holds, "is perfectly balanced" (Croce, 1903, p. 344).[9] He interprets it as a moral tale, in which its author's sympathy is all with the conventional, unimaginative character of Caterina (a view that has been categorically undone in recent Serao criticism).[10] He also notes its debt to "the French [...] especially [...] Flaubert" (*ibid.*, p. 346).[11] In several respects, then, Croce's attention to Serao in this substantial essay secured her longevity in critical discussions of Italian literature of the period, while also placing in question her literary abilities. He notes caustically quite early on that in certain of her works, "The element of reflection, and that other element which could be defined as culture, is almost absent" (*ibid.*, p. 322).[12] He keeps her alive, critically-speaking, but sometimes for the purposes of target practice, and effectively consigns her to the status of a minor writer on the Italian literary scene for most of the twentieth century. In this, I suggest, his response to the writer is highly gendered. It is something of a commonplace in male critics of Serao's work (no matter where they are located) to question, and at times, to negate its value often precisely on the grounds of what is seen as its "feminine" quality. This has the effect of placing her work at a distance from these commentators; effectively, it is "othered." Her female commentators, conversely, tend not to do this; if they note anything about Serao as a woman writer this tends to be viewed in a positive or, sometimes, an empathetic light, as we shall see.

9 "Il romanzo è perfettamente equilibrato".
10 See, for instance, Fanning, "Matilde Serao's Cautionary Tales".
11 "i francesi [...] specialmente [...] Flaubert".
12 "L'elemento di riflessione, e l'altro che potrebbe dirsi di coltura, è quasi nullo".

Gender and (eventually) place are important, then, in Italian critics' writings on Serao; gender is equally central to her English-language reception, while notions of place (and race) turn out to be even more striking in that context, as we shall see.

## VIEWS FROM ABROAD: REPORTS FROM ENGLAND, IRELAND AND AMERICA

Edmund Gosse, who was responsible for Serao's introduction to the British literary scene, through his solicitation of the translation of *Fantasia* (*Fantasy*, 1890), was immensely enthusiastic about her work – and he too focuses on those twin poles of Naples and gender in his reading of her, which predates that of Croce by some thirteen years. Thus, in the English context, too, the same patterns and focal points of reception are in evidence from the beginning – although that reception is not necessarily the same in tone. Gosse wrote the preface to the English translation of *Fantasia*, as well as to that of *Addio, amore!*, and thus he effectively helped to set the tone for Serao's reception in the English-speaking world. In his preface to *Fantasy*, Gosse comments on "the acuteness with which [Serao] articulated the town life of southern Italy" (Gosse, 1890, p. XI), and he also describes her here as "the most important and imaginative writer of her generation" (this last, interestingly, without any qualifications of gender). In the later preface, Gosse reiterates and expands on those same characteristics he has already identified; he opens the preface with the definitive statement that: "The most prominent imaginative writer of the latest generation in Italy is a woman" (*ibid.*) – here, gender is clearly crucial and it warrants Gosse remarking that Serao's skill is exceptional for a woman; he goes on to claim that the source of her imagination (somewhat paradoxically) is to be found in the hardships which she has (unusually, according to him, for a woman) endured. "Madame Serao", he opines, "has learned in the fierce school of privation" (*ibid.*). Gosse, as he continues, shows himself to be fascinated by what he presents as Serao's anomalous approach to her position as a woman journalist: "To give herself full scope [in her] employment, she, I have been assured, cut short her curly crop of hair and adopted on occasion male costume" (*ibid.*). He is intrigued by Serao precisely, in part, because she is a woman, and a woman who is conscious of the limitations imposed on her sex in the normal course of events. Alongside this highlighting of issues of sex and gender in relation to Serao, Gosse returns to the depiction of Naples in her work. Her short stories, he says, "deal with the oddities of Neapolitan life"; she has, he believes, "a fierce [...] passion, [...] the true ardour of the South" (*ibid.*).

This stress on oddness/oddities, passion and ardour (difference, or otherness, in short) reflects a prevailing view of the south of Italy in Britain at that time. William Gladstone's *Gleanings of Past Years*, in which he discussed his view of Naples (and the south as a whole) at length had been published in 1879 (Gladstone, 1879); his *Letters*, in which he had both extolled the energy and lamented at the state of Naples, had already had, in Nelson Moe's words, "extraordinary [...] resonance" (Moe, 2002, p. 131). That same enthusiasm (the positive evaluation of the "passion" and "ardour" of the South), dismay and disapproval (at and of its "oddities", not to mention the "vast, rough crowd" referenced by Gosse here too), an Orientalism in action then,[13] frame this early presentation of Serao's work to a British audience. The South and Naples both are represented by Gosse as violent and uncivilized, wild and unfettered, exotic and lively; there is a discourse of alterity in play here, and Serao's work is read as evidencing these characteristics. As Edward Said noted in an article from 1982, "There is always an Other; and this Other willy-nilly turns interpretation into a social activity" (Said, 1982, p. 3). Othering, I suggest, is operating on two levels here: Naples is othered by Gosse and so too is Serao.

13 Edward Said discusses both negative and positive stereotypes of the other in his seminal work, *Orientalism*. He notes, famously, that alongside a view, and representation, of the Orient as primitive, irrational and violent, there is a tendency to feminize it. The exoticisation of the Orient is intertwined with its feminization (Said, [1978] 1991, pp. 38-41). Parallels with this view of the south of Italy, and particularly of Naples, as "other" and Orientalism are noted by (Moe, 2002, pp. 5-6), and they provide the impetus for Jane Schneider's later volume, *Italy's Southern Question: Orientalism in One Country*. Schneider, before she comes to discuss Orientalism within Italy, makes the general observation that "Italy was certainly affected by Orientalism" (Schneider, 1998, p. 5) – and it is evident that the South, as was also the case in Orientalism from within Italy, was most "othered" by Europeans from the 1700s onwards.

Interestingly, an article on Serao's work as a whole, with specific reference to *Fantasia*, had already appeared before Gosse's (inevitably) brief prefaces to *Fantasy* and *Farewell Love!* [*Addio, amore!*]. This article is unknown and uncommented to date in the context of Serao studies. It is of interest because it is written by one of the translators of *Fantasia*, and because it offers a rather different take from those considered so far, in some respects, on Serao and on her work – a take which I suggest is partly conditioned by the sex of the writer. The article appeared in the 1889 edition of a monthly periodical entitled *The Woman's World*, which was published by Cassells in London, Paris, New York and Melbourne but which was also quite widely read in Ireland (which, of course, had not yet attained independence at this time) in part because, between 1887 and 1890, the periodical was edited by Oscar Wilde.[14] Its author was one Paul Sylvester, the pseudonym of Pauline Schletter, an Englishwoman of German origin.

It is interesting, in itself, of course that Pauline Schletter chose to translate (at least initially, and certainly for her work on Serao) using a male pseudonym and this is presumably indicative of an attempt to stake a claim for greater authority. She worked as a translator from Italian, French and Spanish and was also the author of essays (including on the peasant women of Galicia, and on the modern Spanish novel). Her essay in *The Woman's World* is simply entitled "Matilde Serao" and is six pages in length (the format of the volume, however, is A3 size).[15] The story of the periodical is also of interest to give some context for the publication of this article by Schletter. Wilde was invited by the publishers to edit the journal in 1887 and took on the task in November of that year, immediately changing the title of the periodical from its original, *The Lady's World*, and moving it at once from the category of fashion magazine to one of general (if gendered) interest. He solicited articles

14 Anna de Brémont, in *Oscar Wilde and his Mother: A Memoir* noted that "the magazine caused a flutter in the boudoirs of Mayfair and Belgravia" (De Brémont, 1911, p. 73). The *Irish Times* reported meanwhile that on the evening of the launch under its new editorship "there was not one to be had in the West End for love or money" and that "the most significant reaction of all came from *The Englishwoman's Review*, the organ of the suffragist movement in Britain [...] it ran notices attracting the attention of readers to more progressive articles" ("Art, Fashion, and Gossip", 1887, p. 7).

15 This volume is available in the Special Collections of University College Dublin Newman Library and also in the National Library of Ireland.

on literature, education and suffrage mainly from women writers and was, as Stephanie Green notes in an article on the periodical, "serious about promoting education and professional opportunities for women" in its pages (Green, 1997, p. 111). He was also particularly keen to give "special prominence" to works written by women authors (Fitzsimons, 2015). Schletter's article appears sandwiched between articles on style and culture,[16] but, in the same volume, Wilde contributes an article on modern poets, while there is an essay on Angelica Kauffman by Mrs Francis Moore, on Maupassant by Blanche Roosevelt and two articles on women's suffrage, one in favour by Mrs Fawcett and the other against by Miss L.M.J. Garnett.

Paul Sylvester/Pauline Schletter begins her article by placing Italian fiction of the period against its (better-known) French counterpart. It is not, she holds, of the same high standard overall, missing "the chiselled perfection of form peculiar to" Flaubert (Sylvester, 1889, p. 552); nonetheless, it has, as though to compensate for this, "a photographic memory that, unlike its French prototype, focuses fair as well as foul, the beautiful and the ugly" (*ibid.*). And it is, in part, on this fair/foul dualism that she will focus in her analysis of Serao's work – it will find expression, once again, in an "othering" of the South of Italy in general and of Naples in particular (and, in this respect, is very much of a piece with the view from abroad overall). Italian realism, in general, is, for Schletter "more real and therefore more impartial than Gallic realism" (*ibid.*) and, immediately from the second paragraph, we find ourselves faced with an Orientalist discourse, as Schletter moves directly to consider Serao – whose writings, she tells her Anglophone readers: "present as notable a contrast to the masterpieces of Northern fiction as does a child of the sunny South to his Saxon or Slavonic brother" (*ibid.*). Moving from the South to Italy as a whole, viewed from this northern-European perspective, Schletter remarks on the "din and stress" particular to the new nation-state and then gives a close-up on Naples, claiming that Serao exemplifies "the heart and pulse of the ancient Neapolitan capital" (*ibid.*). She is very much, in Schletter's view, part of the Italian realist group of writers in that she offers her readers: "veritable reproductions of the life of the streets and gardens, the drudgery and recreation [...]

16 Specifically, its immediate neighbours are "A Chat About Japanese Dress" by Mary Reed and "Screens, Ancient and Modern" by Ellen T. Masters.

the every-day joys and sorrows of her native town" (*ibid.*, p. 553). Having mentioned various texts by Serao, including *Cuore infermo* and *Vita e avventure di Riccardo Joanna*, Schletter turns to *Fantasia*, on which she will focus for the remainder of the article, without ever mentioning that she is one of the translators of the soon-to-be-released novel: "for evidence of [Serao's] creative power" (*ibid.*, p. 554). In her analysis of the novel (from which she also quotes at length), she pulls back from a discussion of Naples to a panoramic consideration of the novel as characteristically Italian (strongly and implicitly different from any Northern European "norm," as we might expect by now): "the provincial *élegantes* and their envied and admired sisters from Naples [...] crowd these vivid pages with light and sound and colour, Italian colour and Italian sound, bright, sonorous and clear" (*ibid.*, p. 556). From Naples to Italy, Schletter zooms back into the South at fairly dizzying speed in the next paragraph for a stereotypical description of the character of Andrea Lieti who, for her, is "a genial, good-looking, ease-loving, hot-tempered and hot-blooded athlete, a genuine Southern Italian" (*ibid.*). This description of Andrea, intended positively, offers an example of what Moe describes as European culture [expressing] its attraction for the primitive, natural South (Moe, 2002, p. 195). Passionate and lazy at once, Southern Italians here provide a nice foil for the rational men of Northern Europe. Edward Said noted that, for Lamartine (and other European writers), Orientals are frequently figured as both lazy and passionate (Said, [1978] 1991, p. 178). Schletter, then, in terms of her view of the South and of Serao's realism is very much at one with Gosse in her framing of the South and Naples as distinctly other; she goes further than Gosse, in fact, with her extending of that frame of otherness to the Italian peninsula as a whole.

With regard to gender, Schletter's reading, however, differs from those of the male critics who will follow her. She is especially attuned to Serao's focus on working women, making much of the representations of the telegraph workers in "Telegrafi dello Stato", and linking them specifically with the representation of the woman journalist in *Fantasia*. Here, most unusually in contemporary criticism, Serao's sex is not figured as a weakness or limitation of any kind, but rather as something which piques the reader's (this woman reader's, albeit she strives to bring her own reader with her through her use of the first-person plural) interest as well as her sympathy: "the cause of the sympathy we experience in both instances is not far to seek, nor are extraordinary gifts of divination needed to enable us to recognize one and the same prototype behind each of these sympathetic figures" (Sylvester, 1889, p. 553). This is a synthetic, but revealing, comment – possibly as much as Pauline Schletter in drag could allow herself, but nonetheless indicative of a different positionality from that of Croce and Gosse (and, possibly most interestingly of all, Henry James as we shall see below).[17]

Not coincidentally, I think, Schletter is keen to position Serao alongside the canonical literary figures of the period; the comparators she employs to this end in the first couple of pages of the article are Zola, the Goncourts, Flaubert, Tolstoy, Dickens, Thackeray, George Eliot, Daudet, Keats and Shelley (these last two may seem unlikely, but Schletter finds traces of Keats' "sculpturesque" and Shelley's "colour and fleeting motion" in Serao's *La conquista di Roma*; *ibid.*). Her closing point of reference is Mme de Staël, possibly as popular as Serao in her own time, Schletter opines, but whose works:

> neither picture her time, nor the men and women of any time for us – in which they certainly differ from the imaginative works of the Italian woman of genius who has obtained so firm a hold on the imagination of her clime and day (*ibid.*, p. 557).

Schletter thus claims for Serao a pre-eminence in realism alongside an imaginative capacity that, in her view, should assure this writer of ongoing fame (read canonicity); the article closes: "We can but wish [her works] that length of days which should be the meed of their potent originality" (*ibid.*). This claim for canonicity is interesting, for what we see in action in these debates around Serao's status in both Italy and England is, I would hold, nothing other than the gendered process of canon formation.

Beyond this, Schletter's reading of *Fantasia*, which takes up the bulk of the article, is highly astute. Where other readers (notably Croce, as we have seen, and later James) consider (or want to consider) Serao's

17 Another positive female perspective is that adopted by Edith Wharton in her much later autobiography, where she notes Serao's "wit and eloquence", alongside her "powerful intelligence," and observes that her writing is both imaginative and formed from experience (Wharton, 1934, pp. 575-577).

sympathy to lie with the passive figure of Caterina, Schletter senses something more; she recognizes that Serao is "alternately attracted and repelled" (*ibid.*, p. 554) by this character and she goes on to suggest a possible alternative ending for Caterina (whom she, in line with the views expressed by male critics, finds a reassuring type): "Caterina [...] had surely escaped her punishment had her powers of mind been on a par with [her] capacity for love" (*ibid.*). She wishes for an alternative ending, a more conventional one, one where good triumphs – but she grasps the fact that Caterina is being punished by her creator and that it is lack of intelligence (withheld by that same creator) that leads to this "punishment". This makes her reading of *Fantasia* stand out in terms of its general critical reception.

Finally, then, to Henry James, who was responsible for making Serao known in America and whose essay on her in *The North American Review* of 1901 was instrumental in bringing about the translation of several of her novels in the United States. Christine Richards notes, in her detailed analysis of James's review, that James's reprinting of his essay in his 1914 volume *Notes on Novelists* (James, 1914), "places Serao within the European canon of literature alongside writers such as Balzac, Flaubert, George Sand and Zola" (Richards, 1999, p. 86). This is true, but we have already seen that Pauline Schletter aimed to do the same (and more) in her 1889 article. It is also the case that James, like Croce, focuses on Serao partly in order to set her aside, to mark her work as different, as other (on two counts); as a consequence of James's essay, Serao becomes again an object for target-practice. The essay is, indeed, as Richards has it, "a landmark in the history of the reception of Serao's fiction outside Italy" (*ibid.*, p. 87), but this is due to James's own canonical status rather than to any absence of other writings on Serao prior to his work. Feminist critics (and I include myself here) have been so pleased to find James focussing on Serao to the extent that he does that we have overlooked, or had a blind spot in relation to, the precise nature of his evaluation of her in order to press him into service in the interest of underlining her significance. Now that Serao is better known, it is worth turning back to this essay to analyse it in greater detail. It is overdue a reconsideration in light of the questions around gendered readings and the othering of the South which are central to my argument. Before turning to the *Review* essay itself, however, it is worth pausing to consider James's first mention of Serao, which already encapsulates the gist of what he would say in the article some seven years later. In a letter to his friend Grace Norton of 1894, James asks her whether she has ever heard of "the astounding Matilde Serao," whom he has just met (James, 1920, p. 269); he describes her as "the she-Zola of Italy"(gender is clearly central here) and goes on to say that "she is like a wonderful little burly Balzac in petticoats – full of Neapolitan life and sound and familiarity" (*ibid.*). The description is breathtaking in its gender-coding and switching, and in its linking of gender with place, its neat othering of both the writer and of Naples. The 1901 essay builds on this initial impression, offering a more extended consideration of Serao and of her work in particular. The essay is wide-ranging, both in terms of its demonstration of James's (relative) familiarity with Serao and her writings,[18] and in the way in which he uses her work to illustrate a comparison of fiction in English with that in other languages. James begins, in fact, not with Serao at all, but with a discussion of "the proper" and the notion of propriety in English-language fiction (James, 1901, p. 367). He absolutely refuses to distinguish here, interestingly, between English and American novelists in his discussion, grouping them together on the grounds of their common language, but also, and crucially, on the grounds of cultural sensibility, ranging them on one side of a debate on taste and subject-matter, against an "alien foe" and "outland scorn" (*ibid.*, p. 368). Further complicating the notion of race and culture here, though, appropriately for my purposes, is that of gender. James traces a connection between what he terms "the general mildness" of English and American authors and "the fact that we are likewise so generally feminine" (*ibid.*, p. 370). Is the English novel "proper," he asks, "because it is so largely written by women, or is it, only, so largely written by women because its propriety has been so massively established?" (*ibid.*). Thus, he begins here by lamenting the conventionality (and what he sees as the femininity) of English-language

18 I use the term relative because James virtually boasts of not having read *Il ventre di Napoli* (James, 1901, p. 373) and also bases his critique of *Fantasia* on what he "recalls" (*ibid.*, p. 374); moreover, he feels free to criticize Serao's style despite the fact that, as he admits: "On the question of style, in a foreign writer, it takes a great general intimacy to make us sure of our ground; but I feel myself on the safe side in conceiving that this lady, full of perception and vibration, cannot not only pass for a purist, but must be considered, throughout [...] to pretend but little to distinction of form" (*ibid.*, p. 372).

fiction (though this is not at all where he will end up, as we shall see). He goes on to suggest that it may (paradoxically for him, surely), in the end, be women writers who could move the novel in a different direction, towards a compromise with this notion of propriety; he notes that women writers are beginning to concern themselves with "the sexual" and states: "It is the ladies [...] who would seem to have done most to remind us of man's relations with himself – that is with woman" (*ibid.*, a fascinating comment in itself). He follows this with four pages of discussion on the English-language novel in order to circuitously approach Serao, and it is with "the sexual" in mind that he eventually makes this approach.

In Serao, James sees both the observational skills and realism that are later to be seized on by Croce (and numerous other critics in the wake of both of them), and also the imaginative quality noted positively by Sylvester/Schletter – for which he has much less enthusiasm. Moreover, he also highlights the importance of Serao's origins. She is, for him, because of "her extraordinary Neapolitan temperament, a vivid painter and a rich register of sensations and impressions [...] she reflects at every turn the wonderful mixture that surrounds her – the beauty, the misery, the history, the light and noise and dust" (*ibid.*, pp. 371-373). We are back, then, to that representation of Naples as conceived of in what Moe rightly describes as "superlative, hyperbolic terms" (Moe, 2002, p. 41). The language is reminiscent of that of Goethe in his *Italienische Reise* ([1816-1817] 2008), where noise, crowds and sensuous beauty jostle for pre-eminence. The othering of Naples is indisputable here. As for Serao herself, James enthuses about *Il paese di Cuccagna* (no doubt contributing, in doing so, to its ongoing reputation as Serao's greatest work), but is taken aback by other works she has written. Returning to *Fantasia* (even if he doesn't have it to hand), he finds it "all concentration and erotics" (James, 1901, p. 374), with the exception of the scene at the agricultural show – that scene which aroused sympathy in Schletter and reminded her of Serao's other portrayals of working women – where he sees strong echoes of Flaubert, but manages not to notice the portrayal of the journalist. He defines the Serao of *Fantasia* (in terms that are reminiscent of his first reaction to her in his letter to Grace Norton) as "a lady-novelist [...] flushed with the influence of Émile Zola" (*ibid.*, p. 375). Zola, in turn, is labelled "a lurid warning" even to writers of his own sex, and James also notes that women were "not supposed even to turn his pages" (*ibid.*), to be his readers. Small wonder, then, that he is so taken aback by Serao. *Fantasia* (along with other Serao works such as *Cuore infermo* and *Addio, amore!*) is one of Serao's "novels of 'passion' [which] perfectly meet our speculation as to what might [...] become of our own fiction were our particular convention suspended" (*ibid.*, p. 377). Serao's function here, then, is primarily to serve as a cautionary author. James states clearly she is "to warn us off [...] any [...] lowering of our precious fund of reserve" (*ibid.*, p. 379); she provides an example of "a new kind of vulgarity" (*ibid.*) – a vulgarity all the more pernicious, we can assume, for being practiced by a woman. So, yes, James does make of Serao a figure to be reckoned with – but he has in mind a particular kind of reckoning. For him, she is "this robust and wonderful Serao who is not to be trusted at all" (*ibid.*). Indeed, she awakens in him a "yearning" for her "opposite pole, and there, before we know it, we have positively laid a clinging hand on dear old Jane Austen" (*ibid.*, p. 380). These closing words of James's essay circle right back to its start, to the presumed "femininity" of the English and American novel, which turns out to be a relief in the end after the excesses of Serao. She is altogether too much – in her representations of Naples, which are read through a particular othering lens here, and in herself as a woman writer who not only reads what she should not, but writes it.[19] Serao's status for the foreseeable future is indeed laid out in James's reading. It is interesting, too, that James's cognitive dissonance in relation to Serao's work (his division of it into realist or passionate, rather than any recognition of a hybridity, a generic mix in the writing) is to be repeated in criticism of Serao's work right into the late twentieth century. Richards (1999, p. 89) expresses surprise at his reading of *Il paese di Cuccagna* as unified in form and in this she is absolutely right for *Il paese* is one of the texts where Serao is consciously experimenting with form. The Gothic elements of the plot are all the more arresting for their location in a

19 There's a whole other story, of course, around James's reading of "dear old Jane." Mary Ann O'Farrell astutely notes that James "referring dismissively to 'their "dear", our dear, everybody's dear, Jane' [...] would seem to repudiate his own connection with Jane Austen as an influential forebear" (O'Farrell, 2006, p. 1). Likewise with Serao. Richards details the similarities between James's "In the Cage" and Serao's "Telegrafi dello Stato" in her article (Richards, 1999, pp. 93-99).

domestic (predominantly realist) setting.[20] Serao pushes, deliberately, against generic boundaries repeatedly in her fiction. That this was not generally recognized by critics in her own time says much about their wish to read in specific ways, often following received notions of race, place and sometimes of gender.

## CONCLUSIONS

In this chapter, I have focussed on important voices in English-language criticism of Serao, in an attempt to unravel some of the processes involved in the allocation and transmission of literary status in considerations of her work. Most notable, as I indicated at the outset, is the two-pronged othering that takes place in the work of male critics, an othering based on sex and Southernness. In the works of female critics, it is invariably Southernness alone that provides the basis for a singular kind of othering. The to-ing and fro-ings between the stereotypes to be found in the critical readings of her work are fascinating, and may point forward to similar investigations of English-language othering in the reception of other Italian writers, as well as casting light on particular gendered readings.[21]

Ursula FANNING
University College Dublin

20 See Fanning, 2007, especially pp. 125-127.

21 These processes, I think, continue apace in the critical reception of another, contemporary, Italian writer who has been labelled as extraordinary, Elena Ferrante. Ferrante is regularly presented with special emphasis on her presumed Italian-ness, Southernness and Neapolitan-ness (important in different degrees and in different ways for different critics) in English-language reviews of her work. We are also repeatedly instructed to read her as a woman writer (albeit one who challenges gender stereotypes, in a manner reminiscent of, and yet different from, Serao) and, again, femaleness and femininity are inescapable in English-language critical commentary on her writings. I am currently working on this critical commentary on Ferrante.

## MATILDE SERAO'S FICTION TRANSLATED INTO ENGLISH

Serao Matilde, 1890, *Fantasy* [*Fantasia*], trans. unknown, London, Heinemann.

Serao Matilde, 1894, *Farewell Love!* [*Addio, amore!*], trans. unknown, London, Heinemann.

Serao Matilde, 1901, *The Ballet Dancer and on Guard* [*All'erta sentinella!*], trans. Henry Harland, New York – London, Harper.

Serao Matilde, 1901, *The Land of Cockayne* [*Il paese di Cuccagna*], trans. Richard Davey, London, Heinemann.

Serao Matilde, 1902, *The Conquest of Rome* [*La conquista di Roma*], trans. Richard Davey, London, Heinemann.

Serao Matilde, 1903, *The Land of Cockayne* [*Il paese di Cuccagna*], trans. Richard Davey, New York – London, Pickering and Chatto.

Serao Matilde, 1905, *In the Country of Jesus* [*Nel paese di Gesù*], trans. Richard Davey, London, Heinemann.

Serao Matilde, 1906, *Fantasy: A Novel* [*Fantasia*], trans. Henry Harland – Paul Sylvester, London, London Book Company.

Serao Matilde, 1906, *Farewell Love!* [*Addio, amore!*], trans. Mrs Henry Harland, London, London Book Company.

Serao Matilde, 1909, *After the Pardon* [*Dopo il perdono*], trans. unknown, Irvington, Stuyvesant Press.

Serao Matilde, 1911, *The Desire of Life* [*Evviva la vita!*], trans. William Collinge, London, Stanley Paul & Co.

Serao Matilde, 1919, *Souls Divided* [*Storia di due anime*], trans. William Collinge, New York, Brentano's.

Serao Matilde, 1925, *The Severed Hand* [*La mano tagliata*], trans. David R. Lamb, London, Stanley Paul & Co.

Serao Matilde, 1928, *The Harvest* [*Mors tua…*], trans. William Collinge, London, Nash & Grayson.

# VIENNA DECEMBER 1912

## Leo Spitzer on Matilde Serao[1]

Among the few photographs that allow us to follow Matilde Serao from youth to old age – and to which we have immediate access by typing her name into internet search engines – there is one that shows the writer in the latter stages of life, in which she is captured sitting down, her gloved hands holding an open book that rests on a small table, wearing sumptuous clothes that reflect her social standing, but without a hat.[2] Her striking hair, with tints of white and grey, is drawn back at the neck, but not excessively raised in the elaborate Neapolitan fashion of her youth. She looks at the camera with a calm, affable gaze that is welcoming, but at the same time held in suspense and questioning.

We know that the photograph was taken in 1912 by the Florentine Mario Nunes Vais, a reputable 'amateur' photographer who took portraits of the aristocracy as well as of well-known figures from the spheres of art and society (Vannucci, 1957; Contini, 1978). We can identify the location and the occasion of the photograph, based on a letter sent from Naples by the writer on 25 June 1912, in which she thanks the photographer:

> Dear Friend,
>
> Upon returning to Naples after a visit to Puglia, I found the photographs you kindly sent to me. How I like them! They are real works of art, almost alive and so reflective of my life! Thank you so much, therefore, to the great photographer and artist, and please accept my most affectionate good wishes.
>
> Matilde Serao[3]

---

1 Translated by Sophie Maddison.

2 This photograph may be viewed in Wikimedia Commons at https://commons.wikimedia.org/wiki/File:Matilde_Serao_01.jpg (last accessed 22 January 2021).

3 "Egregio amico, tornando da un mio giro in Puglia, ho trovato, in Napoli, le fotografie da Lei cortesemente inviatemi. Quanto piacere esse m'han fatto! Sono delle vere opere di arte, mentre sono somigliantissime e viventi, quasi, della mia vita! Mille volte grazie,

Apart from the signature, the letter is typewritten on paper, which is headed *"Il Giorno" – Napoli – Il Direttore.* Although this daily Neapolitan newspaper was officially directed by Giuseppe Natale, it was common knowledge that the real director was in fact Matilde Serao and this was an exception in the European context. At the time, Serao was fifty-six years old; she had begun working as a journalist at a young age – starting in Naples before moving to Rome, then back to Naples. Over the years she had gradually become more influential: her continuous journalistic activity was accompanied, as we know, by a considerable output of fiction, which also began in the late 1870s and, by 1912, amounted to roughly forty publications, including novels and collections of short stories. Serao often visited Florence, either as an attendee at conferences or for reasons relating to editorial interests. In that year she was collaborating with the Florentine publisher, Bemporad, and she had written a romantic novel for another Florentine publisher, Salani, *La mano tagliata* (1912), in which she used her narrative skill to produce a risqué yet captivating imitation of the darkest *feuilletons.*

Only two years previously, in 1910, Serao had also had the honour of being officially accepted into the academic canon. A biographical account of the writer appeared in an anthology dedicated to the second half of the nineteenth century in the final volume of the *Manuale della letteratura italiana*, a manual that was widely used and highly regarded in secondary schools as well as universities, and compiled in a distinctly original way by Francesco Torraca, a renowned classical scholar who was well known among European Romance philologists. Serao's biography was followed by several pages taken from the novel *Fantasia* (1883), together with an overview of her previous collection of short stories, *Dal vero* (1879) (Torraca, 1910, pp. 541-550; Melis, 2009, p. 318). When asked by Torraca about her inclusion in the anthology in the summer of 1909, Serao had enthusiastically given her consent in a letter sent from St. Moritz,[4] the famous village in the Swiss Engadine where for a few

dunque, al grande artista della fotografia: e si abbia, anche, i miei più affettuosi saluti. Matilde Serao". This letter, unpublished, is held in the Mario Nunes Vais (Florence 1856-1932) collection in the Alessandro Bonsanti archive at the Gabinetto Vieusseux library, Florence. For more information about the Mario Nunes Vais's photographs held at the Gabinetto Vieusseux library, see: https://www.vieusseux.it/inventari/nunesvais.pdf (last accessed 22 January 2021).

4 "È un onore grande che mi fate e io ve ne debbo gratitudine forte" ["You do me a great honour and I owe you the utmost gratitude"], wrote Serao, in a short but enthusiastic

years the writer had tended to spend the summer months, and where a large part of her recent novel, *Evviva la vita!* (1909),[5] was set. Her fame was increased, at least from the close of the century, by frequent visits to fashionable holiday resorts and Parisian salons, where European and American artists mixed.[6] As for the diffusion of her work, Serao had for some years been widely translated in France (Martin-Gistucci, 1973) and in other European countries.

## THE CIRCULATION OF SERAO'S WORKS IN GERMAN-SPEAKING COUNTRIES IN AND AROUND 1912

In Germany and Austria, too, Matilde Serao was far from unknown. In fact, when considering all translations of her work, we could say that in these countries some of Serao's texts were translated rather early on. In 1890 the Stuttgart publisher Engelhorn (*Engelhorns Allgemeine Romanbibliotek*), which from 1884 onwards had published fortnightly volumes of short stories and novellas by writers from across Europe,[7] released a volume containing two of Serao's short stories, "All'erta sentinella" and "Terno secco", translated by Anna Dulk (1890).[8] It was followed in 1893 by another volume in the same series, containing two short stories, "O Giovannino o la morte" and "Trenta per cento", also

letter on 12 August 1909 from St. Moritz, quoted in Melis, 2009, p. 318, n. 132.

5 The novel was dated at the end "St. Moritz, August 1907 – Naples, June 1908".

6 In St. Moritz Serao also met the art critic Bernard Berenson, who had numerous connections to European and American intellectuals. The Berenson archive at the I Tatti villa (Florence – Fiesole) contains letters written by Serao in St. Moritz in August 1904 and August 1906. See Bernard and Mary Berenson, *Papers, 1880-2002*, Biblioteca Berenson, Villa I Tatti – The Harvard University Center for Italian Renaissance Studies.

7 The series contained collections of stories by writers who were widely read in their native language, including Georges Onhet, Alphonse Daudet, Hector Malot, Rudyard Kipling, François Coppée, Gabriele D'Annunzio and Antonio Fogazzaro. In those years, the publisher made "il più importante contributo alla diffusione di letteratura italiana di consumo" ["the greatest contribution to the diffusion of popular Italian literature"], Balestracci, 2006, p. 395.

8 Anna Dulk – Sehen Pressigny was a renowned translator. In 1888 she had translated Fogazzaro's *Daniele Cortis* into German, again for Engelhorn, and the publisher was very satisfied, cfr. Fogazzaro – Starbuck, 2000, pp. 150, 203.

translated by Dulk (Serao, 1893). These two publications were very timely, when one considers that the stories had only appeared in Italian in volumes by the Milanese publisher Treves in 1889. The same can be said of the collection of stories *Fior di passione*, published in Italy at the end of 1888, and translated by the publisher Schottlaender of Breslau in 1890. As for Serao's novels, let us first note the translation of *Fantasia* in 1886 – not long at all after the Italian publication of 1883 – published by Hermann Costenoble in Jena and dedicated to Hulda Meister von Sacher-Masoch, wife of the writer Leopold von Sacher-Masoch, who was an attentive follower of Italian fiction.[9] Some years later, in 1901, the Balzacian story *Vita e avventure di Riccardo Joanna* was translated in Munich, followed in 1904 by *Il paese di Cuccagna* in Heidelberg and the short volume *Lettere d'amore* in Vienna. In 1908 came the translation of *Dopo il perdono*, in 1910 *Evviva la vita!*, and in 1913 a selection of Serao's work appeared in a collection designed for educational purposes.[10] In terms of the writer's presence in her original Italian in the city and period with which we are concerned – that is, in Vienna up to and including 1912 – the Universitätsbibliothek and the Nationalbibliotek held several of her works, among them first editions of her novel in two volumes *La Ballerina* (1899), *Storia di due anime* (1904), *Dopo il perdono* (1906), *Sterminator Vesevo* (1906), *Lettere di una viaggiatrice* (1908), *Evviva la vita!* (1909), and the incredibly rare conference paper that is difficult to find even in Italy, *L'Italia di Stendhal* (1898). In addition, there were works held in second or subsequent editions, including *Castigo* ([1893] 1911), *Cuore infermo* ([1881] 1908), *Il romanzo della fanciulla* ([1886] 1909), *Le amanti* ([1894] 1907) and *Leggende napoletane* ([1881] 1895).

9 At the time Hulda Meister (1846-1918), the second wife of the Austrian writer Leopold von Sacher-Masoch and a translator from other Romance languages, had translated other Italian works, including Paolo Mantegazza's *India*.

10 This volume, edited by Pia Di Mayo-Gelati, was "Neuere Italienische Schriftsteller", the second of a sub-collection in the "Italienische Lehrbücher" series, designed as an educational tool for those wishing to learn Italian. A brief introduction to Serao's life and works was followed by a seventy-page anthology published in Italian (among the stories selected were *Piccole anime*, *Dal vero*, *Leggende napoletane* and *Pagine mistiche*), with explanatory notes and, finally, around twenty pages of Italian-German vocabulary (it is worth noting that the first volume, which was also published in 1913 and edited by Di Mayo-Gelati, had been dedicated to Leopardi. The third volume, edited by Maria Stura, was dedicated to the work of Giuseppe Giacosa. The fourth, edited by Oreste Antognoni, was dedicated to Gabriele D'Annunzio and published in 1914).

## DECEMBER 1912, VIENNA: LEO SPITZER'S LECTURE ON MATILDE SERAO

It is not surprising, therefore, that in December 1912 a young Viennese scholar, Leo Spitzer – a bright socialite and frequent visitor to France and Italy – chose to dedicate his first lecture as a *Privatdozent*, delivered at the university of his home city which was famous for its cosmopolitan inclinations, to a portrait of Matilde Serao, in whom he was interested for several reasons (Spitzer, 1914; Melis, 2010).[11]

Born in 1887, Spitzer held a Wilhelm Meyer-Lübke degree in Romance Linguistics, which included a thesis on word formation in Rabelais and Balzac published in 1910, and in the years that followed he had continued to study romance languages and literature, focusing in particular on French and Italian (Wellek, 1991, pp. 134-153; Paccagnella – Gregori, 2010).[12] In the same period, through his work *Italienische Umgangsprache* [*Conversational Italian*], which was completed in 1914, Spitzer had immersed himself in an exploration of spoken Italian – a spoken language that was largely mediated by the works of contemporary Italian writers, not least those from the south of Italy such as Roberto Bracco, Salvatore Di Giacomo, Federico De Roberto, Giuseppe Pitrè, Giovanni Verga and, indeed, Matilde Serao (Spitzer, 1922).[13] Subsequent life experiences, linked to his involvement in the First World War, led Spitzer to complete the "Italian triptych" with two further detailed

11 The address, given on 20 December 1912, was only published in 1914, but neither included in a volume nor translated into Italian. Rossana Melis examined it, in part, during her lecture for a conference organized by the Circolo Filologico Linguistico Padovano in 2008. See below n. 12.

12 Of the ample scholarship on the literary critic Leo Spitzer (Vienna, 1887 – Forte dei Marmi, 1960), we refer readers to the general account provided by René Wellek, and the preface to the volume published in 2010 by the Circolo Filologico Linguistico Padovano, following a conference dedicated to Spitzer in Bressanone / Innsbruck in July 2008, Paccagnella – Gregori, 2010. This volume contains Maria Luisa Wandruszka's piece on "l'esprit des femmes" in Spitzerian stylistics (Wandruszka, 2010).

13 There are many quotations from Serao's novels and short stories in *Italienische Umgangsprache*, and in particular from *I capelli di Sansone*, *Storia di due anime*, *La ballerina*, *La conquista di Roma*, *Il ventre di Napoli*, *Addio, Amore!*, *Lettere d'una viaggiatrice*, *All'erta, sentinella!*, and *Il paese di Cuccagna*. See the Italian edition of Spitzer, 2007, pp. 80, 89, 123, 152-153, 164, 187, 213, 218, 229, 230-231, 248-249, 297, 303, 304-305.

analyses of spoken Italian (Spitzer, 1920; Spitzer, 1921). The public address on Serao, held in a lecture theatre at the University of Vienna, was therefore the fruit of Spitzer's in-depth knowledge of contemporary Italian literature, which in turn stemmed from a frequently expressed passion for the Italian nation and its language, and from a "need for vitality" that Italy was able to fulfil (Contini, 1985, p. 10).

At the beginning of the lecture, Spitzer asserted that Naturalism – a literary movement which, he specified, approached the novel as an *oeuvre scientifique* – was "a product of contemporary urban society"[14] (Spitzer, 1914, p. 573). Indeed, it was no coincidence that Naturalism had begun its journey across Europe in a large city, Paris, and that it had been instigated by city dwellers such as Flaubert, the Goncourt brothers and Zola. But immediately afterwards, Spitzer alluded to a geo-anthropological factor that formed a crucial element of his introduction, namely the meridian heat of everyday life in which Italian authors – in contrast to their French contemporaries – were immersed, and which they were able to grasp and express with ease:

> The Italians conveyed local colour with the scientific pretences of the *roman experimental*, in the open air of their own land – from the overheated cultural environment sparked by the electric tensions of Paris to the natural heat of real public life; that which Zola strained to express through knowledge obtained in the library with shark-like voracity, in Italy was within arm's reach, right there in the middle of the street, waiting for an artist to capture it in folkloric material. And within Italy it was once again, and very fortunately, the south that was vividly struck by the Naturalism of Parisian origin; fortunately because the south, with its strong regional character, its dialects that continued to flourish, and its customs that were yet to come into line with those of Europe, offered powerful and genuinely native themes that expressed the *goût du terroir* (*ibid.*, p. 574).

And so, focusing on two of its exponents, Zola and Maupassant, Spitzer explained how there were two strands of Naturalism; one he defined as having a mainly descriptive-didactic character, the other as having a predominantly artistic-stylistic nature. Spitzer linked the Maupassant strand to the realism of Verga – "the one's Sicilian peasants are the other's Norman stepbrothers" (*ibid.*, p. 574), while he likened Serao

14 This and all other original quotations from Spitzer's essay on Matilde Serao may be found in the transcription of the original text in the Appendix below.

to the experience of Zola, noting the importance of both her fervent journalistic activity and, above all, the fact that she was a woman, and a woman of the south:

> Matilde Serao, too, has that documentary, Enlightenment-style trait that we recognise in Zola. Not content, however, with a pseudoscientific objectivity, and as an experienced journalist who over the course of more than 30 years has been the editor of major newspapers, she looks to cast a wide net, to teach and admonish [...] Matilde Serao is not only a documentary writer, she is a woman and a Neapolitan [...] As a woman, and a woman of the south for whom the instincts of life are more important than social habits imbued by heredity and environment, she has removed all traces of determinism from her own realism; in Serao's novels individuals, and in particular many female figures, live through the strength of hate and the power of love (*ibid.*, p. 574).

Spitzer continued to outline a profile of Serao by drawing on general references to the literary-historical categories of Romanticism *versus* Naturalism, while at the same time underlining the inadequacy of those very definitions when applied to the unique characteristics of Serao's realism. He was clear in highlighting the writer's debts regarding Zola, at times making observations – which remain pertinent and are rarely exploited by other critics – that reveal his precocious ability as an attentive and astute reader:

> when, in the journalistic novel *I capelli di Sansone*, the printing machine is anthropomorphized as in Zola, and appears as *a large and mysterious thing*, like a thinking, writing being whose black insides, on a daily basis, produce "a determined and incoercible labour with a precise, inflexible movement" and *hurl out* the newspaper, we witness a mythicization of the machine that in Zola, too, is more characteristic of Romanticism than of Naturalism. In conclusion, we can easily say that: Serao responds to the call of French Naturalism with romantic creations. In Serao's work, the romantic does not only manifest itself in pleasing contrasts and colourful portrayals of passionate characters, it also takes the form of an emotional involvement with the abandoned and the oppressed – the outlaws and outcasts of society. For Serao, those who have been ruined by playing the lottery are not taken as examples for a sociological, evolutionary representation of society, but are poor and oppressed in a way that calls out for the kingdom of heaven, as with Verga's downtrodden Sicilians. And I do not believe that Serao begins by creating an environment in which she immerses a series of characters and plotlines, as Zola claims to do, but that characters and environment take form simultaneously in her imagination and cannot be distinguished from each other (*ibid.*, p. 576).

In order to demonstrate that in Serao it is not only Romanticism and Naturalism "but often also journalism that are interconnected",[15] Spitzer carried out an in-depth analysis of a novel published in 1899, *La ballerina*, which portrays the unrequited love of a poor dancer, Carmela Minino, for an aristocrat, Ferdinando Terzi, who, in a sudden act of love, commits suicide in a small guest house (*ibid.*, p. 576). The dancer watches over Terzi at night and, whilst praying, finally expresses her feelings. After reading the final two pages of the novel, Spitzer observed:

> Let us begin by analysing the 'literary elements' of this scene, towards which the rest of the text builds: the contrasting combination of eroticism and religion, as with the showing of the rosary and the kiss given to the corpse; together with the social contrast between the unattractive, working-class dancer and the high-ranking aristocrat who, handsome even in death, resembles an Oscar Wilde character. This social contrast is overcome by love only in the face of death and is reiterated by the emphatic final sentence, with the juxtaposition of the grand name of Ferdinando Terzi, Count of Torregrande, and the modest one of Carmela Minino. All of this is romanticism and, more precisely, a melodramatic romanticism resembling the works of Victor Hugo, as well as realist Italian operas by the likes of Mascagni and Leoncavallo which today, in theatres all over the world, are a glorious reincarnation of bygone romantic theatre. Naturalism, however, is the source of that desolate description of the guest house room, that drop of blood on the clothing, that judicial inquiry in the presence of someone who loves and is tormented by pain – in short, that inexorability of things alongside the suffering individual and, especially, the subsequent description of the dancer's misery and the wretchedness at work behind the scenes. Both these elements – the melodramatic makeup of the situation as well as its indulgence in naturalistic detail – lead to what I have defined as a journalistic quality: the entire portrayal resembles a *fait divers*, the crude and squalid work of a reporter (*ibid.*, p. 576).

## ENGAGEMENT WITH BENEDETTO CROCE

At this point in his address Spitzer quoted the scholar and philosopher, historian, and literary critic Benedetto Croce. Born in 1866, Croce was a prolific writer who was followed and admired in Italy, but also very well

15 "oft auch Journalismus ineinander verwoben sind".

known in German-speaking countries. In 1903 he had published a long and comprehensive piece on the works of Matilde Serao (Croce, 1903), which appeared in the journal he had recently founded, *La Critica*.[16] The article marked, as is often noted, an important turning point in terms of critical opinion with regard to Serao. Croce discussed in it her work of the 1880s at length but paid very little attention to her novels of later years, during which, he wrote, "she began to move in a completely different direction, operating against her own nature" (*ibid.*, p. 346),[17] therefore following the trend of the so-called psychological novel, whose artistic characteristics Croce was outspoken in condemning. According to the critic, Serao did, however, return to "lived life" (*ibid.*, p. 349) with the short novels *La ballerina* and *L'anima semplice: Suor Giovanna della Croce* (1901). Croce dedicated just a few lines to *La ballerina* which, he asserted, "is long, excessive and persistent; but in the final part gains in rhythm and passion" (Croce, 1903, p. 350).[18] Croce went on to quote the final page of the novel.

Spitzer, who was an attentive follower and admirer of Croce, was inspired by that brief but clear judgement to underline the differing standpoint of the German reader:

> Italian criticism, including that of Croce, has shown itself more willing to accept such a situation than we Germans, who refute descriptions that are dramatic beyond the point of authorial, artistic skill and enter into the realms of sensationalism or the darkest form of Naturalism, cine-drama. Croce, who applauds the final scene of *La ballerina*, recognizes verbosity in the first part. Here, where Serao describes the existence of the little dancer who is exploited by the theatre directors, we are above all moved by the passage describing the crown of flowers she buys for All Saints' Day using the last of her savings, and that she places on the grave of her godmother and former protector (Spitzer, 1914, p. 579).

To support his argument, Spitzer referred to another long article dedicated to Matilde Serao and published in French by Jean Dornis (1907, pp. 157-187),[19] which had accepted the violence of the novel's closing scene with

16 A copy of the journal collection is held at the *Institut für Romanistik* at the University of Vienna.

17 Here, and subsequently, I am quoting from the journal, since Croce only published the essay – with some significant modifications – in the third volume of *Letteratura della Nuova Italia*, published in 1915 (Bari, Laterza), "ella entra a percorrere una via affatto diversa, operando contro la propria indole".

18 "ha lungherie e soverchie insistenze; ma nell'ultima parte acquista passione e rapidità".

19 Jean Dornis was the pseudonym of Elena Goldschmidt-Franchetti (Florence, 1870-1947). In this work, she provided a particularly positive analysis of Matilde Serao.

a far from coincidental nod to the profoundly Italian characteristics by which it was inspired:

> The French Dornis also appreciates the scene, considering it a product of that absolute, *profoundly Italian and almost religious love*. When Dornis cites the words of Christ: "Love is stronger than death, it does not know repugnance," we are moved to wonder whether art can represent a similar "love that provokes repugnance" (Spitzer, 1914, p. 578).

Croce's article – as we have already noted – was certainly the driving force behind Spitzer's conference address. The Viennese critic – through a method that would remain characteristic of his research, namely an inclination towards polemical yet constructive engagement with the research of other scholars – felt obliged to justify his approach to the works of Serao, which was so different from that of the Neapolitan philosopher. If he had not dwelt on the "good works" of the 1880s, he explained, but had analysed *La ballerina*, it was "to demonstrate not the limits of Serao's talent but, in contrast, the reasons for which the German reader's understanding of an art with such strong southern characteristics could not be taken for granted" (*ibid.*). That it was also Spitzer's intention to dispute some of Croce's observations became clear in the next part of his lecture, during which he wished above all "to clarify a problem that is highly disputed in French and Italian criticism: that of the *conversion* of Serao" (*ibid.*).

At this stage Spitzer referred to works published after Serao's visit to Jerusalem in 1893: from *Nel paese di Gesù* to *La Madonna e i Santi*, *L'anima semplice: Suor Giovanna della Croce* and *Storia di due anime*. According to the critic, the fact that these works signalled a shift in Serao's style was contentious. Indeed, he moved away from the position of Croce who, in *La Critica*, had written: "This mysticism was a present given to her, we think, by Fogazzaro. And Serao, the great naturalist, rebelled against her best source of inspiration" (Croce, 1903, p. 349).[20] Again, Spitzer doubled down, turning to another French scholar, Maurice Muret (1906, pp. 75-89):

> While Croce defines Serao's neo-mysticism as a question of fashion, as a 'present from Fogazzaro', Maurice Muret, in his *Littérature italienne d'aujourd'hui*, retorts: we cannot speak of a fracture in the output of Serao; a Neapolitan

20 "Questo misticismo è regalo che le è stato fatto, crediamo, dal Fogazzaro. E la Serao, la forte artista del naturalismo, si è ribellata alla sua migliore sorgente".

> Catholicism dominated her work, before and after her visit to Jerusalem (Spitzer, 1914, p. 579).

Spitzer then reiterated the importance of Serao's Neapolitan origins; of the fact that she had always "demonstrated that *naïve* mixture of paganism and Catholicism particular to Neapolitan faith", even in works that preceded her so-called conversion. This was because, Spitzer argued, "alongside the Naples of Chiaia, via Toledo and the San Carlo theatre, there had always been a Naples of the churches of Santa Maria della Pietà, Santa Chiara and San Gennaro". He concluded: "Serao's Christianity is full of the *vivid sun* of Naples! [...] Serao's religion is not a question of fashion, but a matter of tradition and heart" (*ibid.*, p. 580).

If, in his argument, Spitzer cited Croce, Dornis and Muret, he must also have had in mind another critic with links to German culture, Giuseppe Antonio Borgese. In those years the latter was professor of German literature at the University of Rome and had recently published *La Vita e il Libro* (1910), a volume that contained a review of Serao's *San Gennaro nella leggenda e nella vita*. Constructed in that bright, lively style typical of Borgese, it was in fact a slating that ridiculed the very debate surrounding Serao's 'mysticism', with Borgese himself citing Croce and underlining Serao's provincialism.[21] Spitzer was therefore involving himself in a contemporary discussion, to which he wanted to add the psychological observations that constituted a profound stimulus for his own research.

---

21 "Di là da Sorrento o da Pozzuoli, la Serao si sente all'estero, ed è gran meraviglia se concede qualche fuggevole simpatia a Montecarlo, a Parigi, a Saint-Moritz, a quei tre o quattro punti luminosi della carta geografica, nei quali per un italiano di vecchio stampo si esauriva l'orbe terraqueo e il sistema planetario" ["Away from Sorrento or Pozzuoli, Serao feels as though she is abroad, and it's a wonder she gives even fleeting sympathy to Monte Carlo, Paris or St. Moritz, those three or four bright points on the map where, for an old-fashioned Italian, the world's orbit and the planetary system runs out"] (Borgese, 1910, p. 376).

## A PSYCHOLOGICAL ANALYSIS

If, up to that point, the Viennese critic had analysed the work of Matilde Serao by filtering it through the characteristics of an entire people – and obviously, within all this the influence of the theories of Karl Vossler emerged very clearly – in subsequent analyses he placed a more explicit focus on the writer's personality and, above all, on her contradictory attitudes – as a result of which her works were able to accommodate both Romanticism and Naturalism, religion and paganism, passion and 'strict morality'. It was evident that existential contradictions lay within her life choices. And Spitzer, drawing on contemporary sociological research (Sollini, 1907), immediately drew attention to the most notable and glaring contradiction, which concerned Serao's position regarding female emancipation. This position was predominantly gleaned from female characters in the writer's works:

> Matilde Serao has not led the theoretical campaign against feminism which, in the north of Italy, Neera pursued so tirelessly. But on the other hand, she has never incorporated the Ibsenite woman into her work. On the contrary, she describes the woman who is subjected to the struggles of a profession, as in *Ballerina* or the short story *Telegrafi di Stato*, which brings to light the poverty of the telegraph operator, but not the woman who recognizes a destiny of intellectual advancement. It is indicative that Serao, in her journalistic novel, does not address the life of the female journalist which she knows through direct experience, and to which even in *Fantasia*, when the heroine expresses sympathy with regard to a journalist, her partner responds: *You would still rather be a woman!* In this respect Serao, like the younger Grazia Deledda, is a product of her Latin, conservative background. Serao's women could in most cases be assigned the title of one of her short stories: *O Giovannino o la morte* [...] (Spitzer, 1914, p. 581).

More than any other passage quoted so far, this extract shows us quite clearly the extent to which the critic, in a decidedly raw piece of work, already demonstrated skills of analysis which, in subsequent years, would be deemed "rhabdomantic" (Melis, 2010, p. 501). Here Spitzer, to highlight the writer's contradictory position regarding her own journalistic profession, briefly quoted Andrea, the male protagonist of *Fantasia*, as he addresses one of the two female protagonists, the beautiful and anxious Lucia Altimare. At the opening of an agricultural show in Caserta, which she attends with Andrea and the other protagonist Caterina, Lucia catches sight of a compact group of journalists watching the ceremony, which includes a "young lady in simple mourning dress, pale and sickly beneath the black brim of her hat" (Serao, 1883a, p. 167).[22] Referring to this sole female journalist, Lucia remarks: "I envy her, if she is intelligent. At least she has ambition", to which Andrea immediately replies: "Oh well! You would still rather be a woman" (*ibid.*, pp. 167-168).[23]

Of the entire novel, Spitzer quoted just a single scene – and even then, just a short exchange. But the extract he chose is the very one which – drawing as we can today on the help of biographical information, historical context, and journalistic material – can undoubtedly be considered a key and revealing passage, for the very reason that the writer, who never indulged in direct autobiographical portrayals, had depicted herself in the grieving journalist. In early September 1879 Serao had attended the same agricultural show as a reporter for the daily Neapolitan newspaper *Il Piccolo*; she was grieving because a few weeks previously her mother had died, and she was suffering. And so, in those lines – through a combination of cross-references and mirror images, in which the male and female gaze cross in observation of the young female figure dressed in black and white, an indication of irreconcilable contrasts – she portrayed the very conflict with which she grappled in her own life (Melis, 2011, pp. 163-164).

Spitzer continued to insist upon and drive home his interpretations of Serao's contradictory nature, referring to portraits of the writer and drawing on the observations of Ugo Ojetti:

> Yes, Serao's work indicates health. She is the picture of health – a rather stout, matronly figure; jovial and middle-class, with a healthy way of life. Ojetti has described her as follows: every day this woman writes columns for her own newspaper as well as some pages for the novel she is working on, often remaining in front of her typewriter until three o'clock in the morning. She never misses a public event in Rome, gives lectures, and writes accounts of

22 "giovane, vestita di lutto, semplicemente, pallida e malaticcia sotto la falda nera del cappello".

23 "Io la invidio, se è intelligente. Ha almeno un'ambizione. – Al che Andrea aveva appunto ricordato: – Bah! Preferite sempre essere una donna".

> her travels to Jerusalem, the Riviera, the Tyrol and Paris – and at the same time, she is mother to six children.[24] How strange it is that this woman of action has not become a woman of words; that during an interview, when asked about her attitude towards feminism, she replied: *I don't understand it at all!* How strange, too, that this virile writer (she was described by D'Annunzio, in his preface to *Giovanni Episcopo* dedicated to Serao, as having a *virile industriousness*) who said of herself: *I am not a female writer, I am a writer*, is able to describe female characters, but not male characters, with only a few rare exceptions! (Spitzer, 1914, p. 581).

"How strange", Spitzer kept repeating. In fact, this very strangeness is probably what attracted him more than ever to Serao in 1912, a year already struck by flashes of war. Indeed, Serao's commitment must have stood out to him as a contrast and a contradiction of the "jovial", affable image projected by her physical appearance. And he provided a precise indication of this in the opening pages of his work on the writer, asserting:

> [Serao] looks to cast a wide net, to teach and admonish; from the beginning of her literary career, when she wrote *Il ventre di Napoli*, to her sketches of ordinary Neapolitan life, she gives artistic form to what is a documented appeal to governmental authority. This continues in 1912, as she travels through the cities of Italy as a speaker letting out deep, bellicose cries of *Evviva la Guerra!* Serao has never stopped expressing her own *j'accuse*, and even more so her *je défends* (*ibid.*, p. 575).

## SERAO'S LECTURES ON THE WAR
## *Evviva la Guerra!* (Primavera italica)

Spitzer then recounted a recent event. Between autumn 1911 and 1912, Italy was involved in a conflict with the Ottoman Empire. Thousands and thousands of Italian soldiers were sent to North Africa to invade

24 After her first child, which was stillborn in late May 1885, Matilde Serao had four sons with Edoardo Scarfoglio. Then, after they separated, she had a daughter, Eleonora, with the lawyer Giuseppe Natale. It is probable, however, that Spitzer included the daughter Scarfoglio had with the actress Gabrielle Bessard, who committed suicide while the child was still in infancy. Matilde raised her alongside her own sons and named her after her own mother, Paolina.

Libya, with mixed results. Serao too – like other literary figures before her (we need only mention Giovanni Pascoli and Gabriele D'Annunzio) – had taken the opportunity to speak out on the issue in favour of Italian action, at a lecture given for the first time in Rome on 3 May 1912, entitled *Evviva la guerra!* [*Long Live the War!*] Although the title was reminiscent of a well-known novel of hers, *Evviva la vita!* (1909), which she herself referred to as being 'cosmopolitan', the tone was obviously different. In fact, to quote Spitzer, here she let out "deep, bellicose cries". In July that year the Neapolitan editor Perrella had published the lecture, together with other pieces written by Serao on the same subject, which had already appeared in the daily Neapolitan newspaper *Il Giorno* as well as the *Giornale d'Italia* in Rome. However, if we pay close attention to the volume's design, we can see that the title was in fact split into two: *Evviva la guerra!* was followed by the bracketed subtitle *Primavera italica* [*Italian Spring*]. This subtitle appeared on each page in the upper right-hand margin, while the title was printed on the left-hand side (Serao, 1912, pp. 9-53). If we examine this doubling, we discover that only the innocuous subtitle had been used when Serao delivered the same lecture in Florence's Sala della Filarmonica on 31 May 1912, in front of a huge audience.

This is precisely the occasion discussed at the beginning of this chapter, when Serao had been photographed by Nunes Vais in the striking portrait that captured her good nature alongside her inquiring gaze.[25] The same lecture was given with the title *Evviva la guerra!* in Venice on 26 May. But three days later, in Milan, the title once again became *Primavera italica.*[26] Such variations were clearly opportunistic and varied according to the political climate and the differing levels of support shown towards military intervention throughout the many Italian cities (both northern and southern) in which the lecture was delivered. Even the text itself began by toning down the belligerent nature of the event, immediately shifting attention to the painful aspects of war and the "obscure" dead soldiers:

25 Details of the event, which include a list of speakers, were described at length in the local section of the daily Florentine newspaper *La Nazione* on 1 June 1912, p. 4.

26 For notes on the lecture given in the cities of northern and southern Italy, concluding with Naples on 23 June (with the title *Evviva la guerra!* and attended by Benedetto Croce), see the May and June 1912 issues of the daily Neapolitan newspaper *Il Giorno.*

> Thoughtful and compassionate ladies, courteous and affectionate gentlemen, before exalting the war, let us remember those who have died in Libya. [...] And with yet more affectionate and sorrowful minds, let us remember, amongst the dead of Libya, the simple soldiers, the modest soldiers, the obscure soldiers who, in their hundreds, have given their lives so that the word Italy, from now on and more so now than ever, may also signify indomitable courage, magnificent valour and sublime unselfishness (Serao, 1912, pp. 9, 12).[27]

Serao's commitment was nevertheless underlined with notable emphasis by the Italian press. The cosmopolitan and profoundly pacifist Spitzer (Renzi, 1976, pp. VII-XXXIII) – who was a close follower of the Italian press – was therefore shocked by her clearly oscillating position regarding a subject as tragic as the war.

Serao therefore embodied an Italian nature that fascinated Spitzer, for the very reason that it was contradictory – and for the questions this raised. It was for this reason – and he was very aware of this himself – that he was involved in researching Italian language and literature. In September 1914, dedicating *Italienische Umgangssprache* [*Conversational Italian*] to his mentor, W. Meyer-Lübke, he defined the work as one which, "rather than resolving problems, uncovered problematic issues; rather than distinguishing that which is crystal clear from that which is obscure, it 'illuminated' the obscure aspects of the clear" (Spitzer, 2007, p. 53).[28] Then, when the volume was published in 1922 following the end of the WWI, it contained an afterword in which Spitzer reflected at length on why he had paid so much attention to the language of the Italian people, reiterating remarks he had already made:

> Though rooted in the individual, the Italians never lose sight of all that is social, and they are therefore the subjects of interesting studies from both a sociological and a linguistic point of view. And it is no wonder that, when it comes to Italian discourse, there is an impenetrable interlinking of frankness and pretence, of sincerity and false declarations. This is nothing but the

---

27 "Pensose e pietose ascoltatrici, cortesi e affettuosi ascoltatori, prima di pronunciare la parola di esaltazione, *evviva la guerra,* salutiamo i morti di Libia. [...] E con animo anche più affettuoso e dolente, salutiamo, fra i morti di Libia, i semplici soldati; i modesti soldati, gli oscuri soldati che, a centinaia, han dato la loro vita, perché la parola Italia, oramai e più che mai, significasse, anche, indomito coraggio, magnifico valore, sublime disinteresse".

28 "anziché risolvere problemi, rileva aspetti problematici; anziché scindere ciò che è cristallino da tutto quanto è oscuro, 'illumina' gli aspetti oscuri di quanto è cristallino".

> open manifestation of that very human impulse to affect others through the expression of the self; the role-play at work in every discourse; the staging of the *pathos* which gives voice to human suffering. In this way, that antinomy between *passion* and *calculation*, which one encounters in discourse and which is considered authentically Italian, dissolves into a distinctly human characteristic (*ibid.*, pp. 354-355).[29]

That antinomy characteristic of "Italian discourse", which Spitzer viewed as tightly linked to the impossibility of applying clear and definitive literary categories, would therefore appear to filter down into an understanding of human nature. And as far as the contradictions in Serao's character are concerned, this did not prevent Spitzer from closing his introductory lecture with a reminder of her undeniable artistic talent:

> Never again will we forget the Balzacian César Birotteau, who dies holding his accounting books all in order; Sangiorgi [sic] in *La Conquista di Roma* who, the night before his duel, talks to two sabre swords that shine in the darkness; the agitated people of Naples who, cursing, implore God to liquify the blood of Saint Gennaro. Matilde Serao is an excellent observer of people and of the crowd (Spitzer, 1914, p. 584).

## THE LECTURE IS SENT TO BENEDETTO CROCE AS A SYMBOL OF FRIENDSHIP

Spitzer never released his lecture on Matilde Serao in a published work, probably because he did not consider it to be as good a product as his subsequent scholarship. Nevertheless, although it is raw and disjointed, it contains the seeds – as is often the case with works by young writers – of the theories that were to form the nucleus of his critical

29 "Gli italiani, pur restando ben ancorati al suolo del loro io, non perdono mai di vista l'aspetto sociale, e sono pertanto soggetti di studio interessanti sia per il sociologo sia per il linguista. E non può destare meraviglia alcuna l'impenetrabile intreccio di franchezza e finzione, di sincerità e 'vuota declamazione' proprio del discorso italiano. Esso non è altro che l'aperta manifestazione dell'impulso propriamente umano a fare effetto sugli altri attraverso l'estrinsecazione dell'io, del gioco delle parti insito in ogni discorso, della messa in scena del *pathos* che dà voce al dolore delle creature umane. Così quell'antinomia tra *passione* e *calcolo*, che si riscontra nel discorso ed è considerata autenticamente italiana, si dissolve in una caratteristica propriamente umana".

method (Spitzer, 1960). In every way, that introductory address on the Italian writer – recorded in just a few printed pages, and in the climate of military tension that clouded all of Europe during those years – played a significant role in terms of awareness and reconciliation, and one that we think is worth remembering. Indeed, we have sourced an extract (*Sonderdruck*) from Spitzer's short essay held at the Benedetto Croce library in Naples.[30] On the cover there is an undated dedication: "To the great literary critic who has expressed solidarity with our German culture in recent days, may this illustrate that we too share his love and admiration for the Romanic world / L. Spitzer".[31]

This dedication brings us back to the subject of war. When the article was finally published in Heidelberg, in the sixth instalment of *Germanisch-Romanische Monatsschrift*, it was the end of 1914. For some months, the Central Powers had been at war with France, Britain and Russia, while Italy was at that stage neutral. Within Italy, the debate between interventionists and neutrals was gradually becoming more heated, and public positions were increasingly divided. As early as October 1914 Benedetto Croce, who had strong links with German culture, had joined other Italian intellectuals in signing a letter of solidarity with Richard Delbrück, director of the German Archaeological Institute in Rome, urging greater caution in judging the warmongering activity of Germany. In the months that followed Croce made further statements, which always tended to defend German culture, up until the beginning of the Italian involvement in the war in May 1915. These statements, which appeared collectively in 1919 in the first edition of *Pagine sulla guerra* (Croce, 1919), were first published in *La Critica* or *Italia nostra*, weekly journals founded by Cesare De Lollis – a non-interventionist professor of Romance Philology at the University of Rome (Monticone, 1971) – and always gained some degree of attention, generally being republished in daily newspapers. Although we cannot be certain, it is highly likely that Spitzer, in his dedication, was alluding to an article by Croce entitled "Cultura e politica italiana", which appeared in *Italia*

30 Naples, Biblioteca Benedetto Croce, inventory 12239. The extract is in a miscellaneous volume. We are grateful to Dr Teresa Leo, director of the Croce library, for the information and material she kindly provided.

31 "Dem großen Literaturkritiker, der in diesen Tagen seine Solidarität mit unserer deutschen Kultur geäußert hat, als kleiner Beweis, daß auch wir stets dem Romanentum bewundernd und liebevoll gegenüberstehen. / L. Spitzer".

*nostra* on 27 December 1914. In it, the philosopher emphasized his "profound admiration" for the "political and ethical virtue" of Germany (Croce, 1928, p. 22).[32] And Spitzer – who during those weeks must have received a copy of his lecture on Serao – is likely to have sent this to Croce between the end of December 1914 and the beginning of 1915, by way of a tangible and concrete demonstration of reciprocated sentiment.

We have highlighted this detail because the estimated date precedes, by a number of crucial years, the beginning of direct written correspondence between the Austrian critic and Benedetto Croce – a correspondence that was not made any easier by the conclusion of the war (between 1915 and 1918, Spitzer was working in the censorship offices of Vienna). In fact, subsequent and indirect traces of this correspondence do not appear until the year of peace, 1919 (Colussi, 2009; Colussi, 2010). As is well known, the Neapolitan philosopher was from that point onwards one of the main proponents of Spitzer's work in Italy and, more importantly, he provided psychological support that was far from insignificant when the Viennese critic was expelled from German universities in 1933 because of his Jewish heritage.

## "THE TRUEST MATILDE SERAO"

With regard to the balancing of roles as a writer, a journalist and a woman – in essence, those contradictions to which Leo Spitzer was irreversibly drawn at the time – Matilde Serao's approach was honest and, this time, devoid of hesitation or oscillation; in 1926 she published the long anti-war novel *Mors tua…* (1926). It is a work that casts a courageous and thoroughly female eye on the Great War, the events and outcome of which are harmful for all characters (Fanning, 2002; Fanning, 2006, pp. 134-136). Serao paid heavily for this harsh judgement, with her journalistic reputation suffering until her final days, when she was refused publication of a collection of memoirs in a widely-read Italian daily newspaper.[33]

32 "profonda ammirazione", "virtù politica ed etica".

33 In this regard, we will shortly publish documents held in Italian public archives.

A close Neapolitan friend of Serao's, the journalist and playwright Roberto Bracco, left behind a valuable account of her final disappointments, as well as the strength with which she dealt with them. Born in Naples in 1861, Bracco had known Serao since his youth – in 1881 he worked as a reporter for the Neapolitan daily *Il Corriere del Mattino* (to which Serao also contributed) – and continued to see her until a few weeks before she died, on the evening of 25 July 1927. At that point, he wrote an obituary which was published that year in *Nación*, a daily newspaper in Buenos Aires to which he had been contributing for years (Bracco, 1941).

Bracco was a liberal antifascist who was being watched by the regime, but he was probably able to send correspondence abroad, expressing himself more freely than Italian censorship – or auto-censorship – allowed for at the time. The obituary, which was significantly titled *La più vera Matilde Serao (Dopo la sua morte)* [*The Truest Matilde Serao (After Her Death)*], began as follows: "I like to imagine that she, up there, would be more appreciative of these few commemorative pages if I begin by addressing the novel *Mors tua...*, which was inspired by the Great War and which marked the end of her artistic career" (*ibid.*, p. 101).[34] The article continued by underlining the work's anti-militarist nature and noting how it was received when first published: "Amid scarce instances of praise, which demonstrated a generous lenience towards the meaning – the *thesis* – of the novel, what irrupted were accusations of anti-patriotism, blame and insults, which damaged her reputation (*ibid.*, p. 102).[35] It then recounts the way in which the writer reacted – on a day when he was present – upon reading "a horrendous article that insulted her":[36]

> Seated at her large desk, a loyal servant to the inner workings and instantaneity of journalism, she raised that big strong head of hers, which bore the noble marks of age and was softly framed by the large halo of her white hair. Her energetic attitude was clouded by the veil of tears she was holding back, which dulled the vibrant shine of her wide, black eyes. But her words, like her attitude, were energetic:

34 "Ho l'illusione che possano riuscire più gradite a Lei, lassù, queste poche pagine commemorative se anzitutto mi occupo del romanzo *Mors tua...*, che le fu ispirato dalla Grande Guerra e con cui si chiuse la vita della sua arte".

35 "Tra gli scarsi elogi, che ostentavano una generosa indulgenza per la significazione – per la *tesi* – del romanzo, irruppero accuse di antipatriottismo e biasimi e contumelie, che aggredivano il suo prestigio".

36 "un orrendo articolo che la insultava".

> "They have hurt me. Trodden on me. Torn me to pieces. But no matter! If I hadn't yet written this novel, I would still write it exactly as it is written. And I wouldn't want to die without having spoken about what the war revealed to me, and how it made me feel" (*ibid.*, p. 103).[37]

The obituary closed with a phrase introduced by a negation that therefore cancelled out the following, widely diffused image (Spitzer, too, defined Serao as "jovial and middle-class") – that of her happy and affable "Italian" character:

> That day I did not hear the famous, shrill laugh of Matilde Serao, the laugh that is constantly remembered as a characteristic *leitmotif*, appearing in every account or remark made of her, and with which the most sentimental and passionate Italian writer exuded the bright and noisy happiness of a contented middle-class woman (*ibid.*).[38]

Rossana MELIS
Independent scholar

Maria Luisa WANDRUSZKA
University of Bologna

---

37 "Seduta all'ampia scrivania, fedele confidente dei segreti della creazione e della estemporaneità giornalistica, ergeva quella sua grossa testa virile, nobilmente segnata dagli anni e dolcemente abbellita dalla larga aureola dei capelli bianchi. Contrastava con l'energia dell'atteggiamento il velo di lagrime trattenute che le appannava la lucentezza vibrante dei grandi occhi neri. Ma le sue parole erano energiche come l'atteggiamento: 'Mi feriscono. Mi pestano. Mi dilaniano. Non importa! Se non avessi ancora scritto questo romanzo, lo scriverei così come l'ho scritto. E non avrei voluto morire senza aver detto ciò che la guerra mi ha mostrato e ciò che io ne ho sentito'".

38 "Non udii quel giorno la celebre risata squillante di Matilde Serao, la risata di cui ricorre la reminiscenza a mo' di *leit motiv* caratteristico in ogni profilo, in ogni cenno che si fa di lei e con la quale davvero la più sentimentale e appassionata scrittrice d'Italia profondeva intorno a sé una bonarietà gaia e chiassosa di piccola borghese felice".

## MATILDE SERAO'S FICTION TRANSLATED INTO GERMAN

Serao Matilde, 1886, *Die Märtyrer der Phantasie Roman* [*Fantasia*], trans. Hulda von Sacher-Masoch, Jena, Hermann Costenoble.

Serao Matilde, 1890, *Achtung Schildwache!* [*All'erta, sentinella!*: it includes "All'erta, sentinella" and "Terno secco"], trans. Anna Dulk, Stuttgart, Engelhorn.

Serao Matilde, 1890, *Blüte der Leidenschaft* [*Fior di Passione*], trans. Alfred Friedmann, Breslau, Schottlaender.

Serao Matilde, 1893, *Giovannino, oder den Tod!; Dreißig Prozent* [*O Giovannino o la morte, Trenta per cento*], trans. Anna Dulk, Stuttgart, Engelhorn.

Serao Matilde, 1901, *Riccardo Joannas Leben und Abenteuer. Roman* [*Vita e avventure di Riccardo Joanna*], trans. Maximiliane von Weißenthurn, Munich, Langen.

Serao Matilde, 1904, *Schlaraffenland. Neapolitanischer Sittenroman* [*Il paese di Cuccagna*], trans. K. Manfred, Stuttgart, DVA.

Serao Matilde, 1904, *Liebesbriefe* [*Lettere d'amore*], trans. unknown, Vienna, Wiener Verlag.

Serao Matilde, 1908, *Nach der Verzeihung Roman* [*Dopo il perdono*], trans. Maria Gagliardi, Berlin, Fischer.

Serao Matilde, 1910, *Es lebe das Leben! Roman* [*Evviva la vita!*], trans. Maria Gagliardi, Berlin, Fischer.

Serao Matilde, 1913, *Erzählungen, Skizzen und Sagen,* mit Anmerkungen und einem Wörterverzeichnis von Pia Di Mayo-Gelati [*Stories, Sketches and Legends*, with notes and glossary by Pia Di Mayo-Gelati], Heidelberg, Groos.

Leo Spitzer, 1914, "Matilde Serao (Eine Charakteristik)" ["Matilde Serao (A Character Study)"], *Germanisch-Romanische Monatsschrift,* 6, pp. 573-584.

[p. 573] Matilde Serao
(Eine Charakteristik)[39]
von Privatdozent Dr. Leo Spitzer-Wien.

Die literarische Richtung des Naturalismus, also jene Literaturtendenz, die im Roman eine *oeuvre scientifique*, eine wissenschaftliche Detailbeschreibung sieht, ist ein Produkt der modernen Stadtkultur: denn nur die moderne Industriestadt liefert dem Romancier jene pittoresken Gegensätze, jene vielfältigen Details, die er in der gradlinigen Harmonie des Landlebens vergebens suchen würde: so ist es denn bemerkenswert, daß der Naturalismus von einer Großstadt, von Paris aus seinen Zug durch Europa begonnen hat und daß [p. 574] ausgesprochene Stadt- ja Büchermenschen ihn inauguriert haben, wie der Asketiker seiner Kunst Flaubert, wie die Archivstöberer Goncourt, wie Zola, der von sich selbst zu De Amicis sagte, er würde, wenn er sich in einer fremden Stadt aufzuhalten hätte, die ersten drei Tage im Hotel verbringen, ohne auszugehen, sich Schreibzeug und Bücher besorgen, den vierten Tag vom Fenster aus die Passanten zählen, und schließlich den fünften abreisen, ohne etwas von der Stadt gesehen zu haben.

Die Italiener haben die wissenschaftlich sich geberdende Heimatkunst des *roman expérimental* in das Plein-air ihres Landes versetzt, aus der überhitzten Kultur von Paris mit seinen elektrischen Spannungen in die natürliche Wärme eines wirklichen Volkslebens: was bei Zola mühsam mit "haifischartiger" Gier an Bibliothekswissen zusammengeschafft worden war, das lag in Italien greifbar, auf offener Straße da, nur des Künstlers wartend, der das folkloristische Material aufarbeiten würde. Und von Italien war es wiederum und glücklicherweise der Süden, der vom Pariser Naturalismus am lebhaftesten ergriffen wurde – glücklicherweise, denn im Süden bot das stark und eigentümlich entwickelte regionale Leben mit seinen noch blühenden Dialekten und seinen noch

39 Vortrag, gehalten an der Wiener Universität am 20. Dezember 1912. – Eine vollständige Bibliographie findet sich in Band I. der *Critica*, Nachträge in den folgenden Bänden derselben Zeitschrift.

nicht gemeineuropäisch nivellierten Sitten bodenständige, national echte, kräftige Motive, die den *goût du terroir* atmeten. Die Italiener haben keinen italienischen Zola aufzuweisen (außer den Zola, den sie Frankreich schenkten), eher Talente in der Art der Darsteller französischen Bauernlebens wie Theuriet und Fabre.

Der französische Naturalismus läßt sich grosso modo nach den beiden Häuptern Zola und Maupassant in einen mehr didaktischen und einen mehr artistischen scheiden. Dem artistischen Maupassant entspricht als italienischer Verist – dies ist ja seit dem Halbklassiker Manzoni die etwas umfassende Benennung nichtklassischer Kunstübung in Italien – Giovanni Verga: die sizilianischen Bauern des einen sind Halbbrüder der Normannen des anderen, nur ist der von Flaubert ererbte Unerbittlichkeitsroman des Franzosen in den Händen des Sizilianers (vielleicht gegen seine Absicht, mindestens ohne sein Wissen) zum Mitleidsroman geworden. Und wer entspricht dem Didaktiker Zola in Italien? Nun, höchstens Matilde Serao, eine Frau und eine Neapolitanerin, womit gesagt ist, daß wir weit von den Schrecknissen etwa eines G. Cena, des piemontesischen, also Frankreich näheren Schriftstellers, entfernt sind. Matilde Serao hat auch jenen didaktisch-aufklärerischen Zug, den wir an Zola kennen; nur bescheidet sie sich nicht mit einer pseudowissenschaftlichen Objektivität, sondern als erprobte Journalistin, die durch mehr als 30 Jahre erste Tagesblätter redigiert, will sie in die Breite wirken, belehren und ermahnen: von jenen Zeiten ihrer literarischen Anfänge, als sie *Il Ventre di Napoli* schrieb und durch Skizzen aus dem [p. 575] neapolitanischen Volksleben einen dokumentarisch gestützten Aufruf an die regierenden Gewalten künstlerisch zu gestalten wußte, bis 1912, wo sie als Conférencier die Städte Italiens mit ihrem – vielleicht etwas hohl klingenden – Kriegsruf *Evviva la Guerra!* durchzog, hat sie ihr *j'accuse* und noch öfters ein *je défends* zu sprechen nicht aufgehört und auch in ihre künstlerischen Produktionen hat bisweilen der Journalismus hineingeebbt.

Doch Matilde Serao ist nicht nur eine Didakterin, sie ist eine Frau und eine Neapolitanerin. Als *Neapolitanerin* kennt sie alle Stände dieses Volks, vom Stiefelputzer über den bürgerlichen Parvenu bis zum dekadenten Aristokraten, sie kennt den Volksdialekt, den sie pittoresk in ihre Romane zu verweben weiß, die heimischen Gebräuche und Anschauungen – was Zola seine Bibliothek ist der Serao ihr Gedächtnis: sie hat es selbst vielleicht etwas zu wissenschaftlich gesagt: "Ich schürfe in meinem Gedächtnis, wo die Erinnerungen in aufeinanderfolgenden Schichtungen niedergelegt sind wie die Spuren des geologischen Lebens in der Erdkruste... Seit dem ersten Tag, da ich schrieb, habe ich nie etwas anderes sein wollen und können, als ein treuer und demütiger Chronist meines Gedächtnisses. Ich habe mich dem Instinkt überlassen und glaube nicht, daß er mich täuschte."Und an anderer Stelle verrät sie uns, daß sie die Museen fliehe, vom Jahrmarkt aber sich angezogen fühle. So sind denn ihre Schilderungen nicht Proben eines ungeheuren Gelehrtenfleißes, sondern Mitteilungen eines wohlberichteten Erzählers, der alles aus eigener Anschauung kennt und dessen Wissen nicht dort aufhört, wo seine Quellen ihn im Stich lassen.

Und als *Frau*, als südliche Frau, der das individuelle Triebleben mehr bedeutet als die von Heredität und Milieu bestimmten sozialen Evolutionen, hat sie ihrem Verismo alles Deterministische genommen: Individualitäten und besonders viele weibliche Individualitäten leben in Seraos Romanen des Hasses Kraft, die Macht der Liebe aus; allerdings darf man sich von den Allüren einzelner ihrer Romane nicht über deren Genesis täuschen lassen: wenn im *Paese di Cuccagna* die verheerende Macht des neapolitanischen Lottospiels als eine Art ἀνάγκη Individuen und Familien zermalmt, ja die ganze neapolitanische Gesellschaft zu zerstören droht, wenn gar zum Schluß des Romanes der fallierte Bankhalter einen Rundgang bei allen seinen Opfern macht und überall dieselbe Misère antrifft, so glauben wir mitten in Italien auf einem Stück Zola-Erde zu stehen. Betrachten wir aber *Il Paese di Cuccagna* im Zusammenhang mit den vorausgehenden Werken, besonders mit der Novelle *Terno secco*, so erkennen wir, daß echtbürtige neapolitanische Typen, die der Serao schon längst ans Herz gewachsen sind, sich auf dem Stück Zola-Erde ein Stelldichein gegeben haben, daß *Il Paese di Cuccagna* nichts [p. 576] als eine dem Rahmen des *roman expérimental* angepaßte Zerdehnung der erwähnten, dramatisch konzentrierten Novelle *Terno secco* ist. Oder wenn in dem Journalistenroman *I capelli di Sansone* die Druckereimaschine wie bei Zola anthropomorphisiert wird, als *una cosa grande e misteriosa* erscheint, als ein Wesen, das denkt und schreibt, das aus seinen schwarzen Eingeweiden tagtäglich in "einem bestimmten und unbeugsamen Zeugungsakt" die Zeitung "speit" *(caccia)*, so liegt hier jene Mythisierung der Maschine vor, die ja bei Zola gleichfalls mehr nach der Romantik als nach dem Naturalismus hinweist.

Ja, man kann getrost sagen: Auf den Ruf des französischen Naturalismus hat die Serao mit romantischen Schöpfungen geantwortet. Romantisch ist bei der Serao nicht nur ihre Freude an Kontrasten, ihre Farbenfreude in der Schilderung leidenschaftlicher Charakter – romantisch ist auch das soziale Mitleid mit den Verachteten und Gedrückten, den *outlaws* und *outcasts* der Gesellschaft. Die vom Lottospiel Vernichteten sind für die Serao nicht Exempel für eine evolutionistische soziologische Darstellung, sondern Mühselige und Beladene, denen sie eben so gern das Himmelreich öffnen möchte wie Verga seinen verrotteten Sizilianern. Und ich glaube nicht, daß die Serao, wie Zola nach seiner eigenen Aussage tat, zuerst die Milieus schafft, in die sie dann Menschen und Intrige nachträglich hineinsetzt, sondern Personen und Milieu sind gleichzeitige Erlebnisse ihrer Phantasie, die von einander nicht getrennt werden können.

Ein Beispiel mag veranschaulichen, wie bei der Serao Romantik, Naturalismus und – nun, sagen wir es heraus! – oft auch Journalismus ineinander verwoben sind.

*La Ballerina* schildert die Liebe eines am S. Carlo-Theater in Neapel angestellten Ballettmädchens dritten Ranges, Carmela Minino mit Namen, zu einem schönen, skeptisch-zynischen, aristokratischen Lebemann Ferdinando Terzi conte di Torregrande, eine ideale Liebe, die der häßlichen, armen, kümmerlich dahinlebenden Ballerine alles bedeutet, während der junge Edelmann das Mädchen kaum eines Blickes würdigt: nie ist es zwischen den beiden zu einer Aussprache, ja auch nur zu einem Gespräch gekommen. Da erschießt sich der *conte* wegen irgend eines Liebeshandels in einer Hotel-Pension: Carmela Minino, die das Gerücht vom Tode des Grafen in ihrer Garderobe gehört hat, verläßt das Theater während der Vorstellung, irrt in allen Hôtels herum und fragt nach dem Selbstmörder, den sie endlich in der Pension-Suisse findet. Carmela Minino tritt in das Sterbezimmer ein, es werden uns die von Staub und Rauch verfärbten Vorhänge, der Teppich, dessen Zeichnung verblaßt ist, der grünliche Toilettespiegel, die Kommode mit der Marmorplatte, kurz das Mobiliar dieser *povera, sporca e pretenziosa stanza* geschildert, das große Ehebett ohne Leintücher mit der Decke aus grünem gelbgeflecktem Sarsch, mit spitzenbesäumten Kissenüberzügen, auf denen der Tote liegt, die Blutflecken auf dem Hemdausschnitt des Frackes – natürlich hat sich der *conte* im Frack und weißer Kravatte erschossen – sein Pelz ruht auf einem Sessel, eine Gardenia schmückt sein Knopfloch! "Und trotz des gemeinen Eindruckes, den diese Pension Suisse macht, trotz der ekelhaften Scheußlichkeit jenes Zimmers, trotz alles Blutes, das auf der Brust, auf den Händen, auf dem Bett, auf dem Teppich versprengt war, trotz jenes so schrecklichen [p. 577] Todes, bewahrte jener Tote seine edle Schönheit, die von Gott, von seiner Rasse, von seiner Erziehung, von seinen Neigungen stammte, die weder die Laster des Lebens, noch die Häßlichkeit jenes Endes ihm nehmen konnten". Die Aufnahme des gerichtlichen Protokolls unterbricht die Meditationen der Ballerina, der Wortlaut des amtlichen Protokolls, Gespräche der lauen Freunde des Verstorbenen, Bemerkungen des Hotelkellners werden mitgeteilt. Nachdem sich alle Unbeteiligten entfernt haben, bleibt Carmela mit dem Geliebten allein: "jener Tote gehörte ihr, für eine ganze Nacht, in einem unbekannten, einsamen Zimmer". Sie zündete zwei *steariche*, zwei Kerzen an, und stellt sie auf das Nachtkästchen zu Häupten des Toten. Sie betrachtet diesen *come affascinata da quello spettacolo di funebre beltà, giacente nel suo sangue.* Sie schmiegt einen Rosenkranz, den sie in ihrer Tasche findet, in die Hand des Toten, nachdem sie das daranhängende Madonnenmedaillon geküßt hat. Zweimal taumelt sie von dem Leichnam zurück. Aber "jenes Antlitz berückte sie: sie sah sich um. Sie war allein. Es war tiefe Nacht, tief das Stillschweigen. Und, langsam neigte sie sich über jenen Toten, sie drückte ganz sanft, in einem zarten Kuß, ihre Lippen auf jene stolze Stirn, die stolz auch noch im Tode war". Und sie spricht:

"*Oh amore mio, oh amore mio unico, amore mio bello, voi siete morto e io vivo! oh bellezza mia, oh cuore mio, solo morto io vi poteva baciare! Chi me lo avesse detto, chi, chi, che vi doveva vedere morto! Oh amore mio, perchè campo io, io, perchè ci campo su questa terra, dove voi siete morto!*". Und nach diesen Worten, die mit ihren vibrierenden *io* und *chi* nach dem Organ einer guten Freundin der Serao, der Eleonore Duse, zu rufen scheinen, lautet der letzte Satz der Novelle: "So begann, in der Winternacht, die Totenwacht bei Ferdinando Terzi conte di Torregrande in dem fahlen Zimmer der Pension Suisse, vor dem Blute des Selbstmordes, unter dem Weinen, dem Schluchzen, den gestammelten Liebes – und Schmerzensworten der Carmela Minino, der Ballerine dritten Ranges am Theater San Carlo."

Analysieren wir diese Situation, auf die die übrigen Seiten des Buches nur vorbereiten, nach ihren "literarischen Bestandteilen": die Situation selbst, dieses unheimliche Nebeneinander von Erotik und Religiosität, der Erotik, die den Rosenkranz hervorzieht, der Religiosität, die den Leichnam küßt, ferner der soziale Kontrast zwischen der häßlichen Ballerina dritten Ranges und dem noch im Tode schönen, an Oskar Wildesche Figuren erinnernden Hocharistokraten, ein sozialer Kontrast, den die Liebe erst angesichts eines Toten überwindet und der in jenem emphatischen Schlußsatz mit seiner Gegenüberstellung des pompösen Namens: Ferdinando Terzi conte di Torregrande und des bescheidenen: Carmela Minino möglichst ostentativ herausgearbeitet wird, – all das ist Romantik und zwar melodramatische Romantik im Stile der Dramen Victor Hugos, im Stile der veristischen Opern Jung-Italiens, der Mascagni und Leoncavallo, die heute auf allen Weltbühnen eine glorreiche Nachhut des längst untergegangenen romantischen Dramas darstellen. Vom Naturalismus stammt dagegen jene trostlose Beschreibung des Hotelzimmers, jener Blutstropfen im Frackausschnitt, jene Protokollaufnahme in Gegenwart eines schmerzgefolterten liebenden Wesens – kurz jene Unerbittlichkeit der Dinge gegenüber der leidenden Kreatur, überhaupt die Schilderung der Armut der Ballerine und des faulen Coulissentreibens im Reste des Buches. Und beide Elemente, das Melodramatische in der Anlage der Situation wie das Wühlen in naturalistischen [p. 578] Details in deren Ausgestaltung, führen zu dem, was ich das Journalistische genannt habe: die ganze Schilderung nähert sich einem *fait divers*, dem blutig-traurigen Bericht eines Reporters. Die italienische Kritik, einschließlich Croce, hat sich gegenüber dieser Situation starknerviger gezeigt als wir Deutschen nachzufühlen vermögen, die wir solch krasse Darstellungen bei noch so großer Künstlerschaft des Autors in das Gebiet des Sensationsromans oder der finstersten Nachgeburt des Naturalismus, der Kinodramatik, verweisen. Croce, der der letzten Szene der *Ballerina* seinen Beifall spendet, findet in deren erstem Teil Längen: gerade dieser erste Teil, der die Existenz der kleinen, von der Theaterdirektion ausgebeuteten Tänzerin zeigt, würde uns rühren, besonders die Erzählung vom Kranz, den die Tänzerin zu Allerheiligen mit ihren letzten Ersparnissen ersteht und auf das Grab ihrer Patin und einstigen Beschützerin trägt. Auch der Franzose Dornis konnte die Szene nur genießen, indem er sie als Ausfluß jenes *amour absolu, profondément italien, presque religieux* begreift. Wenn er den Satz der imitatio Christi zitiert: "Die Liebe ist stärker als der Tod: sie kennt keinen Ekel", so bleibt für uns noch immer die Frage, ob die Kunst solch "ekelerregende Liebe" zeichnen dürfe.

Ich habe absichtlich keines der Meisterwerke der Serao, die gewöhnlich angeführt zu werden pflegen, analysiert, nicht die gewissermaßen enzyklopädische Darstellung Neapels *Il Paese di Cuccagna* oder *La Conquista di Roma*, die Epopöe des dritten Rom, der Hauptstadt des geeinigten Königreiches, die von Rom nicht die Kunststadt (wie etwa in D'Annunzios *Piacere*), sondern die bürgerliche Welt der Parlamentarier porträtiert, oder das den Journalisten Italiens gewidmete Werk *I capelli di Sansone*, das den Ahasverus-Fluch, der auf den Journalisten lastet, an drei Generationen zeichnet, auch nicht die kleinen Meisternovellen, wie *La virtù di Checchina*, die Geschichte von der Frau, die tugendhaft bleibt, weil sie, gerade im Begriff, zu ihrem Geliebten zum langersehnten Rendezvous zu gehen, vor dem forschenden Blick des herrschaftlichen Portiers, der seine Pfeife stopft, erschrickt und unverrichteter Dinge umkehrt – ich habe statt all dieser schönen Bücher die *Ballerina* analysiert, nicht um die Grenzen des Talentes der Serao, sondern um die Punkte zu zeigen, wo das Verständnis des deutschen Lesers der süditalienisch-robusten Kunst der Serao nicht immer sicher sein mag, besonders aber um die Verwandtschaft oder Eintracht von Romantik und Naturalismus in Italien darzulegen, und schließlich um einen Punkt aufzuklären, der von der italienischen und französischen Kritik gar heiß umstritten ist: die Frage der *conversione* der Serao. Die Publikationen der Serao nach ihrer Jerusalemreise 1897: die Reisebeschreibung *Nel paese di Gesù*, der erschütternde Roman vom Schicksal einer Nonne, *Suora Joanna della Croce*, deren Kloster aufgelassen wird und die nun in [p. 579] weltlichen Berufen sich versuchen muß, die Plauderei über die drei Marien, das Buch *La Madonna e i Santi*, eine Art Bilderalmanach, die Novelle *Storia di due anime*, alle diese halbgeistlichen Schriften schienen einen Wandel im Denken der Schriftstellerin zu verkünden: Aus der heidnisch-frohen Neapolitanerin wäre eine Nazarenerin geworden. Während Croce diesen Neomystizismus der Serao als Modesache, als "regalo di Fogazzaro" bezeichnet, antwortet Maurice Muret in seiner *Littérature italienne d'aujourd'hui*: kann von keinem Bruch im Schaffen der Serao die Rede sein: ein *catholicisme napolétain* habe immer, vor und nach der Jerusalemfahrt, in ihren Schriften geherrscht. Wir dürfen nicht vergessen, daß es neben dem Neapel der Chiaia, der Via Toledo, des Teatro S. Carlo stets ein Neapel der Kirchen Santa Maria della Pietà, Santa Chiara und San Gennaro gegeben hat, von denen Taine schrieb:

*Ce catholicisme payen est choquant; on y découvre toujours un fonds de sensualité sous une apparence d'ascétisme*, daß gerade die Serao jenes naive Gemisch von Heidentum und Katholizismus in der neapolitanischen Religiosität in ihrer sogenannten vor-katholischen Zeit in der Gestalt jenes alten Grafen Cavalcanti gezeichnet hat, der glaubt, nur ein reines Wesen wie seine jungfräuliche Tochter könne der Gottheit das Geheimnis des Gewinnes beim Lottospiel entreißen, und der beim Fehlschlagen seiner Hoffnungen die Christusstatue seines Hausaltars in entsetzlich heidnischer Rachegier in den Brunnen versenkt, daß eben *La ballerina* auch jenes Gemisch von Erotik und Religiosität zeigt, das uns Nordländern auffiel, daß die Serao in ihrer sogenannten gläubigen Epoche kein Bedenken trug, ihrer tiefreligiösen Schwester Joanna della Croce der Courtisane Concetta Guadagni das Versprechen in den Mund zu legen, sie, Suora Joanna, werde Messen lesen lassen, damit der Geliebte der Concetta, Cicille, dieser treu bleibe! Wie hier die Verirrungen des *catholicisme payen* hat sie mit rührenden Tönen die richtige Herzensgläubigkeit in der *Storia di due anime* in der Gestalt jenes Domenico Maresca geschildert, der mit geradezu zärtlichen Weihegefühlen seine gipsenen Heiligen und Marienstatuen formt. Und gerade in diesem Spätwerk werden Stimmungen verarbeitet, die aus der Jugendzeit der Schriftstellerin datieren, aus der Zeit, da sie als 17 jähriges Mädchen sich wie Ada Negri und Grazia Deledda dem Lehrerinnenberuf widmen wollte, um ihre Familie zu erhalten, und in dem von ihr so oft beschriebenen Viertel zwischen Santa Maria-la-Nuova und Mezzocannone wohnte, dem Viertel der Bilderschnitzer, "wo man das bleiche Antlitz eines halbbemalten hl. Franziskus von Assisi oder die zu lebhaft rote Lippe einer Madonna sehen kann, ein mystisches Viertel mit seinen sechs Kapellen und seinen zehn Kirchen, seinen Prozessionen und Festen, mit großen historischen Palästen und traurigen modernen Wohnungen, ein sehr schmutziges, wenig hygienisches und sonnenloses Viertel".

[p. 580] Von diesen Darstellungen der neapolitanischen Religiosität auf die religiösen Gefühle der Serao schließen zu wollen, halte ich für mißlich. Auch ist *Nel paese di Gesù* nicht etwa mit Chateaubriands *Itinéraire de Paris à Jérusalem* vergleichbar: der Band ist nichts als der Versuch eines aufmerksamen und anpassungsfähigen Beobachters, eines *pellegrino del cuore*, wie die Serao uns selbst sagt, die Seele eines Landes zu erfassen. In den später publizierten *Lettere d'una viaggiatrice* hat die

Serao die kosmopolitische Seele der Riviera, die alte Seele von Florenz, Verona, *Venise la rouge*, die Bergfrische Savoyens und Tirols, die Seele der *città di sogno* Paris ebenso richtig erfaßt, wie eben im *Paese di Gesù* die ehrwürdige Stätte religiöser Erinnerungen. Muret hat Recht: *Entre l'auteur du Pays de Coccagne et celui du Pays de Jésus il n'est en verité qu'une nuance.* In der Einleitung zu *La Madonna e i santi* schreibt die Serao über ein von der Königin-Mutter Margherita gedichtetes Gebet: "teure, zarte, frauenhafte Dichtung, keimend in diesem mystischen Frühling, dem sich nach belebender Sonne verlangend, unsere überzeugten gläubigen Gemüter eröffnen". Das Christentum der Serao ist voll von jenem *vivido sole* Neapels! Der mystische Herbst der Serao ist ein "mystischer Frühling"! Sowie die Barockkirchen in das Straßenbild Neapels, so gehört eine freudige Gläubigkeit zum Charakter der Neapolitanerin Serao und man darf nicht, wie Croce tut, den Ausspruch der gefühlsmatten Donna Angelica in der *Conquista di Roma* "*È così volgare esser atei.* Die Religion ist schön, ist gut, und ist mehr wert als vieles, das die Welt schätzt" auf die temperamentvolle und wohl auch im Glauben enthusiastische Antonia zurückbeziehen. Ihre Religiosität ist nicht Mode-, sondern Traditions- und Herzenssache.

Bekanntlich beobachtet der Italienreisende, daß, in dem Maß als er weiter nach dem Süden vorrückt, die Religiosität eine viel intensivere, daß aber auch der Begriff der Ehre und Zucht ernster genommen wird: das leidenschaftliche Temperament zieht als notwendiges Korrektiv die strengere Auffassung von Sittlichkeit und Sitte mit sich: wie im allgemeinen in Italien, so hat besonders im Süden die Idee der Frauenemanzipation keinen Anklang gefunden; in der *Vita Femminile* von 1907 beschreibt Prof. Sollini das abgesperrte Leben der Frauen in den südlichen Provinzen, das den verheirateten Frauen nicht einmal gestattet, die Freunde ihrer Männer kennen zu lernen, – und ich habe selbst in den Straßen Palermos nicht eine einheimische *signora dabbene* zu Fuß spazieren gehen gesehen. Matilde Serao hat gegen den Feminismus nicht jenen theoretischen Kampf geführt, den im Norden Italiens die Neera ausfocht, sie hat dafür in ihre literarische Praxis das Ibsen-Weib nie aufgenommen, eher zeigt sie die unter der Härte ihres Berufes erliegende Frau wie in der *Ballerina* oder der Novelle *Telegrafo di Stato*, wo die Misère der Postfräulein aufgedeckt wird, nie dagegen die Frau, die in ihrer intellektuellen [p. 581] Entwicklung ihre Bestimmung sieht.

Es ist bezeichnend, daß die Serao das Leben der Journalistin, das sie ja aus eigener Anschauung kennt, in ihrem Journalistenroman nicht behandelt hat, daß sogar in *Fantasia*, als die Heldin des Romans beim Anblick einer Journalistin einige Worte der Sympathie spricht, ihr Partner antwortet: *Preferite sempre di essere donna!* Die Serao, wie ebenfalls die jüngere Grazia Deledda, ist hierin die Tochter ihres konservativen lateinischen Landes: den Frauen der Serao könnte man zumeist den Titel einer ihrer Novellen in den Mund legen: *O Giovannino o la morte* – womit nicht gesagt sein soll, daß sie nicht liebeleere Wesen wie die Angelica der *Conquista di Roma* meisterhaft geschildert hat: aber damit ist die Serao sich selbst nicht untreu geworden: da sie die Frau stets im Hinblick auf die Liebe schildert, muß sie eben auch die Frau schildern, die nicht lieben kann. Fehlen so in ihrer Frauengalerie einige und vielleicht die vergeistigsten Porträts, so sind dafür lauter lebenswahre Gestalten vertreten und ihre Kunst verliert sich nicht in die abstrakte Blutlosigkeit der theoretisierenden Frauenliteratur. Auch hier müssen wir die gewissermaßen physische, fast derbe Gesundheit der Serao konstatieren, die ihre Geschlechtsgenossinnen nicht als unbestimmte und unfaßbare Traumwesen behandelt, sondern aufrichtig und herzhaft das Triebleben als Zentrum ihres Lebens betrachtet. Ja, Gesundheit spricht aus den Werken der Serao, Gesundheit aus ihrem Porträt, diesem etwas behäbigen, jovialen, eigentlich bourgeoisen Matronenbildnis, Gesundheit aus ihrer Lebensführung, die uns Ojetti beschrieben hat: diese Frau schreibt täglich einige Spalten für ihre Zeitung, einige Seiten des Romans, den sie gerade in Arbeit hat, bleibt oft bis 3 Uhr nachts in der Druckerei, fehlt bei keinem öffentlichen Ereignis in Rom, hält Vorträge, schreibt Reisebriefe von Jerusalem, der Riviera, Tirol, Paris – und ist dabei Mutter von sechs Kindern. Wie merkwürdig, daß diese Feministin der Tat keine Feministin des Wortes geworden ist, daß sie auf ein Interview bezüglich ihrer Stellung zum Feminismus antwortete: *Non ne capisco niente!*

Wie merkwürdig anderseits, daß diese männliche Schriftstellerin (von einer *operosità virile* spricht D'Annunzio in der Vorrede zu dem der Serao gewidmeten *Giovanni Episcopo*), die von sich selbst sagen konnte: *Io non sono una scrittrice, io sono uno scrittore*, nur Frauen-, nicht Mannescharaktere zu schildern weiß, sofern sie über bloße Episodisten hinausgehen sollen! Ihre Männer haben eine *à-tout-prix*-Männlichkeit, etwas Unnatürlich-Gespanntes, als ob sie selbst wüßten, daß sie aus einer Eva-Rippe erschaffen sind und diesen ihren Ursprung durch prätentiöses Auftreten zu verbergen wünschten. Man höre nur, wie der Doktor Antonio Amati im *Paese di Cuccagna* charakterisiert wird, er, der als der einzig Tadellose und Aufrechte in der [p. 582]allgemeinen Zerrüttung erscheinen soll: "Jenes eiserne Herz, das alle seine Tränen hatte verschlucken und ohne Erregung an den Tränen aller Arten von Elend hatte teilnehmen müssen, jenes eiserne Herz, das dem Gefühl gegenüber eine kindliche Jungfräulichkeit und Reinheit zeigte, nur langsam, fast furchtsam hatte es sich der Liebe erschlossen!". Rasselt dieser gute Doktor nicht etwas zu viel mit seinem eisernen Herzen, als daß wir ihm glauben sollten? Und tut er in den 479 Seiten des Buches auch nur das Geringste, um die heißgeliebte Bianca Maria Cavalcanti dem furchtbaren Leben, das sie an der Seite ihres lottowütigen Vaters führt, zu entreißen? Am Totenbette des Mädchens murmelt er *teneramente*: *ci vogliono dei fiori, fiori!* Und ebenso ist in der *Conquista di Roma* der angeblich von der bösen Roma besiegte Abgeordnete Sangiorgi nicht Rom, sondern seiner eigenen Weichlichkeit erlegen: der Jüngling, der im ersten Teil des Romanes auf den halbskeptischen Ausruf eines alten Parlamentariers "jemand muß es erobern, dieses stolze Rom!" mit einem selbstbewußten *io!* geantwortet hat, ist im weiteren Verlauf des Romans nicht wieder-zuerkennen: oder sollen wir uns als Conquistador jenen Parlamentarier denken, der statt auf Montecitorio zu sprechen, sechs Stunden lang in einer mit Chinoiserien überfüllten kosigen Junggesellenwohnung auf seine Dame wartet? Ebensowenig werden wir der Energie des Ingenieurs Attilio Franco aus New York in *Pellegrino appassionato* glauben, sondern alle diese Helden mit künstlich herausgepolstertem Biceps, mit jenem Paolo Herz derselben Novellensammlung identifizieren, der nicht nur in seinem durch deutsch-neapolitanische Abstammung erklärlichen Namen, auch in seinem deutschneapolitanischen Charakter ein hybrides Geschöpf ist: "Das, was diesen stolzen und starken Mann gebrechlich wie ein Kind macht, ist gerade dieser breite sentimentale Strom, der seine Kräfte in jeglicher Kampfesstunde vernichtet und erstickt". Wenn darauf mit diesem sentimentalischen Erbe Paolo Herzens germanische Ahnen beschuldigt werden, so ist Deutschland noch allzusehr mit den Augen der Frau von Stael gesehen. Die Serao spricht einmal von *Magdeburgo, città di Westfalia*: ich würde diesen geographischen Schnitzer nicht erwähnen, wenn er nicht symbolisch wäre für die Erfassung Deutschlands durch Italiener; so kompliziert die physische Geographie Deutschlands für den Italiener ist, so schwer findet er sich im Seelenleben des Deutschen zurecht: sind schon Topler senior und junior in dem deutschesten Werk des deutschesten italienischen Schriftstellers etwas altfränkische Gelehrtentypen, so sind die aus Deutschland neu importierten Energie- und Traummenschen der Serao durchaus unnaturalisierte Fremdlinge auf neapolitanischem Boden. Die germanische Sentimentalität macht nicht nur den Halbneapolitaner Paolo Herz zu einem kraftlosen Schwächling, sie lähmt auch die robuste Autorin Serao – die Charakterdarstellerin wie die [p. 583] Stilistin. Man höre nur diesen italianisierten Hauptmann-Flüsterdialog aus dem *Pellegrino appassionato*: – *Paolo? – Chérie? – Non ti pare che sia meglio finire? – Che cosa? – Questo viaggio, insieme. – Ah!... sì. – Io vorrei restare ancora con te – ella aggiunse gentilmente – ma non serve a nulla. – Non serve a nulla. – Me ne vado, allora, Paolo? – Sì. – Tu resti? – Non so. – Vuoi che io resti, Paolo? – No. – Trovi che ho torto? Che faccio male? – No, Chérie : tu hai ragione e fai benissimo. No: non ti serbo rancore. – Mi vuoi bene, un poco, allora? – disse ella, sciocсamente. – Egli rabbrividì: tremò. E disse: – No, niente. – Così, si lasciarono.*

Im Charakter des impetuos-beredsamen Neapolitaners kann solch kondensierte, vieldeutig sein wollende, monosyllabische Redeweise nicht liegen – das Kennzeichen der Unechtheit dieses Stils ist dessen übertriebene Anwendung. Ebenso wie in stilistischer Beziehung manches an die Hauptmann-Ibsen-Schule erinnert, so ist alles Thesenhafte, Konstruierte bei der Serao ein Zweiglein vom grauen Baum der französischen Theorie, auf des südlichen Lebens goldenen Baum gepfropft: die ausgezirkelte Mathematik der Liebe in *Addio amore, Le amanti*, *Gli amanti*, *Pellegrino appassionato* hat schon Croce als der italienischen Kunst fremdes Element getadelt. Derjenige Roman, der am meisten mit der Logik der französischen Thesendramen operiert und eins jener Preisthemen behandelt, wie sie Frankreich allen Kulturländern vorzuschreiben pflegt, die Frage, ob in der Ehe die Verzeihung eines Fehltritts möglich sei (die Frage, die in Frankreich von Jules Lemaître und Paul Margueritte, in Österreich von Schnitzler, in Italien von D'Annunzio im *Innocente*, von Amelia Rosselli in *L'illusione* und endlich von der Serao in *Dopo il perdono* behandelt wurde), ist denn auch von einem Franzosen für die Bühne bearbeitet worden:

Das Stück fiel durch, obwohl von der Réjane an ihrem Pariser Theater gespielt; es war, als ob Frankreich die ihm selbst entlehnte Arbeitsweise verleugnen wollte! Und doch ist gerade Frankreich das Land, in dem die Romane der Serao und Vergas das lebhafteste Echo fanden: das farbige Milieu Neapels, die leidenschaftlichen Konflikte Siziliens behagten dem exotismenfreundlichen Paris mehr als die sonstige [p. 584] italienische Heimatskunst, als das etwas spießbürgerliche Norditalien Fogazzaros oder die trostlose sardische Einöde der Deledda.

Matilde Serao ist kein Dramatiker, vielleicht auch kein ganz großer Epiker: wenn man bedenkt, daß sie selbst ihre großen Romane in kleinen Novellen vorweggenommen hat, *Il Paese di Cuccagna* in *Terno secco*, *I Capelli di Sansone* in der Novelle *Spostati* der Sammlung *Piccole anime*, daß die *Conquista di Roma* in viele verstreute Einzelbeobachtungen und große, allerdings pastose Fresken auseinanderfällt, wird man ihre Stärke mehr im novellistischen Erfassen einzelner, großartig hingestellter Figuren als im Bauen eines architektonisch tadellosen Romans suchen: sie weiß – und dies hat sie nun mit den ganz großen Epikern gemein – Gestalten in symbolsche Handlungen zu bannen, die uns ewig in Erinnerung bleiben. Wir vergessen nie mehr jenen Balzacschen César Birotteau, der mit den in Ordnung gebrachten Geschäftsbüchern im Arm stirbt – wir vergessen aber auch nie den Sangiorgi der *Conquista di Roma*, der in der Nacht vor seinem Duell mit den im Dunkel blitzenden zwei Säbelklingen Zwiesprach hält, noch jenes rasende Volk von Neapel, das von der Gottheit unter Flüchen verlangt, sie möge das Blut des hl. Gennaro siedend werden lassen. Matilde Serao ist eine große Beobachterin der Menschen und der Menschenmassen.

# MATILDE SERAO IN FINLAND[1]

"Matilde Serao is the best-known and most-read Italian woman writer at present, not only in her home country, but also broadly outside its borders. The outward appearance of the book is dainty and elegant" ("Pienoiskuvia elämästä", 1909).[2] The book in question is the Finnish translation of Matilde Serao's *Pienoiskuvia elämästä* [*Fior di passione*, 1888], translated by Frans Oskar Viitanen and published in 1909 in Tampere, Finland. The quote, a kind of advertisement for the book, was printed in the Finnish newspaper *Kaiku* in the section "Kirjallisuutta ja taidetta" ("Literature and art") on 13 October 1909.[3] It shows both Serao's established position in Finland and one of the features typical of the reception of women writers in general: their books were often characterized by "feminine" adjectives, evoking descriptions of women (Russ, 1983, p. 115).

Matilde Serao's reception in Finland first came to my attention in 2010, when working, with colleagues from the COST Action project

---

1 Research for this article was carried out as part of the project "Women's Centres and Peripheries" funded by the Alfred Kordelin Foundation (2016-2017). I would like to thank the editors of the volume, the anonymous reviewers and my colleagues Päivi Lappalainen, Kati Launis, Outi Paloposki and Ulla-Maija Juutila-Purokoski for their insightful comments, Ritva Hapuli, Riitta Sarovuo and Irma Reijonen from the National Library of Finland, Elina Suolahti and, especially, Antonio Parente for their kind help.

2 "Matilde Serao on Italian nykyisin tunnetuin ja enin luetuin kirjailijatar ei ainoastaan kotimaassaan, vaan myöskin laajalti sen rajain ulkopuolella. Kirjan ulkoasu on siro ja aistikas". A similar statement can be found in other newspapers, e. g.: "Matilde Serao is not only the most prominent contemporary Italian woman writer, but one of the most visible ones in contemporary literature in general" ("Matilde Serao ei ole ainoastaan Italian nykyisin etevin naiskirjailija, vaan koko nykyajan kirjallisuuden huomatuimpia" ("Tanssijatar", 1910).

3 *Kaiku* was a Finnish newspaper, published in Oulu in Northern Finland from 1877 to 1949. At the end of the nineteenth century, *Kaiku* was the leading newspaper of the Northern Finnish region and the largest regional newspaper in Finland. In those days, it discussed topical issues like the social position of the working class, the problems of country sharecroppers and migration. Later, its patriotic spirit together with emphasis on the Finnish language as the first (and for many, only) language of Finland's culture, led to a more conservative line.

*Women Writers in History*,[4] on the reception of women writers in *fin-de-siècle* Finland from a comparative European perspective. We looked at the translations of works from the 1890s by European women writers traceable in the Finnish National Bibliography, the *Fennica* database, and found a considerable number of translations of Serao's work into both Finnish and Swedish. When researching the Old Collection of the Turku City Library and comparing it to other library collections in Finland, I found Serao again, this time in a Swedish translation. Her presence caught my attention: I knew Serao's work and her cultural agency were well known and remembered in Naples, but since she seemed to be less known outside Italy by the time of this research project, I did not expect her contemporary Finnish reception to be so rich. Later still I found an essay by Ulla Jokinen, who, when discussing translations from Italian into Finnish around 1910, concludes that the only authors presented to the Finnish audience in a thoroughgoing fashion were Deledda, Fogazzaro and Serao; however, the last "tends to be almost completely unknown" in contemporary Finland (Jokinen, 1986, p. 158).

When more and more Finnish newspapers from the late eighteenth, as well as the nineteenth and twentieth centuries began to become available online, I started looking at Serao's reception in the Finnish press, finding a considerable number of references. During the work on the Collaborative Research Project *Travelling Texts: Transnational Reception of Women's Writing at the Fringes of Europe* (2013-2016)[5] we encountered the reception of Serao's work in the material of various countries, including Slovenia, Spain, Norway, and The Netherlands (Badalić, 2014, pp. 106, 107, 126, 129, 134, 183).

This article will deal with the reception of Matilde Serao in Finland. I understand the term reception broadly, to signify various kinds of

4 "Women Writers in History / Toward a New Understanding of European Literary Culture" was a COST Action IS0901 active from 2009 to 2013. Its main objective was the creation of a strong collaborative international research network (see http://www.cost.eu/COST_Actions/isch/IS0901) (last accessed 12 February 2020).

5 See http://heranet.info/ttt/index and http://travellingtexts.huygens.knaw.nl/ (Project Leader: Henriette Partszsch) (last accessed 30 June 2020). Just like the COST Action project, this project orbited around the *WomenWriters* Virtual Research Environment, which enables reception scholars to see writers' translational reception in a broad European context. The final conference of the project, "Cultural Encounters through Reading and Writing: New Approaches to the History of Literary Culture" (Glasgow, June 9-11, 2016), included the session on Serao held by Katharine Mitchell, Gabriella Romani and Ursula Fanning.

reactions to the primary texts about which we have tangible evidence. It means not only reception through translation; though, indeed, the question of reception often used to be examined exclusively in relation to translated texts. Concern with reception through translation would produce publications such as *The Reception of Jane Austen in Europe* (Mandal – Southam, 2007), where Austen's reception in Finland is mapped through translations of her texts into Finnish (Valle, 2007). As shown by recent research, "Austen was read in Finland in languages other than Finnish, including Swedish, much earlier." (Parente-Čapková – Lappalainen, 2017, p. 264.) Though studies like *The Reception of Jane Austen in Europe* continue to be of major value (see also Schaffer – Brown, 2016), I think it is important to map writers' presence in the literary field in other ways: by analysing their reception in the press in terms of reviews and other articles, advertisements, and obituaries, and, of course, translations (some of them published in serialized form). Such an approach involves employing, in terms of methodology, a compromise between *distant* and *close reading* as well as between macro- and micro levels of literary analysis (see Jockers, 2013; Moretti, 2013). What seems most viable here is a kind of *meso-analysis*, a "middle way" (Saint-Amour, 2019), combining the "distant" reading of larger datasets, available online, with the close reading, in a broad sense, based on a knowledge of the historical and cultural context.

Mapping the reception of an Italian woman author in Finland also makes it possible to trace the "complex routes of travelling texts" (Partzsch, 2014, p. 282) in the long European nineteenth century. As Henriette Partzsch has pointed out, highlighting "the relations between geographical and cultural fringes is an attempt to dynamize the established map of literary exchanges which normally focuses on cultural centres or on the relation of peripheral literatures with centres" (*ibid.*). Through an examination of the presence of Serao's books in major Finnish libraries during the *fin de siècle*, I will reveal the multicultural and the multilingual character of her reception. Library collections are an important source of information about the books that circulated, and, in this respect, they are important sites of reception. I will briefly refer to Serao's later reception (from the 1930s onwards), but my major concern is with the turn of the nineteenth and twentieth centuries, which is when her reception was at its high point.

## TRANSLATIONS AND NATIONAL LANGUAGES IN FIN-DE-SIÈCLE FINLAND

As in all bilingual or multilingual countries, in Finland, reception via translation means translations into more than one ('national') language. First of all, Finland has two 'principal' languages.[6] The territory today known as Finland had been part (an Eastern province) of Sweden from the mid-twelfth century until 1809 when it became an autonomous Grand Duchy within the Russian Empire, and, finally, an independent republic in 1917. Under Russian rule, Finland was able to keep Swedish as its only official language until the 1860s. In 1863, Finnish was put on an equal footing with Swedish, but Swedish retained its position as the language of culture. The Russian language never gained a position comparable with that of Swedish or Finnish in Finland, although, historically, it served as the third official language along with Finnish and Swedish for a relatively brief period between 1900 and 1917. In the nineteenth and the early twentieth centuries Russian was spoken mostly by certain sectors of society such as army officers and public servants (Engman, 2009, p. 237).

Finnish became the second official language in 1863, but it took another two decades before literature in Finnish could compete with that in Swedish, in terms of both original texts and translations. Encouraged by linguistic nationalism, which took over in Finland around the mid-nineteenth century (and caused certain anxiety in the Swedish speaking circles, leading to the birth of the "Finland-Swedish ideology"), more and more writers began to use Finnish as their language of expression, and more and more texts written in Swedish produced both in Sweden and on the territory of Finland were being translated into Finnish.

The translation scholar Pirkko Lilius has called this linguistic situation the "Nordic heritage of the history of translation into Finnish",[7]

6 Nowadays, Finland has two official languages: Finnish and Swedish. Sámi is (since 2003) the official language of several municipalities in Finnish Lapland (Sápmi). In terms of the number of speakers, Russian is Finland's third strongest language, after Finnish and Swedish.

7 "suomennoshistorian pohjoismainen perintö".

stemming from the fact that high culture arrived in Finland mostly via the Swedish language and was translated into Finnish mostly because of a sense of national awakening (Lilius, 2003, p. 23). The practical need to translate from Finnish into Swedish around the turn of the nineteenth and twentieth centuries was minimal: although in that period Finnish-language culture was already well developed, the educated classes could still read Swedish. Many works of foreign literature were read in Swedish translations, which were present in both public and private libraries. Translations into Swedish were published both in Sweden and in Finland. Finnish booksellers would advertise books translated and published in Sweden. As late as the end of the nineteenth century, many Swedish publishing houses sold up to one third of their production in Finland.[8] Books were also sold and read in German, French, English, Norwegian and Danish. Hence the works of authors like Serao travelled to Finland by many different routes.

In the *Fennica* national database, one finds Serao's works translated into both Finnish and Swedish (six translations into Finnish – one work was translated twice – and two into Swedish). This gives us the sense that Serao's presence on the Finnish cultural scene was quite notable. While I will later return to the issue of Serao's translations into Finnish and Swedish in more detail, I would first like to look at the availability of Serao's works in Finnish libraries. I took as examples the National Library of Finland (until 2006, Helsinki University Library) in the present Finnish capital, three libraries in Turku (Åbo in Swedish, Finland's capital until 1812), and I briefly mention some other libraries as well. The library collections in Helsinki and Turku contain rich collections from the period around the turn of the nineteenth and twentieth centuries, that period during which Serao was most intensively responded to in Finland.

8 For more, see Parente-Čapková – Lappalainen, 2017, p. 269, and p. 274, n. 11.

## SERAO'S MULTILINGUAL PRESENCE IN FIN-DE-SIÈCLE FINNISH LIBRARIES

### THE NATIONAL LIBRARY

In the National Library of Finland (whose history dates back to 1640), we find Serao's works in five languages: Italian, Finnish, Swedish, Russian, and French. In the original Italian, there are ten works (one of them in two editions)[9] and one collection of studies about Italian authors. The collection, written by Laura Gropallo and published in Turin in 1903, is called *Autori italiani d'oggi* and comprises chapters on Antonio Fogazzaro, Gabriele d'Annunzio, Matilde Serao and Gerolamo Rovetta.

There are three Serao publications in French. One is the French translation of *Il paese di Cuccagna* (1891) entitled *Au pays de Cocagne: moeurs Napolitaines*, published by Plon-Nourrit et cie in Paris in 1898.[10] There are two copies of *Coeur souffrant* (orig. *Cuore infermo*, 1881), published by Paul Ollendorff in Paris in 1899, translated by Mme Charles Laurent (pseudonym for Nelly Carrère). The third novel is a translation of Serao's *Dopo il perdono* entitled *Après le pardon,* published by Callman-Lévy in Paris and translated by Georges Hérelle (1906). There is also a theatre adaptation entitled *Après le pardon: pièce en cinq actes*, by Matilde Serao and Pierre Decourcelle.[11]

---

9 There are two editions of the novel *Fantasia* (the 3rd edition published in Turin by F. Casanova in 1892, and one published in Florence by Salani in 1920); in the first one, there is an imprint by Ylioppilaskirjasto, the Student Library, the history of which goes back to the mid-nineteenth century. Other books comprise the novel *Addio, amore!* (Milan, Baldini Castoldi & Cie, 1901), *Cuore infermo* (Florence, Salani, 1924), *Il paese di Cuccagna: romanzo napoletano* (Naples, Trani, 1902), a collection of short stories, *Fior di passione* (Milan, Baldini, Castoldi & Co., 1899), the novel *L'anima semplice: Suor Giovanna della Croce* (Milan, Fratelli Treves, 1901), the 7th edition of *All'erta, sentinella* (Milan, Baldini Castoldi, 1904), the 2nd edition of *La Madonna e i Santi (Nella fede e nella vita)* (Naples, Francesco Perrella, 1904), *Il ventre di Napoli (Venti anni fa – Adesso – L'anima di Napoli)* (Naples, Francesco Perrella, 1906), and the novel *Dopo il perdono* (Rome, Nuova Antologia, 1906). The last mentioned belonged, in fact, to the Students' Union Library Collection (Osakuntakokoelma), which used to host the oldest collection of fiction of Helsinki University Library (see, for instance, Hirn *et al.*, 2010, pp. 20-21). The books in this collection had been acquired by university students since the eighteenth century.

10 The translator (not named) was Minnie Bourget (De Montera – Tosi, 1972, p. 182).

11 This adaptation was published in Paris in 1907 in the series *L'Illustration theatrale* (n. 73) – the volume in the library comprises all publications of the series, each including, as a

Most interesting is the German volume of Serao's texts, published in Heidelberg in 1913 by Julius Groos, a publisher specializing in foreign languages and literatures, language textbooks and linguistic works. The title of the book is *Scritti vari: Erzählungen, Skizzen und Sagen* within the series Neue italienische Schriftsteller II (Serao, 1913). The publication is in Italian, with explanatory footnotes in German and Italian: indeed, it says "Mit Anmerkungen und einem Wörterverzeichnis von Pia Di Mayo-Gelati" ["With Notes and a Glossary by Pia Di Mayo-Gelati"]. The Introduction ("Einleitung", pp. III-V) offers some basic information on Serao and brief characteristics of her works, along with a mention of her journalism. The explanatory footnotes that accompany the text are in both Italian and German; sometimes, the languages are mixed within one footnote. The glossary is systematically bilingual (Italian – German) and the volume concludes with a list of Serao's works ("Werke von Matilde Serao"), including information about publishers and prices of the respective volumes. This edition was intended for German speakers learning Italian, as is indicated by the aforementioned publisher's profile, i.e. a specialization in language textbooks. It could also have been used by Italian learners with knowledge of German in Finland, highlighting the fact that at the beginning of the twentieth century, learning a foreign language via another foreign language was commonplace.

Vis-à-vis Serao's texts in various languages in the National Library of Finland, the richest collection is that of Serao's books in Russian, currently hosted by the Slavonic Library, in a special collection of the National Library. There is a Russian translation of one novella by Serao, one volume of her selected short stories in Russian, and her *Collected Works in six volumes* (*Собрание сочинений, Sobranie sočinenij*; the library holds only five volumes, since the fourth is missing). The Russian translations date from 1900-1911, falling within the period 1827-1917, which is when the Library was provided with deposit copies of periodicals and official

vignette, a portrait of the author(s). Before the play itself, there is an introductory text on the theatre production called "Après le Pardon au Théâtre Réjane". The play was, indeed, staged first in Paris in November 1907 and only several months later in Naples. On 18 January 1908, the Swedish newspaper *Nya Pressen* published a rather negative review of the drama by Henning Berger, entitled "Fransk teater" ["French Theatre"], in which Berger comments also on Serao's piece. He calls it "amiable" ["älskvärd"], but, after various critical remarks, he concludes that "Serao's play was bad" ["Seraos pjes var dålig"] (Berger, 1908).

publications published in the Russian Empire (see Ekonen, 2012, esp. pp. 4-7; Knapas, 2012, pp. 91-93, 107). Indeed, all the translations were published in Moscow. One volume published in 1900 and translated by A. Veselovskoj comprises short stories, as the title *Разсказы* [*Razskazy, Short Stories*] indicates. "Или Джiованнино, или смерть: повѣсть" ["Ili Džìovannino, ili smert': pověst'"] is a translation of "O Giovannino o la morte" from 1889, published by Pravda in Moscow in 1903.[12]

There are three translations of Serao's works into Swedish in the National Library. The first is *Straff* [*Castigo*], published in Stockholm in 1893 and translated by E. Weer;[13] this book belonged, in fact, to the Students' Union Library Collection (Osakuntakokoelma – see above n. 9). The second one is *O Giovannino o la morte* [*Giovannino eller döden!*, Helsinki, 1895; translator's name missing]. It is also a part of an anthology of European fiction; the other works in the volume are *Den gamla Adam* by Henrik Pontoppidan and the novelette *Miss Bell* by Charles Foley.[14] In the same series (vol. XXXI, Helsinki, 1891) there is another translation of Serao's work into Swedish entitled *Vänninor* [orig. *Fantasia*].

The National Library holds five translations of books by Serao into Finnish, and one Finnish-language anthology which includes Serao and other authors. The oldest publication is an 1893 anthology, *Nuori Itaalia* [*Young Italy*, ed. Hanna Andersin], the first collection of Italian short stories published in Finnish with works by Luigi Capuana, Giovanni

12 The presence of foreign women writers translated into Russian in the Slavonic Library of Helsinki is a most interesting phenomenon, which has been researched within the project I have been leading since 2018 (*Texts on the Move: Reception of Women's Writing in Finland and Russia 1840-2020,* funded by the Emil Aaltonen Foundation). For Russian translations of Serao's works see also Maria Belova's chapter in this volume.

13 E. Weer was the pseudonym of Ellen Wester (1873-1930), a versatile Swedish translator, who translated at first from German, English, French and Italian, but later specialized in Slavonic languages, particularly Polish.

14 The book was published as the fifty-second volume of the series *Nya Pressens följetongbibliotek*, the serialized novels library of *Nya Pressen,* a Swedish-minded constitutionalist newspaper. Constitutionalists were the political groups or individuals (mostly the liberal "Young Finns" and Swedish-speaking citizens) who, during the *fin-de-siècle* "periods of oppression" (1899-1905 and 1908-1917) in Finland, opposed the laws of the Russian Tsar which introduced policies of Russification. *Nya Pressen was* published in Helsinki 1882-1900. It was shut down during the period of Russification and re-established in 1906, still Swedish-minded and constitutionalist, and even more open to foreign cultural influence.

Verga, Matilde Serao, Edmondo De Amicis and Giuseppe Giacosa.[15] The prose piece by Serao included in this anthology is a Finnish translation of *All'erta, sentinella!* [*Asentoon!*] by Hanna Andersin. Two book translations were published in Finland in 1908: *Tanssijatar: pieni elämätarina* [*La Ballerina*, 1899] and *Korkokeinottelua* [*Trenta per cento*, 1889], both translated by Frans Oskar Viitanen. Another translation by Viitanen dates from 1910: the re-translation of *All'erta, sentinella!* [*Vartia, pidä varasi!*], published by Karisto in Hämeenlinna.[16]

## TURKU CITY LIBRARY – THE OLD COLLECTION

The Turku City Library houses a rich collection of rare and old manuscripts, monographs and other books, known as the Old Collection (Parente-Čapková – Lappalainen, 2017, pp. 265-266). Serao's work here is available in a Swedish translation published in Sweden; this is the same work found in the National Library, the novel *Straff*. The volume is part of the separate Gustav Cyganeus Collection, which is preserved intact within the Old Collection. Gustav Cygnaeus (1851-1907), the owner, was an important Swedish-speaking figure in the cultural life of *fin-de-siècle* Turku. His fiction collection was donated to the City Library in 1907. This collection was influenced by its owner's activity as a "Swedish-minded" journalist, literary and theatre critic, and it comprises a considerable amount of fiction written by women (*ibid.*).[17] Like the Old Collection, the Cygnaeus Collection is multilingual, but many of the translated works of European literature which it contains are translations into Swedish. The fact that Serao's work is included in this collection shows that she had a reputation which placed her as one of the important cultural figures in Finland at the turn of the nineteenth and twentieth centuries.

15 Only Luigi Capuana was brand new to Finnish readers (Suomela-Härmä, 2007, p. 130). In contrast, Serao was one of those authors whose work "suited everybody" ("jokaisen lukijan käteen sopivia tekstejä") (*ibid.*).

16 *Vartia, pidä varasi!* belonged, in fact, to the Library of the Labour Movement [Työväenliikkeen kirjasto] collections. The Library was composed of donations by the Finnish Labour Archives [Työväen Arkisto] and People's Archives [Kansan Arkisto] and enriched by other donations and acquisitions. Most of the library materials concern, directly or indirectly, the history of the Labour Movement, but the library also hosts a large fiction collection.

17 One could speculate as to how much Cygnaeus's wife, the actress and cultural agent Wilhelmina ('Mina') Backlund (1851-1936) influenced the makeup of the collection.

THE LIBRARIES OF ÅBO AKADEMI
AND THE UNIVERSITY OF TURKU

In the library of Åbo Akademi, the Swedish-language university in Turku (officially founded in 1919 but made up of various earlier private collections and donations, from the late eighteenth century onwards), one would also expect to find Serao's works in Swedish. There is an anthology of short stories translated from Italian into Swedish entitled *Från det nya Italien. En samling berättelser* [*From the New Italy: A Collection of Short Stories*], published in Stockholm in 1890. The book comprises texts by six Italian authors,[18] Serao being the author represented by the greatest number of texts (four), translated by Ellen Lundberg-Nyblom (1869-1933), a Swedish translator and writer, with a short preface ["Förord"] written by the translator's mother, the writer Helena Nyblom (1843-1926). There is also the aforementioned volume which comprises Swedish versions of Serao's *Giovannino*, Pontoppidan's and Foley's texts.

The library of the Finnish-language University of Turku, one of Finland's most important scientific and scholarly libraries (founded officially in 1921, but, similarly to the library of Åbo Akademi, consisting of many donations dating back to the previous centuries), has eight books by Serao. They are in Italian, French, Swedish and Finnish. The two Italian books are: *Il paese di Cuccagna: romanzo napoletano* (published in Milan in 1891, i.e. a different edition from the one in the National Library in Helsinki), and the collection of short stories *Fior di passione*, the same edition as in the National Library (Milan, [1888] 1899). The French translation of *Cuore infermo* [*Coeur souffrant*, Paris, 1899] is the same edition as in the National Library. The Swedish translations are the anthology *Från det nya Italien* (Stockholm, 1890), mentioned already in conjunction with the Åbo Akademi library, and the novel *Straff* [*Castigo*, in E. Weer's 1893 translation], present both in the National Library and the Turku City Library (Cygnaeus Collection). Finally, we find three Serao books in Finnish: the anthology *Nuori Itaalia* (1893), containing "Asentoon!" / "All'erta, sentinella!" and two editions of *Tanssijatar*, the Finnish translation of *La ballerina* (translated by Frans Oskar Viitanen).[19]

18 They are: Matilde Serao (four texts), Giuseppe Giacosa (three texts), Contessa Lara (one text), Enrico Panzacchi (one text), Giovanni Verga (one text) and Edmondo De Amicis (three texts).

19 The first one is the 1908 edition as in the National Library, the second one from 1912, published by Isak Julin in Tampere. The copy of the first edition published by K. Kaatra

## OTHER LIBRARIES

Other works by Serao held in Finnish public libraries are almost entirely in Finnish translation: four are held by Helsinki City Library[20] and four by the Tampere City Library[21] (both founded in the nineteenth century); others can be found in other regional public libraries throughout Finland, like those of Lahti, Lappeenranta or Jyväskylä. However, as more and more library catalogues are being digitized and made available online, we learn about smaller collections holding Serao's books in Swedish (e. g. the Catalogue of the Library of Postal Association, holding a copy of *Vänninor*, a Swedish translation of *Fantasia*).[22] The National Repository Library (NRL)[23] holds, apart from several Finnish translations, one translation into Swedish which is not present in the other collections.[24] NRL also holds five original works by Serao, three

(a notable protagonist of the early twentieth century Finnish workers' movement, a poet, editor, and theatre director, who published numerous translations from various languages in his publishing house, see Kivistö – Riikonen, 2007, p. 355) is signed K.A. Koskinen. That signature could point to Kustaa Adolf 'Kössi' Koskinen, another active member of the Finnish workers' movement, who took part in the founding meeting of the Workers' Party of Finland, a predecessor of the Social Democratic Party of Finland.

20 They are *Korkokeinottelua* [*Trenta per cento*] (1908), *Pienoiskuvia elämästä* [*Fior di passione*] (1909), *Vartia, pidä varasi* [*All'erta, sentinella*] (1910) and *Giovannino tai kuolema* [*O Giovannino, o la morte*] (1910).

21 There are the two editions of *Tanssijatar* [*La ballerina*] from 1908 and 1912 respectively. The third one is the Finnish translation of "Una fioraia" from *Piccole anime* (1883), "Kukkatyttö" in Tyyni Tuulio's translation, published in *Italian kirjallisuuden kultainen kirja* [*The Golden Book of Italian Literature*] (1945), also found in many other libraries. For more on Tuulio, see https://375humanistia.helsinki.fi/it/tyyni-tuulio/quasi-un-secolo-al-servizio-della-letteratura (last accessed 30 June 2020).

22 See Katalog öfver Postföreningens i Finland Bibliotek, 1894: https://www.postimuseo.fi/fi/connect-testi/phn-kiertokirjeet/1890-1899/1894/26998-1894-postiyhdistyksen-kirjaston-kirjaluettelo-pdf/file (last accessed 30 June 2020). Libraries of workers' associations have been found in Finland since the 1870s, but with the breakthrough of the socialist workers' movement around the turn of the nineteenth and the twentieth century, their number increased rapidly. According to the rules, their function was to serve and educate not only the members of the associations, but also the general local population. See Mäkinen, 2009, in particular pp. 206-209. Their collections often comprised translated literature.

23 The National Repository Library NRL is a resource shared by all Finnish libraries and information service centres, founded in 1989. See http://www.varastokirjasto.fi/aims-and-function/. In many cases, it is, unfortunately, impossible to trace the origin of the books stored in NRL.

24 It is *Luftslott. Napolitansk sedeskildring* [*Castle in the Air: A Novel of Manners*], a translation of *Il paese di Cuccagna* by Ellen Lundberg-Nyblom, published in Stockholm by Geber in 1892.

of which are not found elsewhere in Finland.[25] The newest holding is the English translation of Serao's *La conquista di Roma* [*The Conquest of Rome*, ed. Ann Caesar], published by Pickering & Chatto in 1991. Perhaps the most extraordinary finding is that of Serao's French edition *Naples: les legendes et la réalité* (Paris, Félix Juven, 1908) in the library of one of Finland's most important twentieth-century public figures, the statesman, general of the Russian Imperial Army and, after WWII, Finland's president, Carl Gustav Emil Mannerheim (see Mannerheim library A-Ö, 2016).

All in all, the presence of works by Matilde Serao in Finland's libraries is notable. Around the turn of the nineteenth and the twentieth century, her works could be found in academic libraries including student libraries, public and private libraries and in collections like those of the Library of the Labour Movement or of professional associations. Thanks to the multilingual character of Serao's work, its presence in Finnish libraries overlaps with its reception through translations in other countries: Sweden, Russia, Germany, France. The Swedish and Finnish language anthologies that include Serao's texts are selections of contemporary Italian prose, where she is included alongside other visible and widely-translated Italian authors like Capuana, Verga, De Amicis or Giacosa, sometimes as the only woman; however, her gender does not seem to be of particular importance. She was also anthologized with other European authors, famous in their own time (like the Nobel laureate Pontoppidan), but – like Serao herself – not so well known outside their countries of origin today.

A most difficult, and sometimes an impossible, task is to determine the origin of the books in the libraries, but it seems obvious that the history of some of the books is related to that of Finnish-Italian relations. In two books present in the National Library, we find the bookplate of the Dante Alighieri Society and the stamp of Istituto italo-finlandese,[26] a cultural institute founded in 1925 with the aim of disseminating and promoting knowledge and study of the Italian language, culture and literature through courses in language and literature, conferences, exhibitions and concerts. The Institute also had a library with Italian

25 They are: *Piccole anime*, Milan, Baldini, 1892; *L'Infedele*, Milan, Brigola, 1897 and *Il romanzo della fanciulla*, Naples, F. Perella, 1909.

26 I thank Riitta Sarovuo for bringing this to my attention.

books, journals, and newspapers, mostly donations from the Dante Alighieri Society of Rome (Santoro 2005, p. 164; Rizzi, 2016, p. 287). One of Serao's books in the National Library was donated by the Helsinki University professor, diplomat and essayist Yrjö Hirn, one of Finland's major cultural personalities during the first half of the twentieth century.[27]

## SERAO'S TRANSLATIONS AND TRANSLATORS IN FINLAND

As mentioned in the introduction, in Finland, translations were published in both Swedish and Finnish. Serao's Swedish translations mentioned *vis-à-vis* the library collections were published in Sweden, but the publications from the Nya Pressens följetongbibliotek, the one entitled *Vänninor* from 1891 and the translation of *Giovannino* into Swedish from 1895, mentioned above, were published in Helsinki and could have been the work of a translator into Swedish who was living in Finland. Moreover, there were two of Serao's short stories published in the Swedish-language press in Finland (translators unknown): "En stor mans hustru" ["La moglie di un grand'uomo"] in 1893 and "En sidenklädning" ["La veste di seta" from *Gli amanti*] in 1899.[28]

Serao began to be translated into Finnish in the early 1890s, and several of her works were published in the press. The first of these appears to be "Kawaltaja" ["A Traitor"], a translation of her "La settimana delle Novelle (Anniversario)" from *Fior di passione* (1888), republished in 1897 in *Donna Paola* as "Molti anni dopo". "Kawaltaja" was published as a serialized novel in five instalments in the newspaper *Aura* in Turku on

27 Hirn (1870-1952) was specialized in aesthetics, but he was a most versatile scholar, who also worked in psychology, sociology, arts, and literature, with a special interest in French literature. He was a member of Finland's delegation to the Paris Peace Conference in 1919 and, after Finland became an independent republic, Hirn worked at the Finnish Embassy in Paris.

28 Both short stories were published in regional newspapers: "En stor mans hustru" was published in *Bjorneborgs Tidning*, 4 July 1893 (and republished in Östra Finland, 18 September 1893); "En sidenklädning" came out first in *Björneborgs Tidning* (7 February 1899) and, a week later (14 February 1899), in *Wasa Nyheter.*

7, 9, 10, 13 and 16 June 1891. This was a general trend in publishing fiction in *fin-de-siècle* Europe: even Finnish authors published their writings serially in newspapers and magazines (Suolahti, n.d.; Parente-Čapková – Lappalainen, 2017). In 1893, Serao was represented in the above-mentioned anthology *Nuori Itaalia*. As Elina Suolahti pointed out, "[w]ith its title recalling the eponymous Young Italy association of Giuseppe Mazzini, the collection reflected Finnish aspirations for independence at a time when the nation was still under the domination of the Tsarist Russian empire" (Suolahti, n.d., p. 1). The anthology was very probably inspired by the Swedish collection of short stories translated from Italian entitled *Från det nya Italien. En samling berättelser* (1890, mentioned earlier). In both anthologies, we find Serao, Giovanni Verga, Edmondo De Amicis and Giuseppe Giacosa. Though in the new century most of Serao's translations came out in book form, some of them appeared first in journals, such as "Novella greca" (the title was unchanged from the Italian original; *Aika*, 7, 1 April 1908) or *Giovannino tai kuolema*, published as an attachment in *Helsingin Kaiku*, 3, 22 January 1910 (both translated by Frans Oskar Viitanen; this illustrated weekly, *Helsingin Kaiku* is a different journal from the *Kaiku*, mentioned above).

Hanna Andersin (1861-1914) was the first translator of Serao's work. Andersin was born into a Swedish-speaking family (her father was a Counsellor of State), but she became passionate about Finnish and learned several foreign languages. She was a teacher, headmistress, author of textbooks and scholarly articles, and translator. She taught French, German and English, and became the first principal of Finland's first grammar school for girls, founded in 1906. She was internationally-oriented, passed her matriculation examination in Finland, and later undertook five study trips abroad (1883-1911). She compiled fiction reading lists, wrote textbooks and articles about language teaching and other linguistic topics for journals both in Finland and abroad, making her one of the first female linguists in Finland (Sainio, 2001). Her passion for languages led her to study foreign literatures, to write articles about literary works and to translate and adapt various works into Finnish. Andersin was a versatile cultural agent, typical of the *fin-de-siècle* women who fitted the description of cultural transmitters as developed by Petra Broomans: she "often takes on various roles in the field of cultural transmission: translator, reviewer, critic, journalist, literary historian, scholar, teacher, librarian, bookseller, collector, literary agent, scout, publisher, editor of a journal, writer, travel writer, or counsellor" (Broomans, 2009, p. 2).

Andersin was not directly involved in day-to-day politics, but she was a convinced Constitutionalist and interested in what was happening around her. She was particularly concerned about women's rights (Sainio, 2001). It was not surprising that she wrote mostly for *Valvoja*, an important liberal cultural journal of *fin-de-siècle* Finland, which gave space to women's emancipation, among other contemporary issues. In *Valvoja*, she published detailed work on contemporary Italian literature in an extensive article "Etelä-Euroopan nykyisen kaunokirjallisuuden alalta. Italialaista nykykirjallisuutta" ["On Contemporary Southern European Fiction: Contemporary Italian Literature"; see Andersin, 1892]. In the first section of the article, "Italialaista romanikirjallisuutta" ["On the Italian Novel"], dedicated to the "so-called verists' school" ("n.s. *veristien* koulu"; *ibid.*, p. 550), she introduced Serao after Luigi Capuana, Giovanni Verga, Carlo Dossi and Cesare Tronconi, and discussed her as "the most productive author of all the protagonists of *verismo*".[29] She mentions Serao's short stories, but concentrates on her novels, with much emphasis on *Fantasia* (*ibid.*, p. 563). Andersin also mentions Serao's *Il ventre di Napoli*, comparing her, in the usual manner, to Zola, and then discusses her latest works, seeing Serao as increasingly turning her attention to the "evils which torment Italian society" (*ibid.*, p. 565).[30] In this respect, particularly interesting is Serao's novel *Il paese di Cuccagna*, in which Serao deals with the Southern passion for the lottery. Andersin describes Serao's superb ability to create characters and depict both individuals and crowds, which, again, allows her to compare Serao with Zola. In the closing paragraph, Andersin states that though Zola might be a good point of comparison, as far as the depiction of the crowd is concerned, Serao (like Verga) shares her ability to empathize and sympathize with her characters with Alphonse Daudet and George Eliot. She sees this as the reason why Serao's books have been so widely distributed, "both in her home country and abroad, where they are read quite a lot and translated into other languages. Her imagination is perhaps

29 "tuotteliain kaikista 'veristeistä'".

30 "niitä paheita, jotka kalvavat italialaista yhteiskuntaa".

sometimes rather too lively and in places the language rather too dense, but this does not seem to be an obstacle to their [the books'] success" (*ibid.*, p. 567).[31]

After Andersin, Serao's next translator into Finnish was Frans Oskar Viitanen (1881-1942). Another journalist and a prolific author who published various historical works, this very patriotic and rather right-wing figure became the most prolific translator of Serao's work. A farmer's son from Western Finland, Viitanen attended secondary school (lyceum) in the town of Pori and, from 1900, he studied philology at the University of Helsinki. In 1905, he began to work as a journalist at *Aamulehti*, a patriotic newspaper of the city of Tampere, founded in the 1880s in order to strengthen the position of the Finnish (speaking) people and to improve the position of the Finnish language. Later on, *Aamulehti* was aligned with the Finnish National Coalition Party [Kansallinen Kokoomus, founded in 1918], one of the four largest political parties in Finland, on the centre-right of the political spectrum. *Aamulehti* obviously suited Viitanen's political orientation, since he later joined the National Coalition Party and represented it in the town councils of Lahti and Pori, where he then lived. While living in Lahti, he worked at the *Lahti* newspaper of the same political orientation, and while living in Pori, he wrote for the National Coalition Party paper, *Satakunnan Kansa*.

Viitanen's translations of Serao's œuvre began with *Tanssijatar: pieni elämäntarina* [*La ballerina*, 1899] in 1908. The book was published by Kaatra in Tampere, and sold well, since a new edition was issued in Tampere in 1912 by Isak Julin, as already mentioned. Viitanen's next translation was *Korkokeinottelua* [*Trenta per cento*, orig. in *Racconti napoletani*, 1889], also published in Tampere in 1908, by Osuuskunta Wäinämöinen. In 1909, his Finnish version of *Fior di passione* (orig. 1888), entitled *Pienoiskuvia elämästä*, was published by Väinämöisen kirjakauppa in Tampere. The short story "Novella greca", from *Fior di passione*, as we saw earlier, was published a year earlier, in 1908, in the periodical *Aika*. In 1910, Viitanen published both his re-translation of "All'erta, sentinella!" (from *Racconti napoletani*, 1889) as *Vartia, pidä*

31 "Eikä sentähden ole ihmeteltävää, että hänen kirjansa leviävät niin laajalle sekä hänen isänmaassaan että ulkomaillakin, joissa niitä verrattaen paljon luetaan ja käännetään muihin kieliin. Niissä löytyvä ehkä joskus liian vilkas mielikuvitus ja paikoittain liian tuuhea kieli eivät siis näy suuresti ehkäisseen niiden menestystä".

*varasi!* and, finally, "Giovannino tai kuolema!" from *Racconti napoletani*, published in Helsinki by Emil Vainio (within the series *Helsingin Kaiun kertomuskokoelma*, 11).

Viitanen accompanied his translations of Serao's works with prefaces and information about the author, signed 'the translator into Finnish.' He used basically the same preface (Viitanen, 1908a, 1908b) for *Tanssijatar* [*La ballerina*] and *Korkokeinottelua* [*Trenta per cento*]. The text is untitled, and Viitanen introduces Serao with an emphasis on her journalistic activities. He writes that some of Serao's work was among the best modern Italian narrative. In his eulogy, Viitanen points to the authority of literary historians such as the German Romance scholar Berthold Wiese, the Italian Erasmo Pèrcopo, and Serao's translator into German, Alfred Friedmann. He foregrounds Serao's merits in her depiction of life in Naples, but emphasizes that though she is a realist, she "stays far from the extremes of this current".[32]

Though I have concentrated on Serao's *fin-de-siècle* Finnish reception,[33] when speaking about her translators, I should also mention the distinguished writer, translator and scholar Tyyni Tuulio (1892-1991) who, as we saw earlier (see n. 21), translated Serao's short story "Una fioraia" from *Piccole anime* (Serao, 1883) as "Kukkatyttö", and included it in *Italian kirjallisuuden kultainen kirja* [*The Golden Book of Italian Literature*], which she herself edited, published by one of the major twentieth-century Finnish publishers, WSOY, in 1945, as part of the book series "Maailmankirjallisuuden kultainen kirja" ["The Golden Book of World Literature"]. Like Hanna Andersin, Tuulio too was a many-sided cultural agent and transmitter. She herself wrote both fiction and scholarly works and translated literature and scholarship from various languages. Her translations from Italian included Dante, Petrarca, Lampedusa and Pirandello; she also translated Luigi Salvini's volume on contemporary Italian literature (*Uusi Italian kirjallisuus 1870-1915*, 1935).

---

32 "Vaikka hän onkin realisti, pysyttelee hän kumminkin etäällä tämän suunnan äärimmäisyyksistä" (Viitanen, 1908a, p. 4; Viitanen, 1908b, p. 4). Viitanen's characterizations of Serao were often repeated in the Finnish press, including his quotations from distinguished academics and foreign translators of Serao's works, particularly Swedish and German *connoisseurs* of Italian literature (e.g. "*Tanssijatar*", 1910; "Matilde Serao", 1910).

33 There were also two Serao short stories published in 1930 in the journal *Kiki. Suomalainen novellilukemisto* [*Kiki: Finnish Short Story Readings*], nn. 5 and 7 respectively: "Sovinto" and "Lulu järjestää asian" ["Sovinto", "Il trionfo di Lulu" from *Dal vero* (1879)].

## SERAO IN THE FINNISH PRESS

A search for Serao in the Digital Collections of the National Library of Finland, which hosts the country's digitized newspaper, magazine and journal archives yields 380 references in newspapers (published in Finland 1771-1930), and 84 references in journals (including the possible errors that come up in a "fuzzy search"). Most of these are advertisements or short mentions of books published, both in Swedish-language and in Finnish-language newspapers of diverse political profiles, including some left-wing newspapers.[34] In 1908, the Social Democratic newspaper *Kansan Lehti* even pointed out that Serao engaged in a "war against the faults and wrongs of society" (*Kansan Lehti,* 1908).[35]

The Swedish-language press, of course, advertised Serao's translations into Swedish which were published both in Sweden and in Finland. Most of these advertisements appeared in the Swedish-minded newspaper *Nya Pressen* which also published reviews: already in 1892, a review of *Luftslott* (*Il paese di Cuccagna*, published in Sweden) had appeared. The critic E.G., most probably Ernst Grånsten (1865-1942), an influential Swedish-speaking cultural and political figure and in 1920, Minister for Finance, was a lawyer, banker, journalist and a prolific and feared literary critic, who expressed his dissatisfaction with the fact that Italian literature had been so rarely translated into Swedish – there were works by De Amicis, Farina and Giacosa, but Leopardi and Carducci were still waiting for their translators. E.G. welcomes Serao's sharp analysis of Italian society, her psychological insight, the way she never betrays the qualities of "real, true art"; E.G., 1892). She does not avoid misery and suffering, but she does not preach, and she is never pompous, unlike the authors of the "Nordic literature of indignation" ["den nordiska indignationsliteraturen"], especially that "of feminine origin" (*ibid.*).[36] Instead,

34 We find advertisements of Serao's works also in radical and/or working-class newspapers such as *Eteenpäin, Sosiaalidemokraatti, Työmies*, and even in *Työkansa*, a Finnish Socialist newspaper published 1907-1915 in Canada.

35 "romaaneissaan [Serao] usein nousee sotajalalle yhteiskunnan virheitä ja epäkohtia vastaan".

36 "Realism of indignation" was a term used about Nordic realism, often in a negative way. The term points to the anger and indignation that literary texts were to provoke

Serao's work emanates sympathy for the object of its author's interest, a sympathy which makes her style, otherwise restrained, "tremble with unspoken suffering", but which elevates and comforts the reader (*ibid.*).[37]

Generally, we can say that compared to the Finnish-language papers, the Swedish-language press paid more attention to Serao's personal life, informing its readers about Serao's separation from her husband,[38] and discussing her as a woman journalist. In the article "Kvinnan i tidningsvärlden" ["Woman in the World of the Press"], for example, the critic G.H.T. focuses on female journalists in Europe and in the U.S.A. Serao is presented in a complex and rather contradictory way: she is the publisher of *Il Giorno*, where the staff is all male; according to G.H.T., this does not prevent the paper from engaging in an "energetic battle for women's political rights" nor from cultivating connections with women's movements in various countries. However, in her newspaper, Serao does not neglect to stress that woman is most powerful as a ruler of the house, and the home, nor that woman's power lies in the womanly care she dedicates to these (G.H.T., 1907).[39]

The *fin-de-siècle* Finnish-language press also drew attention to Serao's Italian origins (often labelling her 'the darling of the Neapolitans'). In Viitanen's aforementioned preface, reprinted in various newspapers, Serao's "pessimism" is, according to the author, compensated for by a "breath of the Southern-Italian joy for life" (Viitanen, 1908a; Viitanen, 1908b,

---

in their readers (see Isomaa, 2012, p. 11). In the Finnish context, E. G.'s mention of the "feminine" literature of indignation evokes the harsh critical response to the work of the Finnish realist, playwright, and prose writer Minna Canth (1844-1897), the author of *Työmiehen vaimo* [*The Worker's Wife*, 1885, the first Nordic drama situated in the *milieu* of the urban proletariat].

37 "Men hon deklamerar icke: ingenting ligger henne fjärmare än det ihåligt storvulna, som inom den nordiska indignationsliteraturen, särskildt den, hvars ursprung är feminint, så ofta stöter en I stället genomandas hennes framställning af en sympati för skildringens föremål, som gör rättvisa åt alla, – en sympati, som stundom bringar den förnämt reserverade stilen att skälfva af undertrykt lidelse, men som både lyftar och värmer".

38 See, for instance, the article published in 1902 in *Hufvudstadsbladet* (47, 18 February, p. 5), Finland's most popular, highest-circulation Swedish-language newspaper during the second half of the nineteenth century.

39 "Hon har endast manlig personal till sitt förfogande, hvilket dock icke hindrar, att tidningen för en energist kamp för kvinnans politiska rättigheter och lifligt följer med kvinnorörelsen i olika länder. Matilde Serao försummar likväl icke att i sin tidning framhålla, att kvinnans största makt ligger i hennes herravälde öfver hemmen, och i den sant kvinnliga vården af dessa".

p. 4).[40] Occasionally, there were also comments on Serao's gender: Viitanen points out that there have hardly been any Italian women who used the Italian language better than Serao (*ibid.*).[41] These features are to be found also in the partly negative review of Serao's work (in *Tampereen Sanomat*, 1909) signed by the initials "vtt". Discussing *Pienoiskuvia elämästä* [*Fior di passione*], the critic ironizes on Serao's themes and style: "the lady", as this reviewer calls her, does not deal with any topical issues, just with love, which she "adores" – "of course she does, being Italian". Serao's style is "beautiful", exuberant, with typically Italian "rhetorical pathos", but her way of writing about love is too "chaste" and "respectable" – in other words, a bit dull, as we can read between the lines. However, the way in which she creates her characters through focussing on external features is "accurate in a feminine way", a statement that other newspapers and journals reprinted several times (vtt, 1909).[42]

In Finnish-language journals, there are several reviews which discuss translations of Serao's texts in more depth. Two notable reviews came out in 1908 in the journals *Valvoja* and *Aika*. As mentioned earlier, *Valvoja* was a liberal journal, while *Aika* was more conservative: indeed, one of the most powerful reviewers in *Aika* was the poet, journalist, and university professor Veikko Antero Koskenniemi (1885-1962), a very influential figure in early twentieth-century cultural life in Finland, politically conservative, a lover of classical antiquity and a devoted friend of Italian culture.[43] He did not speak Italian, but travelled to Italy and was able to read the language thanks to his knowledge of Latin and French (Saarenheimo, 2000, p. 63). He signed his reviews with his initials, V.A.K. In his review of *Tanssijatar*, he first sums up the plot and then praises Serao's style, especially its "restraint" ("hillitty"; V.A.K., 1908, p. 273). Koskenniemi likes this "steady slow motion", though it might be *too restrained* – he would wish for more of a dramatic take. Nevertheless, he considers *Tanssijatar* a "very laudable example of the (woman) writer's good ability to tell stories. There is good reason to

40 "hänen pessimismiäänkin miedontaa jonkinlainen henkäys etelä-italialaisen elämänilosta".

41 "tuskin kukaan Italian naisista on käyttänyt kieltä kauniimmin kuin hän".

42 See the short advertisements of *Pienoiskuvia* and *Korkokeinottelua* in *Lahti* newspaper, 196, 19 December 1909, p. 3, quoting the *Tampereen Sanomat* paper.

43 Koskenniemi's authority is obvious also from his short review of *Vartia, pidä varasi!*, published in *Kirjastolehti*, in December 1913 (Koskenniemi, 1913), where he recommends the book for public libraries.

include Matilde Serao in the canon of literary stars in Italy" (V.A.K., 1908, p. 274).[44] However, at the end of his review, Koskenniemi introduces his reader to another Italian writer still unknown in Finland, Grazia Deledda, and mentions her novel *La via del male*, which he believes could find readers in Finland.

In the same year, a review of *Tanssijatar* and *Korkokeinottelua* [*Trenta per cento*] was published in *Valvoja,* signed by the initials Y.K., most probably, Yrjö Koskelainen (1885-1951), a writer, editor, and literary critic; originally of patriotic orientation, he developed gradually into a strongly right-wing thinker and politician. He specialized mostly in Scandinavian and Italian literature, having studied Italian language, literature, and theatre in Italy (Muiluvuori, 2016). Y.K. is the one who emphasizes, most of all, the 'essentializing' features of Serao's writing, gendering it very strongly and explaining its characteristics with her "Italianness". He emphasizes that Serao is an extremely popular Italian or Neapolitan writer, mostly of "summer reading for Italian women in pale dresses from middle-class homes" (Y.K., 1908, p. 564).[45] Serao's ethnicity/nationality and gender determine the reviewer's approach to her work: "Matilde Serao is a woman and an Italian, two things that define her work as does a law of nature" (*ibid.*).[46] According to Y.K., Serao, as a woman, pays attention to private matters; the sentimentality of her style is an expression both of her femininity and of her being Italian. *Tanssijatar* is "a true Neapolitan story" ("aito napolilainen tarina") and has too much local colour. Y.K. then goes on to compare the Italian and Nordic "nature" in terms of issues such as feelings and the relationship between city and countryside. Serao's sentimentality is of a specially (Italian) kind, since it is based in the everyday life of the city. One cannot deny Serao's compassion for the unfortunate, writes Y.K., but she does not "rise" to the heights of the Nordic authors. She does not deserve to be called a pessimist – as a writer, she is just mediocre, though she is quite a pleasant narrator – "[a]t least by Nordic standards" (*ibid.*, p. 566).[47] At the end of the review, Y.K. rather harshly criticizes "Mr Viitanen's"

44 "erittäin kunnioitettava näyte tekijättärensä hienosta kertomataiteesta. On täysi syy pitää Matilde Seraoa muistissa, kun määrittelee kirjallisten tähtien asemaa Italian taivaalla".

45 "keskisäädyn kodeissa ja vaaleapukuisten italiattarien kesälektyyrinä".

46 "Matilde Serao on nainen ja italialainen, kaksi seikkaa, jotka jo luonnonlakina määrittelevät hänen tuotantoaan".

47 "Ainakin pohjoismaalaisen arvostelulla mitattuna".

translation, which he accuses of clumsiness, errors, and misspellings of Italian names. The review ends rather unexpectedly, with the statement that the reviewer would definitively join the admirers of Matilde Serao.

A review of *Pienoiskuvia elämästä* [*Fior di passione*] under the pen name L.W-r. was published in the originally nationally-minded and socially-oriented weekly *Raataja* which,[48] however, became a conservative, antisocialist paper in 1908. L.W-r.'s review came out in 1909. The reviewer sounds a bit uncertain, repeating the phrase 'in my opinion' several times, and mentions Serao's capacity for compassion towards her characters, which means she [Serao] must be a person with a good heart. Without ironizing Serao's 'sentimentality', L.W-r writes about the wide range of female characters that Serao depicts in her prose, praising the author's psychological insight. At the end of this positive review, L.W-r. thanks the "meritorious translator"[49] (L.W-r., 1909, p. 269).

## CONCLUSIONS

Matilde Serao's reception in Finland was very rich, especially when understood broadly, and taking into account the presence of her books in public, academic and private libraries. Working with large datasets such as the digital collections of the National Library of Finland and online library catalogues in various languages enables us to combine close and distant reading, carrying out a kind of a transnational *meso-analysis* of Serao's reception. The material relating to Serao's reception in Finland is so vast, that it could yield a much larger study, or even several studies. Questions connected to the library collections, the issue of Serao's reception in the periodical press and a closer look at the translations and their authors remain as interesting and important issues for further investigation.

As mentioned earlier, Serao's reception in Finland began in the early 1890s with serialized translations of her prose works in the Finnish press

48 The name of the paper, *Raataja. Yhteiskunnallinen Viikkolehti* translates as "Drudge: A Social Weekly".

49 "ansiokkaalle kääntäjälle".

and peaked towards the end of the 1900s, when several of her works were translated into Finnish, reviewed in Finland's major journals and advertised in a wide range of publications. The fact that Serao's books were widely sold and read is also indicated by the retranslation of one of her texts and the republication of another in a second edition. Though two of her novellas were published in Swedish in Helsinki, at present there is no information available about Serao's possible translators into Swedish on Finnish territory. Apart from the translations into Finnish and Swedish, Serao's books were present in Finland's libraries in languages which were read by many people in those days. This shows that translations into the 'national/majority language(s)', while very important in reception, do not usually tell the whole story. A special case are anthologies aiming to bring the 'pearls' of foreign literature to Finland. As Juhani Niemi (2007, p. 371) has pointed out, the first decades of the twentieth century can be called "the golden age" of literary anthologies However, as shown by the *Italian kirjallisuuden kultainen kirja* [*Golden Book of Italian Literature*], Serao was also anthologized later, though this publication from 1945 remained the last of this kind.

Serao was received mostly positively by both the Swedish and Finnish speaking publics in Finland, as well as by publishers, newspapers, and other cultural agents such as libraries across the political spectrum (including publishers active in the workers' movement), in cultural centres and in provinces. There are many notable contradictions in the ways in which Serao's writing was characterised: she was praised for her analysis of Italian society and for her psychological insight and ironized as an author of light reading for women, who avoided topical issues. She was mentioned as a journalist who cared about women's political rights, but who also emphasized woman's domestic role. Her style was depicted as 'restrained', but also as 'exuberant' or 'sentimental'.

The differences between the political profiles of Serao's key translators are telling. Her proximity to Naturalism and *verismo* was of interest for cultural transmitters dedicated to topical issues and interested in social problems, like Hanna Andersin. However, Serao's tendency to abstain from denouncing the centres of power (Wood, 1995, pp. 50-51), which most probably alienated her from being more readily embraced by the pronouncedly left-wing public, made it easier for conservatives like Viitanen or Koskenniemi to appreciate her work. They followed

Georg Brandes in maintaining that Nordic literatures do not have and do not desire Naturalism, which is a trend typical of the 'sick' French and Latin spirit. They would label Serao a realist, who remains "far from the extremes of the [realist] current"[50] (Viitanen, 1908a, p. 4; Viitanen 1908b, p. 4). This meant they had no problem praising her rather neutral faculty of having psychological insight and compassion for the poor and the unfortunate. On the other hand, the critic E.G. would use Serao to attack Nordic and Finnish realist/naturalist authors, especially women writers.[51]

Situating Serao in the nationalist context of the Young Italy movement was also a strategy that appealed to patriotic feelings across the political spectrum. In the early twentieth century, when Finland's own national movement was reaching its zenith, translated works of foreign literatures were published as part of the project of educating the nation, in the spirit of popular enlightenment (Niemi, 2007, p. 371); they were read as a pretext for reflection on national issues. To critics like Y.K. the confrontation of Serao's "Italianness" and "Neapolitan spirit" with Nordic qualities also offered an opportunity to praise what Matti Klinge (1990, esp. pp. 7-57) has called the "Nordic self": a kind of identity constructed in hierarchical opposition to the Southern European identity, which was simultaneously exoticized and demonized. At the same time, critics like E.G. would welcome Serao as another voice from Italy, whose literature deserves more attention. The fact that Serao's works were promoted by institutions like the Dante Alighieri Society or the Istituto Italo-finlandese show that she was seen as an appropriate representative of Italian culture in Finland.

The essentializing features of Serao's reception concerned her nationality, her local identity, and her gender. Serao's Neapolitan colour is often exoticized, intensifying the kind of temperament ascribed to the Italians in general. For some critics, the fact that Serao was a woman was a pretext for gendering her work and ironizing her 'sentimentality', the 'feminine' or 'amiable' features of her texts, and her concern with

50 "etäällä tämän suunnan äärimmäisyyksistä".

51 The role of critics' evaluation of the realist/naturalist mode in Serao's reception in the Nordic countries would deserve a separate study. Feminist literary scholars in various Nordic countries have pointed out that (apart from the controversial role of naturalism in Nordic literary histories), "naturalism was a literary method and an aesthetic which was especially suited to women writers" (Lappalainen, 2007, 37). For more on Finnish realism and naturalism, see Lappalainen (*ibid.*) and Rossi, 2007.

petty private matters, while others praised her way of depicting female characters. The most insightful critique remains the article on Serao's work written in *Valvoja* by the versatile cultural agent Hanna Andersin (1892). Nevertheless, Serao's problematic relationship with feminism did not make her attractive for contemporaries who were engaging with women's emancipation.

After 1910, Serao's reception in Finland was very sporadic. In 1927, a long obituary by a notable Finnish historian and diplomat Liisi Karttunen was published in *Helsingin Sanomat* (Karttunen, 1927),[52] nowadays the largest subscription newspaper in Finland and in the Nordic countries. As we saw earlier, two translations of Serao's short stories were published in 1930 and a translation of her short story by Tyyni Tuulio (1892-1991) was published in 1945. Karttunen and Tuulio serve as further examples (after Cygnaeus, Hirn, Koskenniemi and Mannerheim) of important Finnish public figures who included Serao in their libraries, translated her work or dedicated critical writings to her.

Nowadays, Serao's work seem to speak mostly to readers and students interested in Italian culture (see Wessman, 2001, and the rich collection of Serao international research in Finland's university libraries, including links to online texts).[53] Serao's most recent translation into Finnish came out in the journal *Settentrione. Rivista di studi italo-finlandesi* published at the University of Turku.[54] Hence Finnish scholars have

---

52 Liisi Karttunen (1880-1957) worked for many years in Italy both for the Finnish embassy (after 1917), and as a researcher (Palosuo, 1991). In her obituary for Serao, Karttunen highlights Serao's worldwide fame and depicts the author's life through its hardships and its deserved success. She skilfully frames Serao's career as prose writer and journalist in the context of Italian cultural life at the turn of the twentieth century, emphasizing her friendship with Eleonora Duse (Karttunen, 1927). Shorter obituaries on Serao were published in several other newspapers.

53 See the National Library in Helsinki (https://kansalliskirjasto.finna.fi/Search/Results?lookfor=Serao%2C+Matilde&lng=en-gb&op=%EE%A8%B5) and the very rich contemporary collection of the University library of Tampere (http://utafi.summon.serialssolutions.com/en-UK/#!/search?ho=t&l=en-UK&q=Serao,%20Matilde). Searching in the Finna database (https://finna.fi/?lng=en-gb) (last accessed 30 June 2020), which provides free access to material from Finnish museums, libraries, and archives, we get ninety-four hits for Serao, including Serao research and some newspaper reviews. The searchable material has, of course, been growing steadily, with the rapid digitization of the periodical press and other sources.

54 This is the most recent translation and, at the same time, the only Post-War translation of Serao's work into Finnish that I have found. It is Jukka Nyman's translation of "Maggio e il miracolo di San Gennaro" under the title of "Toukokuu ja

a good opportunity to study another 'difficult woman writer', given the contradictory nature of both Serao's authorial personality and her writings *vis-à-vis* (not only) gender.

Viola PARENTE-ČAPKOVÁ
University of Turku

## MATILDE SERAO'S FICTION TRANSLATED INTO FINNISH[55]

Serao Matilde, 1891, "Kawaltaja" ["A Traitor"; orig. "La settimana delle Novelle (Anniversario)"], trans. unknown, *Aura*, 7 June, pp. 3-4; 9 June, pp. 3-4; 10 June, pp. 3-4; 13 June, pp. 3-4; 16 June, pp. 3-4.

Serao Matilde, 1893, *Asentoon!* [*All'erta, sentinella!*], trans. Hanna Andersin, Helsinki, Otava.

Serao Matilde, 1893, *Nuori Itaalia* [*Young Italy*], ed. and trans. Hanna Andersin, Helsinki, Otava (includes "Asentoon!" ["All'erta, sentinella!"]).

Serao Matilde, 1908, "Novella greca" ["Novella greca"], trans. Frans Oskar Viitanen, *Aika*, 7, 1 April, pp. 264-270.

Serao Matilde, 1908, *Korkokeinottelua* [*Trenta per cento*], trans. Frans Oskar Viitanen, Tampere, Osuuskunta Wäinämöinen.

Serao Matilde, 1908, *Tanssijatar: pieni elämätarina* [*La Ballerina*], trans. Frans Oskar Viitanen, Tampere, Kossi Kaatra.

Serao Matilde, 1909, *Pienoiskuvia elämästä* [*Fior di passione*], trans. Frans Oskar Viitanen, Tampere, Väinämöisen kirjakauppa.

Serao Matilde, 1910, *Giovannino tai kuolema!* [*O Giovannino o la morte*], trans. Frans Oskar Viitanen, (part of a newspaper book series) *Helsingin Kaiku*, 10, Helsinki, Emil Vainio.

Serao Matilde, 1910, *Vartia, pidä varasi!* [*All'erta, sentinella!*], trans. Frans Oskar Viitanen, Hämeenlinna, Karisto.

San Gennaron ihme" (Serao, 1994a), accompanied by an introduction by Raffaella Sforza (1994).

55 The list of publications in newpapers is meant to reflect only a selection of the translations mentioned in the essay; this is also the case for the translations into Swedish.

Serao Matilde, 1912, *Tanssijatar: pieni elämätarina* [*La Ballerina*], trans. Frans Oskar Viitanen, Tampere, Isak Julin.
Serao Matilde, 1930, "Sovinto. La moglie di un grand'uomo", *Kiki. Suomalainen novellilukemisto* [*Kiki: Finnish Short Story Readings*], 5, pp. 1-16.
Serao Matilde, 1930, "Lulu järjestää asian" ["Il trionfo di Lulu"], *Kiki. Suomalainen novellilukemisto* [*Kiki: Finnish Short Story Readings*], 7, pp. 83-102.
Serao Matilde, 1945, "Kukkatyttö" ["Una fioraia"], *Italian kirjallisuuden kultainen kirja* [*The Golden Book of Italian Literature*], ed. and trans. Tyyni Tuulio, Helsinki, WSOY, pp. 577-582.

## MATILDE SERAO'S FICTION TRANSLATED INTO SWEDISH

Serao Matilde, 1890, *Från det nya Italien. En samling berättelser* [*From the New Italy: A Collection of Stories*; it contains Serao's "La settimana delle novelle (Anniversario)" / "En *öfverlöpare*", "Novella d'amore" / "Kärlek", "Salvazione" / "Räddning", "All'erta, sentinella" / "Fången på Nisida"], trans. Ellen Lundberg-Nyblom, Stockholm, Fahlcrantz.
Serao Matilde, 1891, *Vänninor* [*Fantasia*], trans. unknown, Helsinki, Nya Pressens Följetongbibliotek (vol. 31).
Serao Matilde, 1892, *Luftslott. Napolitansk sedeskildring* [*Castle in the Air: A Novel of Manners; Il paese di Cuccagna*], trans. Ellen Lundberg-Nyblom, Stockholm, Geber.
Serao Matilde, 1893, "En stor mans hustru" ["La moglie di un grand'uomo"], *Björneborgs Tidning* 51, trans. unknown, 4 July, pp. 2-3.
Serao Matilde, 1893, "En stor mans hustru" ["La moglie di un grand'uomo"], *Östra Finland*, trans. unknown, 17 September, p. 2; 18 September, p. 2.
Serao Matilde, 1893, *Straff: roman* [*Castigo*], trans. E. Weer [pseud. of Ellen Wester], Stockholm, Hökerberg.
Serao Matilde, 1895, *Giovannino eller döden!* [*O Giovannino o la morte*], trans. unknown, Helsinki, Nya Pressens Följetongbibliotek (vol. 52).
Serao Matilde, 1899, "En sidenklädning" ["La veste di seta"], trans. unknown, *Björneborgs Tidning*, 7 February, pp. 2-3.
Serao Matilde, 1899, "En sidenklädning" ["La veste di seta"], trans. unknown, *Wasa Nyheter*, 14 February, pp. 2-3.

# MATILDE SERAO IN THE HOLY LAND

During the summer of 1893 Matilde Serao travelled to Jerusalem and wrote about her journey in a newspaper series, published in the daily *Il Mattino*,[1] and later collected in a volume, *Nel paese di Gesù. Ricordi di un viaggio in Palestina* (1898).[2] By 1910 her travel book had sold more than 24000 copies, a considerable number even by today's standards (Palermo, 1972, p. 42), and had been translated into several foreign languages, including French (1903),[3] English (1905) and Spanish (1910). By the time it came out in England in 1905, with the title *In the Country of Jesus,* Serao was already known to English-speaking readers thanks to critical essays featuring her work, for instance an article in 1889 by Pauline Schletter,[4] and the 1901 Henry James's "note" on Serao, which famously introduced her to the American readership.[5] Some of her novels had already been translated into English, among them: *Fantasy* (1890), *Farewell Love* (1894), *The Land of Cockayne* (1901), and *The Conquest of Rome* (1902),[6] all printed by the London-based publisher

---

1 The first article reporting Serao's journey to Jerusalem was published by *Il Mattino* on 18 May 1893, with the title "Matilde Serao in Terrasanta" ["Matilde Serao in the Holy Land"], which announced that Serao had left the previous day for Alexandria, Egypt. A second article, "Nel Paese di Cleopatra: Navigando" ["Journeying in the Country of Cleopatra"], followed on 6 June 1893. The last article, "Speranza" ["Hope"], came out on 25 September 1899. For a list of all published articles, see Della Badia, 2011, p. 156, n. 50.

2 The first print of *Nel paese di Gesù* is dated 1898, but actually came out in 1899, see n. 18 in this chapter. To avoid confusion I kept the date that appears on the first printed edition and that is reported in most library catalogues.

3 The French translation, *Au pays de Jésus: souvenirs d'un voyage en Palestine,* published in Paris by Plon-Nourrit et Cie reached its 12th edition in 1906.

4 On Schletter's article see Ursula Fanning's chapter in this volume.

5 On Henry James's essay on Serao see Fanning's chapter in this volume; Richards, 1999; Sambuco, 2015.

6 According to Anthony Gisolfi, Serao was first mentioned to a British readership in an article published by *Blackwood's Magazine* in 1885, where she along with Giovanni Verga, Salvatore Farina, and La Marchesa Colombi were discussed and recommended to British readers (Gisolfi, 1968, pp. 120-121, 133).

William Heinemann.[7] With *In the Country of Jesus,* Serao capitalized on and further expanded her success in English-speaking countries, as her travelogue to Jerusalem was published in several editions both in England and the United States.[8]

In light of the theme of this volume – Serao's international profile, reception, and networks – this chapter will focus on the production and subsequent English translation of *Nel paese di Gesù*, a narrative of gender and religious self-definition, which, on the one hand, as already noted by Patrizia Sambuco, redefined traditional gendered notions of space and boundaries, but on the other, reenforced stereotypical views of her work as an Italian and Catholic woman writer.[9] If, in fact, in a 1899 review, *Nel paese di Gesù* was interpreted in Italy as a case of "wise literary evolution" and Christian expiation for a literary career spent in futile and mundane writings (Nediani, 1899, p. 382),[10] on the international scene, *In the Country of Jesus* reconfirmed, indeed emphasized, Serao's profile as a southern and Catholic woman writer, who "accepts the legends, illusions, and delusions – all that poetry of spirituality which the religious imagination of saints has added to the land and life of Jesus" (by an anonymous reviewer, "In the Country of Jesus", 1906, p. 1226). Serao's self-portrayal as a fervently religious Catholic woman, placed within a narrative of women's new mobility, proved to be appealing to an international audience, but it also provided fodder for an exoticizing and essentializing interpretation of her work. As other chapters of this volume illustrate, Serao's work was often

7 William Heinemann founded in London a publishing house which, still existing today as part of Penguin Random House, was considered one of the most prestigious presses in England. He published translations of works by major European authors. See Britannica, The Editors of Encyclopedia, 2021, https://www.britannica.com/biography/William-Heinemann (last accessed 25 January 2021).

8 My research was limited to Britain and the United States where I could access archival material. I was able to identify five different editions of *In the Country of Jesus,* three printed by the Scottish publisher Thomas Nelson and Sons, the first without a date (although library catalogues reported it as published in 1897, an implausible date given that the original book had yet to come out), the other two dated 1919 and 1930; one by the New York publisher Dutton, dated 1905; and an illustrated edition by the London publisher Heinemann also dated 1905. This last one was probably the initial publication, of which all others were a reprint, most likely illegal.

9 In her analysis of Serao's travel writings, *Lettera di una viaggiatrice* and *Il paese di Gesù,* Sambuco argues that Serao expresses in both texts a fundamental need to break free from gender-defined constraints of domesticity and, at the same time, to counteract accusations of eccentricity as a woman traveling alone (Sambuco, 2015, p. 132).

10 "sana evoluzione letteraria".

viewed by foreign readers, as the expression of an essentially Neapolitan and Catholic literary voice. In *Nel paese di Gesù,* Serao herself encouraged such a reading, as she positioned herself within a presumed Southern European Catholic identity, defined in contrast to a Northern European one, in particular to that of Britain, which for Serao represented the emblem of the failings of modernity.

## TRAVEL LITERATURE ON THE HOLY LAND

Matilde Serao embarked on her journey to Jerusalem as a lone "journalist-pilgrim"[11] in a moment of personal crisis (Di Bitonto, 2009, p. 125).[12] The term pilgrimage is fitting, as the author narrates her journey to Jerusalem as part of a religious vow,[13] but also as an opportunity to travel less beaten paths of modern and consumeristic tourism. "There is a very common traveler, you can meet anywhere [...] they are many, like the stars in the sky", Serao wrote in her preface, complaining about the burgeoning tourist industry, and concluding that only few people – and she counted herself among them – know "how to go to Palestine" (Serao, 1898, pp. IX, 329).[14] Stylistically a mixture of different genres – guidebook, autobiography, and devotional book – Serao's *Nel paese di Gesù* was initially written as a journalistic reportage of a journey to Palestine she took in the summer of 1893, to then turn, over the course of four years and several rewritings,[15] into a much more ambitious

11 "giornalista-pellegrina".

12 She and her husband, the journalist Edoardo Scarfoglio, were facing several legal challenges to their newly founded newspaper, *Il Mattino*. On a more personal level, around the same time, Edoardo Scarfoglio began an affair with the French singer Gabrielle Bessard, which created a rift in their marriage (Banti, 1965, pp. 186-193).

13 Serao ends her travelogue with these words: "I kept my word, and my vow is now fulfilled" ["E ho tenuto il giuramento e sciolgo, oggi, il voto"] (Serao, 1898, p. 364).

14 "Vi è un viaggiatore comunissimo, che s'incontra dappertutto [...] è numeroso come gli astri del firmamento"; "Pochi sanno come si va in Palestina". Unless otherwise noted, all translations into English in this essay are mine. As I will discuss later in this chapter, the 1905 English translation of Serao's travelogue presents several problems of textual accuracy.

15 The publication of the volume turned out to be challenging for Serao, who spent more time than anticipated in reworking the articles already published in *Il Mattino*. In a

writing project, defined by the author as "not the most artistic of my books, but the most human" (Serao, 1898, p. 364),[16] one that expressed with sincerity ("not the most beautiful, but the most sincere")[17] (*ibid.*) the transformational power of her journey. The laboriousness of the rewritings indicates the difficulties she was encountering in finding the appropriate format, style and tone for a book that had the potential of reaching a wider public of readers than that initially offered by the readership of the daily *Il Mattino*.[18] Indeed, her travel book to the Holy Land, more than any other book she had written previously, reveals Serao's ambitions to engage not only a national, but also an international public of readers. An experienced and successful writer at that point in her career, she understood what it took to create a travel narrative with an international appeal, making specific narrative choices, which enhanced her gendered and national identity. She also engaged with contemporary debates taking place beyond national borders, whether on artistic expression or the recently established, but fast-growing, tourist industry. Describing herself, finally, as a "pilgrim of the heart," a sort of traveller of the human soul, which anticipated Zygmunt Bauman's distinction between tourist and pilgrim, Serao created a travel narrative, focused on self-discovery and the exploration of the "soul" of a country – an undefinable but, according to the author, nevertheless essential aspect of every country.[19]

For Bauman, a tourist is someone whose goal is to be on the move, rather than to "arrive" somewhere, while the pilgrim leaves footprints, engraved for good, so that "the trace and the record of past travels are kept and preserved" (Bauman, 1996, p. 23). The tourist, like the vagabond, has no specific goal, it is the moving around not the destination

---

letter Serao wrote to her friend Gegè Primoli, she complained that she had to rework it and correct it four times (cited in Di Bitonto, 2009, p. 125).

16 "non il più artistico dei miei libri, ma il più umano".

17 "non il più bello ma il più sincero".

18 The first edition of *Nel paese di Gesù* was published in Naples by Angelo Tocco in 1899 and not in 1898 as appears on the printed volume. According to Daniela De Liso, the book's proofs (and printing plates) were ready in 1898 but the publication was delayed (possibly because Serao was still making changes). The volume was finally published in the Autumn of 1899 and the publisher chose not to reset the plate that had been prepared a year earlier for the title page. See De Liso, 2019, p. 181.

19 "Ogni paese ha un'anima, lo sapete. Dove essa risieda, mai? Chi lo dirà? Inafferrabile eppure reale" (Serao, 1898, p. XI).

that matters; for the pilgrim, instead, the significance of travelling can only be in the pilgrimage, and the destination is where the meaning resides (Bauman, 1997, p. 91). Serao presents a similar juxtaposition – albeit less neatly distinct – between those who travel to London, Paris or Venice, destinations that "do not leave any trace on the soul of those who reached them",[20] and those, instead, whose journey is connoted by a spiritual experience which leave an enduring mark on one's life (Serao, 1898, p. 329). Another useful concept elaborated by Bauman is the fact that the two juxtaposed figures – pilgrim versus tourist – represent the modern and postmodern human condition: the former as a metaphor "for the modern life strategy preoccupied with the daunting task of identity-building", and the latter as a metaphor "for the postmodern strategy moved by the horror of being bound and fixed" (Bauman, 1996, pp. 25-26). The pilgrim, in other words, evokes life's distress, seeking meaning in one's troubled life; the tourist tends to shed it, as the whole point of vacationing for the tourist is to forget the stress of modern life.

Seen through this interpretive lens, Serao's travelogue presents a modernist reading of identity-building and mobility, especially of female mobility, that reveals Serao's anxiety and ambivalence towards some of the novelties brought by modernity, including tourism, which she practised throughout her life, visiting some of the most exclusive European destinations, but towards which she was becoming increasingly, if ambiguously, critical. Tourism, like other forms of consumerism connected to leisure, represented for Serao a source of modern alienation, a contemporary trend towards commodification, which she thought left the tourist without "a brain, but a gallery of pictures, his spirit is nothing but *a panorama* in which he constantly wants to change the images" (Serao, 1898, p. x; my emphasis).[21] Walter Benjamin has eloquently written about the illusionary nature of "panoramas", as "scenes of a perfect imitation of nature", and about "the gaze of the alienated man" who fetishizes the new as the ultimate destination of the modern era (Benjamin, 2008, pp. 99, 104). Serao too was concerned in her writings about the fetish of modernity in women's life, but her ambition, unlike Baudelaire's – featured in Benjamin's analysis of nineteenth-century

20 "non lasciano alcuna traccia nell'animo di chi li compì".

21 "un cervello, ma una galleria di quadri: il suo spirito non è che un panorama, di cui egli deisdera sempre cambiare le immagini".

Paris – was not to represent the life of a *flâneur* or, better, in her case a *flâneuse* – an alienated free-roaming woman travelling on her own in the phantasmagorias of the Holy Land – but to portray, and even poeticize, the spiritual struggle of a woman contending with modernity. Serao's travel narrative, developed in the tradition of the exempla – whereby each chapter illustrates her *via dolorosa* – and written with flowery language and moralizing tones, provided an account of Serao's soul-searching at a specific moment in her life but also a sort of blueprint for modern female mobility, and an escape – a 'dream' as she would put it in a later essay[22] – from the trappings of modern life. With a message, therefore, of salvation rather than alienation, Serao sets up Jerusalem as her travel destination and a promise of new beginnings and reconstituted wholeness in her life. "Destination", as Bauman aptly pointed out, "the set purpose of life's pilgrimage, gives form to the formless, makes a whole out of the fragmentary, lends continuity to the episodic" (Bauman, 1996, p. 22).

Serao's narration of salvation from modern life does not translate, however, into a mystical narrative. Her religiosity is an important aspect of her book, but not the central one. Critics have already written about the authenticity of Serao's religious feelings in her travelogue.[23] What has not been sufficiently highlighted by critics is Serao's modernist approach to her travel writing, her sense of loss in portraying the modern human condition, especially as it affected women's lives, and her seeking of new ideas with which to represent what she perceived as the confusing and contradictory aspects of modernity. While she rejected mass tourism and other aspects of modernity (she was critical, for instance, of the railroad),[24] she encouraged travelling by exalting the spiritual and moral transformation that a journey may bring. Written

22 See Serao's *Sognando* (Serao, 1906b, p. 37) where she defines dreaming as a mysterious elixir that has the extraordinary capacity to transform society ("forza capace di sollevare montagne" [a force capable of moving mountains]).

23 On the different critical interpretations of this aspect of Serao's travelogue, see De Liso, 2019, p. 186.

24 "The train is too fast, you know everything but see nothing. You cannot catch a line or color, you don't understand anything; and dispirited and with tired eyes, you fall back on your wooden seat, exhausted and overwhelmed by the vulgarity of the railway" ["Il treno è troppo rapido, voi sapete tutto ma non vedete nulla, voi non afferrate né una linea né una tinta, voi non capite più niente: e con gli occhi stanchi, lo spirito disgustato, voi ricadete snervato sul vostro banco di legno, lasciandovi vincere dalla soffocante volgarità di questa ferrovia"] (Serao, 1898, p. 55).

as a sort of know-how manual (*galateo*) – a burgeoning genre in the late nineteenth century – Serao's travel book to Palestine is rich in detail on best practices on how to visit even the most remote corners of Palestine, but also provides guidance for the traveller pursuing not only leisure but also self-improvement. And if nineteenth-century leisure suggested pleasurable idleness, a journey to the Holy Land promised a path towards meaningful personal transformation.

Although religious pilgrimage to Palestine had long existed, it was only towards the latter part of the nineteenth century, with the opening of the Suez Canal in 1869, technological and infrastructural developments – railroad and steamship – and the development of the Thomas Cook travel company that the Middle East became a tourist attraction for Western travellers, missionaries, and explorers (Ben-Arieh, 1979; Brendon, 1991; Cohen-Hattab – Katz, 2001). Writers too from all over the Western world flocked to Palestine and wrote about their journey. Travel books about the Holy Land – whether inspired by religious or artistic intentions – became enormously popular at the time. Mark Twain, for instance, wrote *The Innocents Abroad, or The New Pilgrim's Progress* (1869), which according to Hilton Obenzinger (2009, p. 146) was perhaps the most popular travel book in American literature; and Herman Melville based his *Clarel: A Poem and Pilgrimage in the Holy Land* (1876) on his 1857 visit to Palestine. Paul Bourget, a conservative French writer very popular in his own time and today largely forgotten, did not write a book about Jerusalem, but he visited the Holy Land in 1893, a month before Serao,[25] who mentions him in her travelogue, as will be further explored in this chapter.

Bourget wrote *La Terre promise* [*The Promised Land*] (1892), a book with a misleading title for a novel set in Sicily, but nevertheless influential on Serao's future writings. As for Italian writers who travelled and wrote about the Middle East, Cristina Trivulzio di Belgiojoso published in 1855 in the *Revue des deux mondes* the account of her travels to Anatolia and Jerusalem, *La Vie intime et la vie nomade en orient* [*The Intimate and Nomadic Life in the Orient*], written in French and translated into Italian only much later.[26]

25 In the chapter in which Serao recounts her climbing the mount Tabor in Galilee, she noted: "I sign my name at the eight-third place, after Paolo Bourget who was here a month before me" ["Segno il mio nome all'ottantatreesimo posto, dopo Paolo [*sic*] Bourget che vi è passato un mese prima di me"] (Serao, 1898, p. 281).

26 According to the Opac SBN catalogue, the first translation into Italian, *La vita intima e la vita nomade in Oriente,* was printed in Milan by Facchi in 1921.

An "accidental orientalist", according to Barbara Spackman, Belgiojoso presented with her travel narrative an early example of a transnational representation of identity (Spackman, 2017, p. 4). Towards the end of the nineteenth century, Angelo De Gubernatis, a major literary figure and an academic specialized in the study of the Orient, went to Palestine and wrote *In Terrasanta* [*In the Holy Land*] (1899), a book mainly focused on the political and diplomatic issues affecting the Middle East (De Caprio, 2000, p. 96). Finally, several priests and friars wrote about the Holy Land – among them, Gaspare Olmi, *Il mio quarto pellegrinaggio in Palestina* [*My Fourth Pilgrimage in Palestine*] (1876), Giuseppe Maria Filanti, *Il mio viaggio in Oriente* [*My Voyage to the Orient*] (1881) – inaugurating a fertile season of Catholic travel books which were supposed to harmonize religious content with the modern techniques of fictional writing (Piazza, 2012, pp. 319-322). None of these Italian travel books on the Holy Land were translated into English and even in Italy they had a limited circulation. Serao's travelogue to Palestine was the only book among Italian contemporary publications of this genre to circulate widely both nationally and abroad. Its success may be explained both by her being already a recognizable name among a wide public of readers, and by the hybrid style, format, and content she used for a book she was already imagining translated into foreign languages as she was completing it.[27]

In *Nel paese di Gesù,* Serao clarifies from the very beginning that her travel book is different from other similar books. Serao, in fact, wrote a book, which for its style, content, and language – neither technical nor purely religious or fictional, but rather a mixture of all these elements – was intended to be not only instructional but also entertaining. Not surprisingly, she uses the terms "pilgrim of the heart and of the imagination" to define the ideal traveller, underlining the relevance, indeed necessity, of the imaginative element to reveal the otherwise inexplicable spiritual and magical nature of her journey (Serao, 1898, p. 245).[28] What

27 "I hope that from some Italian region, be it near or far, from some big city or small unknown town, where my book will be translated, a soul will be irresistibly attracted to this journey and [...] will embark for Palestine, with a heart full of trepidation and affection" ["Io spero che, da qualche regione italiana, lontana o vicina, da qualche grande città o da qualche borgo sconosciuto, da qualche paese straniero, ove il mio libro andrà tradotto, qualche anima si senta irresistibilmente attratta da tal viaggio e [...] s'imbarchi per la Palestina con cuore ansioso e affettuoso"] (Serao, 1898, p. 342).

28 "pellegrino del cuore e della fantasia".

distinguishes, therefore, her book from other similar books is its use of a mixture of different elements traditionally treated separately. Serao's travelogue shared the practical concerns of Thomas Cook's guidebook *Tourist Handbook for Palestine and Syria* (1891) on how to reach Palestine, where to sleep or eat (Sambuco, 2015, pp. 208-209), De Gubernatis's recognition of the importance of Jerusalem as the centre of the Christian world (De Caprio, 2000, p. 95), as well as the mystical reflections of religious travel literature. Writing with a hybrid style, using fictional elements seemingly straight out of a gothic novel,[29] Serao set out to narrate the many aspects – commercial, moral, religious, and artistic – of her travel experience.

*Nel paese di Gesù* is divided into nine sections, comprising forty-six chapters – that span the time from when she left Italy in the Spring of 1893 until she completed her book in the Autumn of 1897, as indicated at the end of her preface. Each section describes a specific moment in her journey to Palestine. The first two sections narrate her travels to Jerusalem via Egypt and her reckoning with the challenges of travelling in the Middle East. The following three sections are set in Jerusalem, "the sublime residence of the spirit, it is on earth, the image of Paradise" and are the most mystical in tone and religious in content. The next three sections are devoted to her travels to Jericho, the Jordan river, and the Dead Sea, which recount her most adventurous moments: "there is not a single traveller in Palestine, young or old, man or woman, solitary or in company, who does not go to Jericho [...] which gives immediately the thrill of adventure" (Serao, 1898, pp. 44, 188-190).[30] Here she portrays herself as an unconventional woman travelling alone and behaving in ways that at home might have still been considered inappropriate according to contemporary expectations of female behaviour. She writes about travelling with a gun ("I have a gun, and I am in constant fear that it will shoot in the suitcase") and smoking ("I did not visit Nazareth before five in the afternoon, after I'd slept, read, smoked, dreamed, and written"), an activity which in her conduct book *Saper vivere* (Serao,

29 In her description of her visit to Jericho, for instance, Serao mentions the British gothic novelist Ann Radcliffe (Anna Ratcliffe [*sic*] in Serao's text) and her *The Mysteries of Udolpho* to convey "l'immediato brivido di avventura" she experienced there (Serao, 1898, pp. 190-191).

30 "non vi è un solo viaggiatore di Palestina, giovane o vecchio, uomo o donna, solitario o in compagnia, che non vada a Gerico, immancabilmente [...] che dà l'immediato brivido dell'avventura".

[1900] 1989, p. 179) she described as common for women, but that not long before, would have scandalized even the most liberal-minded Italians. In the nineteenth century, few Italian women travelled across Italy, and even fewer travelled outside Italy or wrote about it.[31] Serao considered herself an exceptional woman by Italian standards, and with her travel narrative she was not addressing exclusively an Italian readership but also a foreign one, more accustomed to the idea of a woman travelling on her own. The overall image of Serao that emerges from her travelogue is one that communicated women's independence and freedom, although Serao's self-portrayal suggested also an essentializing discourse about identity that asserted a supposed primacy of countries of "Latin" origin. Serao praised the work of monks and nuns and "the poor Latin Church, the only one which, thanks to Franciscan friars, has been resisting fearlessly for centuries [...] the only one that upholds the prestige of Christian Charity" (Serao, 1898, pp. 106-107), for instance, as well as her Italian (and European) Southern identity, expressed in terms of her religious fervour or capacity to sustain hot climates and dangerous environments: "But I am a southerner" she replies to people surprised at her willingness to visit Jerico (*ibid.*, p. 185).[32] The last section, finally, concludes the volume with Serao's expressed hope that if only one person in Italy or abroad ("where my book will be translated", *ibid.*, p. 342)[33] will go to Palestine her efforts would not be in vain. It was her certainty that her book would find a readership abroad that provided Serao with the impetus to expand her initial serialized reportage into a travelogue.

31 Italian travel literature features fewer women than other literary traditions. Nevertheless, critics of travel literature have recently drawn attention to women travellers in Italy, previously ignored, and to their travel writings, often included in diaries, letters, and journalistic reportage. For the nineteenth century, besides Cristina di Belgioioso and Anna Nizzoli, several other women left travelogues, such as Caterina Percoto, Dora D'Istria, Aurelia Cimino Folliero Della Luna, and Caterina Pigorini Beri, who, however, wrote mainly about travelling in Italy. See Scriboni, 1996; Ricorda, 2011.

32 "la povera chiesa latina, la sola che per mezzo dei frati francescani, resista, da centinaia di anni, impavida [...] la sola che tenga alto il prestigio della carità cristiana"; "Ma io sono meridionale!"

33 "ove il mio libro andrà tradotto".

## SERAO'S SHIFTING PROSE IN A EUROPEAN CONTEXT

The making of *Nel paese di Gesù* marks a transitional moment in Serao's career and falls into a period – 1890-1905 – which critics have traditionally identified as the initial phase of her artistic downfall.[34] Few critics have recognized, however, the centrality of this book in Serao's stylistic and narrative shift.[35] As mentioned earlier, Serao accorded to her travelogue to Palestine a special place among her writings as a most meaningful and sincere work she wrote during a difficult time in her life, both personal and professional. In a letter to her poet friend, Alfredo Catapano, she confided in 1904 that she went to Jerusalem as a writer but also as a woman in a mid-life crisis, which resulted, upon her return to Italy, in a legal separation from her husband and in a significant shift in her fictional writing style.[36] Her visit to Palestine, coincided, in other words, with the beginning of her rethinking her narrative choices, of her growing scepticism towards Naturalism, and her decision to infuse her work with a stronger spiritual and psychological

34 Scappaticci, for instance, considers *Il paese di Cuccagna* (1891) the novel that marked this shift, while Pancrazi sees 1905 as the beginning of her sentimental production (Pancrazi, 1944, p. IX; Scappaticci, 1995, p. 103). In my monograph *Postal Culture*, I argued that when analysed thematically rather than stylistically, Serao's career looks like a continuum of similar artistic preoccupations and general pessimism about the realities of women's lives (Romani, 2013, pp. 113-114). See also Fanning for critical reassessment of Serao's Gothic narratives. Fanning, 2007, pp. 119-141.

35 Giulio Ferroni (1991, p. 447) mentioned Serao's travel to Palestine as the beginning of Serao's infatuation with spiritualism in his *Storia della letteratura italiana*.

36 "I do not want to use the psychological reasons which moved various writers to go to the Holy land [...]. Surely they were different from mine. I went to Palestine first as a woman then as a writer. Oh, those days! My youth was declining, I was just about thirty-five years old [...] was thinking too much and from those thoughts I was saved by faith which gave peace again to my tormented soul [...] And I prayed Jesus to let me age without pain" ["Non voglio usare le ragioni psicologiche che mossero verso la Terrasanta scrittori diversissimi [...] Certo furono diverse dalle mie, per la semplice ragione che io, in Palestina, vi andai prima come donna e poi come scrittrice. Ah quei giorni! La mia giovinezza tramontava, da un lustro passata la trentina [...] ragionavo e troppo: e dai ragionamenti potè camparmi solo un atto di fede che valse a ridonar la pace alla mia anima angosciata [...] pregavo Gesù di farmi invecchiare senza dolore"], quoted in Martin-Gistucci, 1973, p. 294.

component, as she explained in an article, published on 8 July 1894 in *Il Corriere del Mattino,* in which she defined herself, along with Antonio Fogazzaro and Paul Bourget, as "Spiritual Knights" (Serao, [1894] 1992). She wrote:

> Those who believed that Naturalism as a form of art had established itself forever, aggrandized and exaggerated their little discovery to the point of delirium. They did not understand what rebellion they would cause among those who looked at life and its reasons with calmer eyes [...] it matters that in the silence of one's profound thoughts, each of us searches anew for the dried-out springs of our internal life and finds the way to replenish them, and, not finding them, searches, searches again, always searches. [...] it matters that our spiritual impulses reawaken, superior, supreme, pacifying, and consoling! Truth is elusive. It is important to find it again (*ibid.*, pp. 57-58).[37]

The mention of Paul Bourget, as a co-religionist in her poetics of renewal, is not a coincidence; she felt great mystical affinity with him as she was seeking new artistic inspirations. A French author of psychological novels, critical essays, travel literature, and poems, Bourget was politically conservative, and well known for his critical positions towards Positivism and his belief in the moralizing effect of literature (Singer, 1976, p. 11). Serao read his work and shared many of his theoretical and fictional preoccupations. Already in 1884 in a letter to Gegè Primoli she expressed interest in him: "Bourget the idealist [...] I hope to meet him" (Martin-Gistucci, 1973, p. 461).[38] She finally met him in 1892 during a summer vacation in the Alps. That same year, he had published *La Terre promise,* a drama set in Palermo about a man confronting a moral dilemma when, soon after finding the true love of his life, he discovers he had a son from a previous relationship with a married woman. Although thematically unrelated to Serao's travelogue, the preface presents a sort of manifesto of the author's ideas which strongly

---

37 "Coloro che hanno creduta instaurata, per sempre, una forma d'arte nel naturalismo, si sono esaltati della loro piccola scoperta e hanno esagerato sino al delirio, non hanno compreso quale ribellione avrebbero causato a quelli che guardano con occhio più quieto la vita e le sue ragioni [...] importa che nel silenzio delle proprie cogitazioni, ognuno di noi ricerchi nuovamente le sorgenti disseccate della sua vita interna e trovi modo di farle ripullulare e, non trovandole, cerchi, cerchi ancora, cerchi sempre [...] importa che le ragioni dello spirito ci riappaiono, superiori, supreme, pacificatrici, consolatrici! Tutta la verità è altrove. Importa di ritrovarla".

38 "Bourget l'idealiste [...] J'espère bien le connaître".

influenced Serao's future writings, including her *Nel paese di Gesù.* In explaining his psychological method, Bourget argued that literature was a most adept vehicle to examine and explain the human soul:

> An expression which is very simple, clear, and exact, and for which our contemporaries have substituted the much more pedantic and rather equivocal word psychological. I say equivocal, for this term seems to claim the study of the human soul in the name of a special school, whereas its study is common to all literature [...] Is not the description of the most plastic landscape a transcription of a condition of soul? And in like manner does not a drama which teams with adventures admit of sensations and sentiments in consequence of the soul? Balzac in his criticisms has more acutely denominated analytical novels 'novels of ideas', thus signifying that their authors had concerned themselves particularly with the phenomena of the internal life (Bourget, 1895, p. 7).[39]

As a traveller seeking to explore the human soul and renewal in artistic inspiration, Serao must have found meaning in Bourget's words well beyond her journey to Palestine. Serao highly admired him, felt inspired by his work ("That delicate wondering in the regions of one's spirit", Martin-Gistucci, 1973, p. 461),[40] and actively promoted his ideas in Italy. She published an Italian translation of *La Terre promesse,* first in *Il Mattino* and later again in *La settimana* (*ibid.*, p. 465). His wife, Minnie Bourget translated into French Serao's *Il paese di Cuccagna*, and Serao dedicated to Paul Bourget her *L'anima semplice: Suor Giovanna della croce* (1901). Theirs was a relationship that she actively cultivated and that aided her entrance into the intellectual circles of Paris. As a result of this and other close relationships with French intellectuals, by the late 1890s she was well known in Paris, indeed almost a celebrity,

39 "d'un terme très simple, très clair et très exact, auquel les contemporains ont substitué le nom beaucoup plus pédantesque et assez équivoque de psychologique. Je dis équivoque, car cette appellation semble revendiquer l'étude de l'âme humaine au nom d'une école spéciale, tandis que cette étude est commune à la littérature tout entière [...] Même la description du paysage la plus résolument plastique n'est-elle pas une transcription d'un état de l'âme et, pareillement, le drame le plus emmêlé d'aventures ne comporte-t-il pas à un degré quelconque des sentiments et des sensations, par conséquent de l'âme encore? Balzac, dans des pages de critique trop peu connues, – car elles sont d'une portée supérieure, comme tous les fragments de théorie ébauchés par ce gran spirit d'un don philosophique égal à son don évocateur –, avait plus finement dénommé les romans d'analyse des romans d'idées, signifiant par là que leurs auteurs sont surtout préoccupés de phénomènes de la vie intérieure" (Bourget, 1892, pp. III-IV).

40 "Quel délicat vagabondage dans les regions de l'esprit!".

something she considered a consolation in life for the disappointments she was receiving at home (*ibid.*).

Writing *Nel paese di Gesù* with an international audience in mind meant for Serao principally writing it for a French public of readers who could not only identify with her religious message of Catholic faith, but also with her repeated jabbing at English travellers. Criticized for travelling in a group with the Thomas Cook tourist agency, stealing relics ("English tourists constantly took away pieces of the living rock [of Jesus' tombstone] and would have slowly destroyed it"),[41] and keeping their old daily routines and meal habits ("a mediocre and abundant breakfast"),[42] the English travellers are depicted by Serao as the quintessentially disruptive modern tourists (Serao, 1898, pp. 68, 231). Serao envisioned the "Latin" spirit of French or Italian travellers as the antidote to the frenzy of modern life. "Oh! the abomination of the railway's desolation is not for us" she wrote implying by us the Latin type of traveller, "it is made for a people that gives to time a monetary value, for a people who are always in a rush and wants to go everywhere at maximum velocity, even to the sacred Sepulchre [...] the railway is for the Englishman!" (*ibid.*, p. 56).[43]

Despite Serao's negative portrayal of the English traveller, her travelogue was translated into English, and was reviewed and advertised in various newspapers, among them the *London Evening Standard*, *London Daily News*, *Daily Telegraph*, *The Yorkshire Post*, *The Morning Post*, *The Globe*, and the *New York Times*. The *London Evening Standard* of 1 December 1905, for instance, described *In the Country of Jesus* as "a vivid narrative [...] uniquely descriptive and devout [...] Matilde Serao writes with a beautiful reverent fervour" ("In the Country of Jesus", 1905, p. 16); while the *Manchester Courier* on 10 January 1906, reported that "Miss Serao is one of those trusting natures which accept the traditions and legends of the Roman Catholic Church without scruple" adding that she was a "keen observer" ("Matilde Serao", 1906). Overall, contemporary

41 "I turisti inglesi portavano via continuamente dei pezzetti di pietra viva e l'avrebbero lentamente distrutta".

42 "colazione abbondante e mediocre".

43 "Oh, l'abominazione della desolazione di questa ferrovia non è per noi, essa è fatta per il popolo che assegna al tempo il valore del danaro, per il popolo che ha sempre fretta, che vuole andare dappertutto con la massima velocità, anche al Santo Sepolcro [...] è per gli inglesi, la ferrovia!".

reviews in British newspapers point to her Catholic experience of the Holy Land but also praise her for "beauty of diction, a sublime, unhesitating acceptance of the traditions of the place, together with a faculty for keen observations, this gifted Italian authoress has presented us with a book at once stylish, readable, and frank, which it would be difficult to over-estimate" ("Matilde Serao", 1905).

## THE ENGLISH TRANSLATION OF SERAO'S *NEL PAESE DI GESÙ*

*Nel paese di Gesù* was translated from Italian into English by Richard Davey, an English journalist, novelist and playwright.[44] Although structurally faithful to the original text (*In the Country of Jesus* is also composed of nine sections), Davey's translation took many liberties with the content of the book, providing an abridged version of the original text, for reasons that Davey explained in his translator's note:

> Many works have been written on the land of Jesus, but few have attained the great popularity of Matilde Serao's "Nel Paese di Gesù". A simple record of a journey through the land consecrated by the Life and Passion of Christ, it has in less than two years passed through thirty editions. A fervent Catholic, Signora Serao sees the Holy Land through very orthodox glasses, and unhesitatingly accepts not only the Gospels, but the ancient traditions of her Church: and in this she is most probably right, for what is tradition if not unwritten history? She makes no pretence to historical or archeological learning but accepts all she sees and hears with the naïve faith of a true daughter of her Church. [...] Her faith is all the more welcome in this age of scepticism, because it is so honestly and so frankly expressed. Would that it were possible to transfer to our colder and terser language some of the fiery ardour of the original! But, unfortunately, much that is beautiful in the Italian of Signora Serao would

44 His full name was Richard Patrick Boyle Davey. He was born in Norfolk in 1848 but was educated in Italy and in the 1870 moved to the US. He later returned to England where he worked for the *Morning Post* and the *Saturday Review*. He is the author of several historical novels on female figures of the past (Lucrezia Borgia, Mary Tudor, and Jane Grey), plays and art books, such as, for instance, *The Work of Botticelli* (1903). He travelled to the Middle East and wrote *The Sultan and his Subjects* (1897). He died in 1915. See Plarr, 1899; Sutherland, 2009.

> sound exaggerated in English. "Nel Paese di Gesù" is so essentially Italian that it defies close translation. I have done my best, however, to transfer to the English version at least something of the charm of these rapidly sketched impressions of a journey undertaken by one of the most gifted women of our time (Davey, 1905, pp. XIII-XIV).

Deemed too verbose, too Italian, and too Catholic for the average English reading taste, Serao's *Nel paese di Gesù* was repackaged by Davey into a cultural product, which, thematically in vogue, could meet the expectations of an English-speaking readership. With different degrees of intervention, Davey summarized or skipped portions of the original text written by Serao, maintaining the overall meaning but excluding what was considered inappropriate. The following examples illustrate the method used by Davey, which Translation Studies scholars have defined as the "hermeneutic model", that is a way, not uncommonly used in the nineteenth century, of treating translation "as an interpretation of the source text whose form, meaning, and effect are seen as variable, subject to inevitable transformation during the translating process" (Venuti, 2000, p. 483):

> Gesù, richiesto, insegnò ai suoi discepoli come si pregava congiungendo le mani e pronunciando la sublime preghiera che consola, che invoca perdono: *Padre nostro*! (Serao, 1899, p. 115)
>
> [Jesus at their request taught His disciples to pray. Joining His hands, He uttered the divine supplication, the "Our Father"! (Serao, 1905, p. 89)].
>
> Un dolore profondo, sgorgante dall'anima spasimante, vide il vagone della piccola ferrovia che doveva strapparmi velocemente, per sempre, da Gerusalemme. Guardavo, guardavo dal finestrino, con occhi fissi e desolati, Sionne, alta sui suoi colli, come si guarda il viso di chi non si vedrà più: e bene avevo pensato, pregando che niuno mi avesse accompagnato alla stazione quella mattina (Serao, 1898, p. 363).
>
> [As the train was carrying me away, I looked back upon the high hills of Zion. I was glad indeed that I was alone with my grief, and that I had had the courage to refuse to allow anyone to see me off (Serao, 1905, p. 293)].

Davey highly admired Serao, as he made clear in his note, but considered her language redundant or excessive at times, and therefore unnecessary. What he omitted to add in his note, however, was that he also excluded from his translation any expression of criticism towards

English travellers. There are innumerable instances in *Nel paese di Gesù* of Serao berating English tourists (English or English-speaking? Serao never makes a distinction between English, British, Irish or American), which are not to be found in the translation. The following examples illustrate my point:

> Qui in un vasto prato che attornia una palazzina, due o tre famiglie inglesi giuocano al tennis, al crocket, mentre sul limitare del parco, un gruppo di giovanotti inglesi galoppano, lanciando i loro focosi cavalli (Serao, 1898, p. 31).
>
> [Here, on a vast lawn, you will see English families playing lawn-tennis or croquet; further on in the park British youth are playing polo (Serao, 1905, p. 19)].
>
> Coloro che, viaggiando, vogliono levarsi alla medesima ora del loro paese di dimora, vogliono mangiare gli stessi cibi, divertirsi allo stesso modo, costoro non sono dei viaggiatori: è per questo, come dimostrerò un'altra volta, che gli inglesi non sono dei viaggiatori e che pur vagabondando per tutto il mondo, stanno sempre fermi allo stesso posto. Chi ritrova il suo the e i suoi crostini al burro, dappertutto, non si muove dalla sua stanza da pranzo! Il viaggio è fatto dalla vita ordinaria che si capovolge (Serao, 1898, p. 330).
>
> [Those who will only get up at their usual hour and will eat only the same food they do at home, might just as well remain in their own dining rooms: they are not travellers in the true sense of the word. If one wishes to thoroughly enjoy Palestine, it is necessary to resign oneself to an entire change of habits, a topsy-turvydom, so to speak, of our ordinary mode of life, and this, after all, is not without his compensations (Serao, 1905, p. 267)].

The translator of *In the Country of Jesus* (all editions reported the same translation) aptly converted Serao's Anglophobic sentiments into a narrative that minimized Serao's disparagement of English tourism in Palestine, and enhanced readers' understanding of Serao as a Catholic writer rooted in her national and religious traditions. In the end, Davey's translation only favoured Serao's intentions of distinguishing her "Latin" soul from the English character.

## CONCLUSIONS

At the beginning of the nineteenth century, travel to the Middle East extended the European tradition of what was until then known as the Grand Tour, with the "Orient" becoming in the eyes of Western travellers a place of mystery, exoticism, spiritual and sensual rejuvenation. Not surprisingly, imagination, indeed a dream-like evocation of the East (as an Orientalist projection of the West) played a major role in travel narratives of the time (Brilli, 2009; Said, [1978] 1991). Matilde Serao also portrayed Palestine as an imaginative place, as she was less interested in the realities of the inhabitants of the Holy Land[45] than in what travelling meant in cultural, literary, and existential terms for Western women living in the modern era, such as herself. There is not space here to expand on Serao's Orientalism – a topic that Sambuco has already addressed in her essay – or on Serao's "Meridionism",[46] which would require a whole new chapter, but it is important to mention the fact that because Serao was writing about Jerusalem not only as an Italian or Neapolitan woman, but also as a member of an "imagined community" of Southern Catholic Europeans, questions arise about her self-perception as a woman travelling abroad but also positioning herself beyond national borders.[47] In other words, from Serao's travel writings emerges a transnational dimension of the author's identity which suggests that Serao embraced the idea of a Mediterranean identity that could counterpose the prevailing modalities of modernity offered by the Northern European model. Finally, if Serao's *Nel paese di Gesù* was popular among readers at the time, it has from the very beginning been neglected by critics. And, yet, Serao's travelogue to Palestine not

45 In this regard, see Cavaglion, 2016, pp. 26-28.

46 "'Meridionism' would make an apt term for that discursive formation that accompanied the fall of the Mediterranean, through which Europe auto-produced itself as a superior civilisation not only in contra-distinction to the West Indies – as Quijano (2000) claims or, later, the Orient – as Said (1978) claims – but also against its 'inner Indies' or 'inner Orient'. Both Orientalism and Meridionism are but two of the discursive formations belonging to the progeny of the colonial matrix of power, which was generated with the rise of the Atlantic world", Cazzato, 2017, p. 72.

47 On the notion of Mediterranean "imagined communities" see Fogu, 2020, pp. 6-7.

only provides relevant insights into a crucial phase of her career as a writer, but also illustrates how interconnected she was with an international network of authors, translators, and readers. Considering this, the too-often used definition of regional author for Serao seems grossly inadequate.

Gabriella ROMANI
Seton Hall University

# MATILDE SERAO IN THE SPANISH PRESS AT THE TURN OF THE CENTURY

The periodical press offers a rich archive for scholars working on women writers' historical significance. However, periodical studies have not received the attention they deserve for a number of reasons: scholars have faced numerous obstacles in locating, accessing and travelling to archives; even the traditional concept of high/low culture may have hampered research. Luckily, at present in Spain researchers can benefit from the massive digitization of the nineteenth- and twentieth- century Spanish press, which has been under way for a decade. The sheer number of digitized newspapers is relevant for any researcher. The *Digital Newspaper Library* (*Hemeroteca Digital*) contains around 40 million pages and more than 2,000 titles, while the *Virtual Library of Historical Spanish Newspapers* hosts around 2,400 newspapers, which corresponds to more than 8 million images.[1]

We can confidently use these archives as reliable sources from which to retrieve a significant number of references to women writers in general, and here we explore how the periodical press of the time encouraged Spanish readers to approach Matilde Serao's work. Our aim is to study the comments on, reviews, and advertisements of Serao's work in the Spanish press at the turn of the twentieth century. Unlike traditional reception studies, our focus is not on the translations of Serao's work. Therefore, we will analyse a large collection of clippings as we assume that most readers only had access to those fragments, rather than to the author's entire work. Moreover, we assume that nineteenth and twentieth-century publishers relied on predictable responses from their readership, such as shared beliefs about gender roles, which were likely

1 BNE, *Hemeroteca Digital*, http://www.bne.es/es/Catalogos/HemerotecaDigital/docs/tabla_nuevostitulos.pdf (last accessed 29 November 2019) and "Estadísticas", *Biblioteca Virtual de Prensa Histórica*, http://prensahistorica.mcu.es/es/consulta/estadistica.cmd (last accessed 29 November 2019).

reinforced by the stereotyped content of the images and by dissemination strategies.

Finally, it is worth noting that, even though the press was predominantly the space of male expression, women did have a voice there.

## METHODOLOGY

First of all, one must keep in mind that "A literature differs from another less for its text than from how it is read" (Genette, 1976, p. 123).[2] Researchers are heirs to the phenomenology of reading, to "Rezeptionsästhetik" in the sense of appropriation, and to hermeneutical conflicts of interpretation, but, at present, we can take some steps forward: broader, more empirical fieldwork is possible as a result of digital libraries and digital tools.

Secondly, the "sacred original source text" will be displaced from the centre to become just one of many positions in the system. Teachers, referees, and journalists express, convey, and make public all the conditioning factors of literary circulation. Institutional conventions provide the normative expectations which are the basis of social behaviour. Rather than using source texts, the present research applies the so-called "target-oriented" approach (Even-Zohar, 1990; Hermans, 1999; Luhmann, 2000).

Matilde Serao will not be treated as a source, since her source function is present in the volume as a whole. Instead, the focus will be on the reading guidelines to Matilde Serao's work that are present in the digitized Spanish press during the so-called "Spanish Silver Age" (1898-1936) (Bordonada, 2013; Romero, 2014). Those were the years of Federico García Lorca and Luis Buñuel. It was a period of notable literary, artistic, scientific, and cultural production which was tragically interrupted by the civil war and by the subsequent dictatorship in 1939.

Thirdly, since both translations and criticism are culture-sensitive,[3] and seek to influence and manipulate the development of a literary

2 "Une littérature diffère d'une autre moins par le texte que par la façon dont elle est lue".

3 See Vermeer's *Skopos* theory (Vermeer, 1996), focusing on the goals of the translation as the most important criteria guiding translators' decisions, and Lefevere, 1992 who was

system, the "quality" of the assessments will not be an issue here. Instead, their "models" will matter: which words, terms, and model texts were being promoted? Which ones were being criticized?

More precisely, researchers are well aware of the performative dimension of press discourse, which urges people to buy, to read and instructs them on how to be. It is a ritualized practice: "It accumulates the force of authority through the repetition or citation of a prior and authoritative set of practices" (Butler, 1997, p. 51); it creates a discursive order by disseminating these practices; it is conservative so as to guarantee communication.

Finally, the present work proposes to situate the periodical press somewhere between long-term cultural memory and transitory communicative memory based exclusively on daily communication.[4] Both types of memory provide formative and normative impulses through which a group (re)produces its identity. The periodical press *bridges the gap between the two types of memories* by means of repetition, formalization, specializations which became institutionalizations. Like oral communication, the periodical press is redundant in its expression: it is an example of phatic communication.

The periodical press also stands somewhere between the archives and the canon, namely between society's reference memory, which is a passive but expansive repository, and the necessarily reductive and restrictive drive of working memory, which is an active, second-order memory (Assmann, 2010). A nineteenth- or twentieth-century journal can be considered a predictable repository which creates past memories, thanks to its extensive and accessible data retrieval system, as one might say in the twenty-first century.

---

interested in translation-control mechanisms in terms of poetics, patronage and ideology.

4 The distinction was established by Assmann – Czaplicka, 1995, but both notions can only be strictly separated in a theoretical context, since, in the actual memory-practice of individuals and social groups, their forms and methods are linked together: this is our challenge.

## FROM DATA TO NARRATIVE

During the inception of this project, the researchers decided to approach the concept of language as a list of chosen words, or more precisely, as clusters of words which tend to go together in a sequence. Our quantitative work thus dealt with word frequencies and three measuring criteria: abundance, consistency, and interrelationship.

The macro-analysis was performed according to the following procedural steps. First, all the translations published by Spanish newspapers, magazines, and publishers, between the end of the nineteenth and the beginning of the twentieth century, were found (see the bibliography "Matilde Serao's fiction translated into Spanish", below). Second, more than 800 references to Matilde Serao were retrieved in 138 digitized periodicals from the *Hemeroteca Digital* and the *Virtual Library of Spanish Newspapers*;[5] the first quotation dated back to 1884 while the last one was made in 1939. A timeline comparing the dates of the Spanish translations and the number of references provides a first overview of discursive peaks regarding Matilde Serao in Spain: the period between 1905 and 1909 and again in 1927, the year of her death and obituaries. But it is notable that there is no correlation between the publication of translations and the references in the Spanish press, possibly because Serao was, in any case, well known in Spain (Fig. 1):

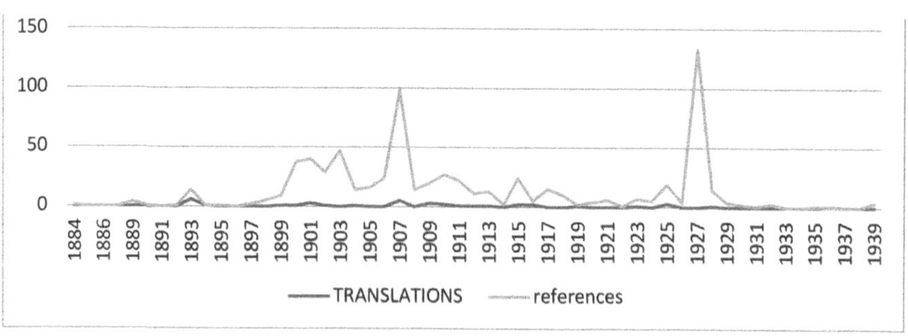


FIG. 1 – Translations and references to Matilde Serao.

5 Our corpus was built only on the basis of these Digital Newspaper Libraries. This corpus of almost 50,000 words is available at the *E-print Collection* of the Complutense University (Iasci – Sanz, 2018). All our bibliographic references and quotations can be verified there.

The digitized periodicals were sifted through with a simple search query: Serao's name and its variants; the occurrences and their understandable context were transcribed by means of automatic OCR, but also manually, due to the irregular quality of the printed characters. The excerpt corpus was compiled chronologically, and it was prepared for publication. Then the entire text was formatted for examination with electronic text-analysis tools: keywords and graphs, frequencies and collocations; all of these allow a kind of topographic overview.

Voyant Tools and SketchEngine provided a word cloud where the terms that occur more frequently have a central position and the largest dimensions.[6] Here (Fig. 2) is the cloud visualizing the forty-five most frequent words of the corpus:

FIG. 2 – The forty-five most frequent words from the Serao corpus.

The first item of relevance is the fact that Serao is defined primarily as an Italian, related to Italy, especially to Rome and even more often to Naples, with a total of 93 references. Secondly, what stands out is her

6 These are the words in English and their frequency: Serao (727), Matilde (695), novel (147), Italian woman (129), novelist (120), female writer (118), Italy (114), work (96), great (96), life (87), book (80), novels (74), woman (71), works (63), literature (58), Spain (55), Alert (54), books (53), Italian (52), passion (52), house (51), Rome (51), Sentinel (49), women (48), art (44), she (44), flower (44), female author (41), pages (41), Paris (40), writers (38), Neapolitan (36), country (36), today (35), Naples (35), Deledda (34), literary (34), newspaper (34), theatre (34), world (33), name (33), Maucci (32), death (32), heart (29). The colour of words and their absolute position are not significant. See "Cirrus" in *Voyant Tools Documentation*, http://docs.voyant-tools.org/tools/cirrus/ (last accessed 29 November 2019). Also, SketchEngine. Language corpus management and query system, https://www.sketchengine.co.uk/ (last accessed 29 November 2019).

presentation as a novelist. This second result persuaded the researchers to try to compare the various representations of Serao as novelist, writer, woman, and author in a line graph of the relative frequencies across the corpus. However, the result did not seem conclusive: at the end of the nineteenth century the press tended to insist on the fact that she was 'a woman' and 'a female novelist', while at the beginning of the twentieth century it underlined her professional role as 'a female writer'.

For this reason, it was decided to use a collocation graph (Fig. 3) which shows a network of higher-frequency terms that appear in proximity to each other:

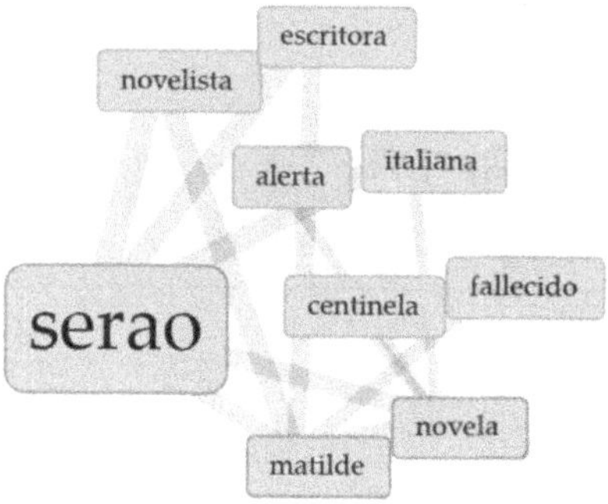


FIG. 3 – Collocation graph with higher-frequency terms from the Serao corpus.

This graph actually showed something that had not been noticed at the beginning: the absence, in quantitative terms, of the journalistic dimension of Matilde Serao's work and, alongside it, the absence of her most committed, militant, pro-empowerment aspects. In fact, there are only 24 occurrences of the word 'newspaper' and these are mainly references to the professional conflict between Matilde Serao and her husband (24 occurrences): this referenced the claim made by Serao that she was unfairly dismissed from *Il Mattino* and her taking a case to court. Her characterization as a female novelist is what prevails, especially in connection with the novel that is advertised most frequently, *¡Centinela alerta!* (*All'erta, sentinella!*), and in the context of the many tributes paid to her at her death on 25 July 1927, which accounts for the privileged position of the past participle "died". She is described primarily as a journalist only by reporters who sign their articles and, in these cases, the reporter's militant position in support of women is clear.

If one increases the number of the most frequent words, in the top one hundred words, we find the first names and family names which co-occur with Matilde Serao: Grazia Deledda (34 occurrences), Gabriele d'Annunzio (27), Antonio Fogazzaro (25) and Emilia Pardo Bazán (23). What is noteworthy is the co-occurrence of the four writers as related to Matilde Serao in the period between 1900 and 1910, a co-occurrence which tends to disappear insofar as the references to D'Annunzio decrease while in the 1920s the references to the 1926 Nobel prize-winner Grazia Deledda increase. There is also a decrease in the references to Fogazzaro and Bazán, the writers considered the most "costumbristas", namely those focused on local customs.

At this point, it is worth entering into some detail and analysing what is actually being said about those writers in relation to Matilde Serao. It is as though briefly quoting famous writers was on some level enough to canonize the Neapolitan as a great writer. In fact, in the act of reading, readers tend to fit their interpretation into a contextual series and repertoire, assigning meaning as they classify.

First, in the initial references to her narrative production, Matilde Serao is depicted as a representative of Italian realism together with Giovanni Verga, Luigi Capuana, Anna Vivanti, and Grazia Deledda. Within that literary movement, and also on the Italian and European literary scene as a whole, originality and literary fame are what account for the frequent co-occurrences of D'Annunzio's and Serao's names in the Spanish press from 1898 to 1915, along with with positive comments on their prompt translations into Spanish around 1907. The idea that Serao's narrative occupies the highest place in the literary hierarchy of the period is shared by various influential journalists. She is appreciated in Paris as much as is D'Annunzio: they are published by the same publishing houses in Italy and Spain, are ranked as two of the best and the most creative Italian and European novelists and appear among the international celebrities of the time; fame also explains Serao's less-frequent associations with Fogazzaro and Deledda. Apart from her celebrity, some critics also mention their common themes explored by these writers, such as love, and common character-types like the degenerate stock type. Only one journalist explicitly contrasts D'Annunzio's more refined style and pagan perspective with Serao's human love and less inflated passions; rather, their difference is generally implied. As a matter of fact, Serao is unanimously depicted as a novelist focusing on regionalism, and on the character, customs, and soul of Neapolitans, just as is the case for Deledda and Verga with Sardinians and Sicilians, respectively. Matilde Serao's narrative is also mentioned when journalists report on Naples, as in the case of the eruption of Vesuvius, the local mafia known as the Camorra, and the Neapolitan addiction to the lottery. Finally, she appears as a skilled interpreter of the human heart in a generous, compassionate sense, and influential critics of the period define this as a specifically feminine trait. This last feature appears to be furthest removed from the consideration of D'Annunzio's individualistic and atheistic paganism.

As regards Serao's association with Grazia Deledda, journalists explicitly define both of them primarily as women writers ("escritoras"). In particular, they underline the fact that Matilde Serao's talent, which is designated female, is characteristic of Italian women of letters whose huge number has no equivalent in other countries such as England or France. The 1926 Nobel prize award to Grazia Deledda was said to glorify and reward that legion of contemporary Italian women writers, who, in a typically Italian way, focused on both universal and local themes. In fact, both Grazia Deledda and Matilde Serao represented life and local colour in a less cruel and pessimistic vein than did either French naturalism or Verga's verism. In the first years of 1900, Matilde Serao began to be associated with idealism, which meant having a positive outlook on life and believing that, in the long run, good will prevail. The influential historian and scholar Rafael Altamira y Crevea (Ángel Guerra) considers this perspective to be a distinctive trait of women's writing, together with the theme of human passions (Guerra, 1904). Unlike Serao, however, Grazia Deledda is seen as less sentimental and as narrating a harsher reality which is considered to be more masculine. Matilde Serao's romanticism of reality, full of overwhelming Southern feminine passions, becomes a popular leitmotiv reiterated and praised by later critics.[7] In 1904 Ángel Guerra sees Serao's work as an original

7 In 1900 the critic Fernando Araujo Gómez designated the romanticism of reality as a merit of Serao's fictional works (Araujo, 1900). A 1901 reviewer of *All'erta, sentinella!* pinpoints Serao's ability to move readers to compassion towards less fortunate fellow

contribution to the renaissance of Italian narrative made up of her work and that of other women writers such as Neera and Grazia Deledda along with talented male novelists, including Farina, De Amicis, Fogazzaro, Capuana, and D'Annunzio.

As regards Fogazzaro, just as happened with D'Annunzio and Deledda, journalists associated him with Matilde Serao primarily because both were renowned writers of Italian literature.[8] When they give more details, the journalists mention the authors' common sentimental view of life and their values based on Christianity, a perspective which was very relevant to Matilde Serao's reception in Spain.

Secondly, Matilde Serao was often considered "the Italian Pardo Bazán" (Alas "Clarín", 1898),[9] on the basis of a simple equivalence and contrast: Pardo Bazán represented "Galician Costumbrismo", Matilde Serao "the colour of Neapolitan places"; one possesses "spiritual depth" and the other "a passion for the picturesque since she is a Southern lover of the sun" (Guerra, 1927a). According to these categorizations, Serao belongs to different series or groups of women writers: Matilde Serao, Emilia Pardo Bazán and George Sand (Soriano, 1902), Emilia Pardo Bazán, Blanca de los Ríos and Matilde Serao (Z., 1902), or even: "The countess Pardo Bazán is as good as the best women writers in the world: Clara Viebig in Germany, Matilde Serao in Italy, Eurica Maudel Mazetti in Austria, Selma Lagerloff in Sweden, Raim Michaelis in Denmark" ("La condesa", 1921).

In lists of recommended reading for women, we find Judith Gautier, Matilde Serao, Concepción Arenal, Carolina Invernicio, Pardo Bazán, Carlota Braerné, or, among those women writers who "cannot define

beings ("Libros populares", 1901b). The critic Zeda sees in the compassionate attitude towards the suffering of lower social classes a distinctive trait of the modern novel (Zeda, 1904). In an article dedicated to Italian literature of the period, Ángel Guerra writes extensively on the Southern passions that characterize it (Guerra, 1904). Blanca Valmont praises Serao's feminine capacity for compassion (Valmont, 1907).

8 Leopoldo Alas "Clarín" recommends both Fogazzaro and Serao (Alas "Clarín", 1898). Like Serao, D'Annunzio and others, Fogazzaro is praised in the periodical *La España moderna* ("Cómo ha nacido", 1900, p. 165). Luis de Terán dedicates an entire article to Fogazzaro (Terán, 1902a). Ángel Guerra acknowledges his importance (Guerra, 1903, pp. 1-2). Like Serao, Deledda and D'Annunzio, Fogazzaro was widely read in Paris ("La poetisa del dolor", 1903, p. 168; "El país de Jesús", 1910; Blanck, 1910); like D'Annunzio, Serao, Deledda, and Neera, he was seen as a beacon of the Italian novel ("Ojeada", 1904).

9 According to Ángel Guerra, Emilia Pardo Bazán was superior (Guerra, 1905a).

themselves as feminists" (Añaza, 1912), we encounter Mme de Staël, Mme Girardin, Rosalía de Castro, George Sand, Concepción Arenal, the Countess Pardo Bazán, Matilde Serao, Sofía Casanova and Carmen de Burgos. Serao also appears together with Gip (Sibylle Riquetti de Mirabeau, 1849-1932), George Eliot, the Bell sisters, Lady Blessington, Lady Fullerton, Caiel, Clara Viebig and Gabriela Reuter. Finally, in the obituaries on her death in July 1927, Matilde Serao was presented as a figure straddling two centuries. It may be for this reason that her name is associated with those of D'Annunzio, Emilia Pardo Bazán and Galdós, and also with Antero de Quental, Guerra Junqueiro and Eça de Queiroz. Some critics considered her to be close to Bourget, Tolstoy, and Dostoyevsky (Zeda, 1900, p. 1), while others found her to be quite different from them (Monterrey, 1903, p. 495).

All in all, the most frequent arguments in support of the reading of Matilde Serao in Spain are the following: she was well known everywhere, except in Spain; she was being published, translated, and celebrated in Paris, but not so much in Madrid, so that translating her work into Spanish became a matter of justice, in a period in which the Republic of Letters centred on Paris and, consequently, Paris signified the world. The positive reviews (and even a bad one) in the Parisian press (and not in Rome) are repeatedly used to demonstrate the quality of Serao's work. The press also covered her trips to Paris and the cultural events she attended, and even reported her intention to apply for French citizenship ("Serao", 1902). The extent of her popularity, confirmed by Parisian newspapers, was nonetheless generally considered to be exaggerated and undeserved. Even reviewers like Ángel Guerra o Jacques D'Auvergne (a likely pseudonym) criticized the excessive attention that Parisians paid to Northern writers and claimed (in 1904), or already appreciated (1906), a greater interest in Southern authors.

The reviews of the theatre adaptation of one of Matilde Serao's short stories also appeared in timely fashion and paid special attention to her "large and distinguished" public, as in the case of the opening performance of *Los caballitos de madera* in 1925 (an adaptation of *I cavallucci di legno*), when all the critics approved of this comedy "just for ladies", because "it is honest, entertaining and [because in Paris it is] recommended as a *spectacle de familles*" ("Una matinée", 1925). However, when "the interesting and sensational" movie *Mi vida por la tuya* was advertised in 1915, something had changed for the public: what stood out was the role of "the famous actress Maria Carmi" and no longer the character of the female novelist ("Diversiones públicas", 1915).

A theme which deserves attention in the Spanish reception of Matilde Serao is the press's growing attention to her Catholicism after the Spanish translation in 1910 of her account of a journey to Palestine, which led to her characterization as a Christian novelist. Except for an extremely critical article published in a left-wing newspaper (Ferrandiz, 1910),[10] *El país de Jesús* [*Nel paese di Gesù*] generally received positive reviews, primarily because of its religious content. Most critics saw her travel book as an example of a deeply religious faith, and portrayed Matilde Serao as a talented orthodox novelist with a sincere neo-Christian spirit, implicitly placing her in contrast to D'Annunzio, the champion of neo-paganism. Between 1911 and 1927, Ángel Guerra published five articles on Matilde Serao, where he invariably underlined her mysticism and charted her spiritual development in books like *El país de Jesús* [*Nel paese di Gesù*], *L'anima semplice: Suor Giovanna della croce*, *La Madonna e i santi*, *La Bailarina* [*La ballerina*] and *Santa Teresa*. He even welcomed her production, like the production of other European writers, as an indication of a timely resurgence of Catholic ideals in Italy after Fogazzaro's death.

Such a characterization is quite remarkable considering the fact that Matilde Serao was at the time of the publication of *El país de Jesús* [*Nel paese di Gesù*] a separated woman with a daughter born out of wedlock from an extramarital relationship with the journalist Giuseppe Natale, whom she would marry on the death of her husband, Edoardo Scarfoglio, in 1917. Interestingly enough, the press is rather reticent about Matilde Serao's filing for separation in 1902 and about her subsequent relationship. As a decision taken independently by a woman, this news was reported with the greatest neutrality and Matilde Serao's heterodox self-confidence was downplayed with a cryptic explanation: it was the result of an alleged scandal caused by her husband.[11] In some respects, the Spanish press seemed to be protecting Serao's image.

10 The article practically tears the book to pieces for its fake religiosity, its utter lack of religious, historical, and artistic culture and defines it as of scant interest.

11 Serao's decision to separate from her husband was accounted for by referring to a scandal caused by Scarfoglio, which was a significant shock in Neapolitan society. In 1918, only

## FROM NARRATIVES TO DATA

Our examination of Serao's impact shall now shift from a macro-analysis to a micro-analysis. And with good reason, because big numbers also imply more or less harmful exclusions and silencing. Hence we will focus here on the anomalous.

Using procedures akin to those employed by European historiography of the last forty years, initially major groupings were privileged, insisting on repetitions and their variants, on observable regularities, which can be measured, and on the transformations that can be detected within long-term timeframes, thanks to simple and simplified indicators that refer to a limited number of features. In this way, our approach is close to that of the so-called French 'Annales school', which analyses social and economic history rather than events.

However, one can also privilege the unique case, the exceptional, the accidental, the break that interprets each individual path as independent links, shifts and likely distinctions, so that the unusual can become normal.[12] In the present case, micro-reading may be necessary in order to analyse two of the most important female journalists of the period, who appreciated the role of the Italian novelist and also closely followed the Italian feminist movement: Carmen de Burgos and Concepción Gimeno de Flaquer.

Carmen de Burgos authors the only article in which a female writer, who is also a translator and a journalist, considers Matilde Serao to belong to the category of European female journalists. Burgos is aware of "the very important role that women can play in the press" and of the fact that "this may be the most important driver of women's education" (Burgos, 1905). Besides these latter issues, Burgos also sees journalism as "the most recent and popular literary form of progress; it branches out, it extends and reaches the freedom of the press and it becomes

---

after Scarfoglio's death and Serao's marriage to Natale, did the Spanish press mention the name of Matilde Serao in relation to the latter: an article talks about funds generously given to the paper *Il Giorno* by Luca Cortese ("El aventurero italiano", 1918).

12 This is akin to the micro-history of Italian historians Giovanni Levi and Edoardo Grendi. See Revel, 1996.

the instructor of the crowd" (*ibid.*).[13] This is the general sense one also perceives when reading the famous lecture on the pedagogical task of female journalists delivered by Carmen de Burgos on 31 December 1905. This speech illustrated how Burgos considered Serao's different roles to be coterminous: women's progress and women's rights in Italy had to do with new professions that complemented rather than denied traditional female roles. In other words, the narrative profile of Serao, which is regarded as primarily feminine, is not necessarily in contrast with her journalism. In both cases, what is at stake is the didactic function of writing. And if there is a difference between male and female journalists, it has to do with themes that each is better equipped to handle. Burgos suggests that politics or crime are for men, and human suffering is for women because women possess the skills to understand and change pain: psychological insight and compassion, and the ability to educate gently and sensitively.

These ideas are not very different from those expressed by the writer Margarita Leclerc Herreros in an article provokingly entitled "Is Woman Superior to Man?".[14] Leclerc sees Matilde Serao (and Grazia Deledda) as part of an "army of selfless women" (Leclerc Herreros, 1928) who reinforced the idea that perfect intellectual equality is a fact of nature, and also a social ideal. In the pleiad of emancipated women of letters from different countries which Leclerc drew up, Matilde Serao and Grazia Deledda appeared as equals and as rivals of D'Annunzio and Fogazzaro. The current era of moral matriarchy, Leclerc said, was moving towards the construction of social happiness, which was based on the defeat of female subjection and enslavement, on the restoration of women's basic right to self-determination, and on social harmony between women and men.

Concepción Gimeno de Flaquer, whose articles revealed a comprehensive knowledge of women writers, was the first journalist to define Matilde Serao as "a modern woman" and then as a public speaker, a novelist, and a truly southern reasoner. Like Carmen de Burgos, she

13 "última y más popular forma literaria del progreso; se ramifica, se extiende, alcanza la libertad de la prensa y llega a ser cátedra para la multitud".

14 "Esa santa revolución francesa hizo surgir de todos los rincones de Francia a un ejército de abnegadas. [...] No de Francia, en todos los países ha surgido la mujer cuando ha sido preciso. [...] Matilde Serao y Grazia Deledda, que rivalizaron con Fogazzaro y D'Annunzio".

praised Serao as a journalist who knew how to transform the press into a power (Gimeno, 1899; 1900b; 1902). Only afterwards did she celebrate her as a Neapolitan novelist, a public speaker, and finally as a writer who was truly feminine. The articles penned by male journalists, on the contrary, mentioned Serao's work as a journalist only briefly: Matilde Serao appeared in a few articles primarily as a reporter who interviewed aristocratic women and royalty on women's issues (mourning, marriage, the social role of a diplomat's wife) or as the angry wife of the director of *Il Mattino di Napoli.*[15] No wonder that when the floor was given to Matilde, she introduced herself as a journalist first (Monterrey, 1903, p. 495). Very few, in fact, dared to underline that it was in the field of journalism where she exercised her militancy, and that "in the magazine called *Emporium*, she carves pages of vigorous rebellion, and, leaving aside Platonic quietism, she knocks on the doors of the rich and wealthy with a loud wake-up call" (Castro, 1904).[16] She was also acknowledged as a theatre critic.

Concepción Gimeno de Flaquer reiterated the fact that the mission of her sex was, first of all, to fulfill the roles of mother and wife and to take care of domestic chores. Time dedicated to the cultivation of intelligence and the uprooting of ignorance came second. Besides, the goal of instruction was not simply individual achievement, namely personal independence and rational discernment, but also one of social returns, because an educated wife reinforced the conjugal bond by honouring her husband, and she helped social development through the education of future generations. For Concepción Gimeno, therefore, women's emancipation meant exercising the right to participate in and benefit from education and work, in order to fully contribute to social progress

15 In 1903, various national and regional newspapers made brief references to the letter of resignation that she sent to *Il Mattino*. Only in a few cases did they refer to Serao as the founder of a different paper and as a director of the magazine *La Settimana*, while her husband was invariably mentioned as the director of the newspaper. Moreover, the news of her resignation was interestingly the target of ironic comments on the conjugal problems of the couple and the lawsuit filed by Matilde Serao against the director became the vengeance of a woman against her husband ("Escritora vengativa", 1905; "Menudencias", 1903. In 1927, at her death, in various obituaries, her different roles as a founder, cofounder and director of papers were mentioned, although the fact that her fame came from her novels was frequently underlined.

16 "en la revista *Emporium*, páginas de vigorosa rebeldía, y dejándose de quietismos platónicos, llama, con fuerte aldabonazo, a las puertas del dinero y del bienestar".

as responsible citizens, to live in dignity (gaining men's true respect instead of hypocritical gallantry) thanks to the acquisition of knowledge and skills, and to improve their communities through self-sacrifice and discipline, as in the case of Saint Theresa.

No wonder that one columnist accused journalism and female journalists of being the cause of such great evils as feminism and of all of women's achievements in the twentieth century: "Presently, three of the greatest female writers in Italy are journalists", "the brightest and the most famous is Matilde Serao," who "is a journalist. But not a journalist dealing with elegant issues. [...] She continues to criticize in powerful articles full of rage" (Soiza, 1907).[17] And when Ángel Guerra once concisely acknowledged Matilde Serao's fierce political battles in the pages of *Il Mattino di Napoli*, this facet got overshadowed by the prevailing narrative of her Christian apostolate (Guerra, 1911). With the same attitude of disavowal, when the writer Eduardo Zamacois praised the didactic power of the contemporary press and of literature, he did not mention Serao the journalist and virulently attacked her romantic novels as lowbrow (Zamacois, 1929).

Burgos, Gimeno, Nenkel, and Leclerc were the only women who supported the idea of Serao as a committed woman fighting for emancipation. All of the other female reporters supported the prevailing discourse: Blanca Valmont (Valmont, 1907) and Margarita-María de Monterrey (Monterrey, 1903), for example, flatly rejected the epithet feminist for Matilde Serao. Other reporters, who signed with only their initials, considered Matilde Serao to be a "Feminist in the noblest sense of the word", whose talent in 1917 continued to be her "love for God, family, country, humankind and, notably, for the weak" (J.D., 1917, pp. 184-185).[18] When the twentieth century is considered as the century of women writers, typists, and emancipationists, Matilde Serao is

17 "La célebre escritora napolitana Matilde Serao, que goza actualmente, entre todas las mujeres que escriben, de mayor fama en el mundo. De las tres escritoras de Italia de las que hablo, la mejor, la que más brilla, la que más fama tiene es Matilde Serao. Nadie que haya leído a Matilde Serao sin conocerla, creerá que su figura física, que sus ademanes, que su manera de vivir, pueden ser las mismas que sus libros suponen. Matilde Serao es periodista. Pero no periodista de temas elegantes. [...] Sigue criticando en poderosos artículos llenos de furia".

18 "El secreto de su talento es el amor: amor a Dios, a la familia, a la Patria, a la Humanidad y, señaladamente, a los desvalidos, y ese amor le dicta sublimes páginas y le sirve de guía en todos sus actos. Feminista en el más noble sentido de la palabra".

included in the first group. Indeed, the use of the word 'feminism' in derogatory terms by some journalists constituted an attempt to distort and violate femininity, which is described as natural and therefore in need of protection. Nevertheless, Serao's participation in the 1908 Feminist congress of Rome was noted in several articles (Gimeno, 1908; "Congreso feminista", 1908).

## FRAMEWORKS OF INTERPRETATIONS

Three main narratives on Matilde Serao's production emerged in the Spanish press, motivating the public to read her works according to specific interpretive approaches.

First of all, reporters criticized the French echoes of the Naturalistic school, since naturalistic writers "did not hate human miseries; on the contrary, they were pleased to study and represent them" and that was part of "the character of masculinity that women use to add to their literary art" (Guerra, 1905b).[19] Serao was seen "not even a single time [as being] caught in the vertigo of evil" ("Literatura", 1900, p. 173),[20] which was typical of the pessimistic and the naturalistic school period. She was a realistic writer then, but "alien to Tolstoy's and Ibsen's positive suggestions", "without the black, desperate sadness of the materialistic hypothesis" ("Actualidad extranjera", 1903),[21] "entirely unrelated either to the vast goodness preached by Russian novelists, or with socialist ideals", different from the French and from "the harshness that characterized its supreme pontiffs", "in a very original and sometimes strange language" (Monterrey, 1903, p. 494-495) which could shock cultural salons, but also added charm.[22] Therefore, Matilde Serao became the prototype of an Italian realism. Likewise, a female

19 "Causa extrañeza así, al pronto, este carácter de masculinidad que suelen poner en su arte literario las mujeres".

20 "recorriendo sus obras, no se la encuentra ni una sola vez cogida por el vértigo del mal, más ó menos enmascarado por traidoras apariencias de belleza y de bondad".

21 "Matilde Serao no tiene la tristeza negra y desesperada de la hipótesis materialista".

22 "La compasión de la escritora por las miserias humanas no tiene parentesco alguno con la amplia bondad predicada por los novelistas rusos. Tampoco profesa Matilde Serao el

reporter from Paris, Blanca Valmont, agreed with this description and praised "the moral truth" in Matilde Serao (Valmont, 1907). Ángel Guerra's idea of the Italian novel corresponded to what Blanca Valmont thought was a prerequisite for the novel written for a female readership: it had to teach through compassionate realism because this warded off the excessive pessimism, begrudgement and hatred of naturalistic writers, and thus protected female readers by cultivating their sensitivity, moral principles, and offering a consoling idealism.[23] Such a definition of the novel rested more or less explicitly on the view that women's proper social roles were those of mothers, daughters and wives in the domestic space, as Ángel Guerra made clear in his review of what he emphatically praised as Serao's masterpiece, *Mors tua…* (1926): a book against the war "written by a woman, a woman with a mother's heart" (Guerra, 1927b).[24]

Secondly, the critics who signed their articles insisted on the sun and the colour associated with the adjective "Southern", on the passion and happiness of the south, on the picturesque quality of Neapolitan life. Ángel Guerra noticed that she "could copy, with the grace and art of an inimitable realist, Neapolitan life in its typical and picturesque details", "this sentimental overflowing, this excess of Southern passion that is wild when it gets excited" (Guerra, 1904, pp. 55, 52).[25] In fact, this was a well-established opinion, already supported by the French

ideal socialista. […] En Italia, nunca ha tenido el naturalismo la crudeza que caracterizó a sus pontífices magnos".

23 Blanca Valmont clearly states that this is a necessity for female readers (Valmont, 1907). In an obituary on Matilde Serao's death, the journalist mentions this female compassion when praising Serao's last novel *Mors tua* (1926) as "a woman's and mother's book", where Serao harshly criticizes the horrors of the war hidden behind patriotism, thus irritating the fascists (F.M., 1927). This idea of women's writing is the same that we find in the magazine called *Las novelas femeninas*, a collection of stories written by women such as Matilde Serao, Fernán-Caballero and Carolina Invernizio that could educate and provide female readers with art, moral principles, entertainment and elegance, and which were advertised everywhere in 1907, 1908 and 1913.

24 "No hay que olvidar que es una novela escrita por una mujer, una mujer con corazón de madre".

25 "ha sabido copiar, con gracia y arte de costumbrista inimitable, la vida napolitana en lo que tiene ésta de típica y pintoresca", "ese desborde sentimental, esa plétora de meridional pasión que es brava cuando se exalta". All the journalists emphasize Serao's philosophical pessimism tempered by the optimistic happiness of Southern Italy (Terán, 1902b, for example); or the "very funny stories of Neapolitan life" ("Libros populares", 1901a).

philosopher Auguste Comte as reported in the Spanish press: the "excellent depiction of Neapolitan customs" (Comte, 1905).[26]

Thirdly, Serao was worth reading for what were considered the typically feminine features of women's writing, as well as for women's analytical skills. Critics insisted on the fact that "women perceive the subtlest psychological nuances with unusual insight" (Zeda, 1903) [27] and especially Matilde Serao, who could "reveal the female soul" ("Literatura", 1900, p. 171).[28] Various critics from Madrid or from other places defined her writing as "touching" and full of "compassion", characteristics that male writers were capable of as well, such as in the case of Dostoyevsky, Tolstoy and Gorky in Russia; Zola in France, Galdós in Spain, and, surprisingly, Matilde Serao in Italy. Hence the merging of characters with the narrator and the female author who "love, hate, cry, because she herself knew how to cry, to hate and to love" (Monterrey, 1903, p. 495),[29] and who showed "the great drunkenness of the happy woman who was loved, who is still loved and who still loves, surrounded by her kids, a good mother and a generous friend" ("Literatura", 1900, p. 172).[30] Finally, in 1907 Blanca Valmont stated: "Matilde Serao's intelligence is basically feminine" (Valmont, 1907).[31] Therefore, it is no wonder that her books were recommended for well-educated ladies ("¿Qué libros se leen?", 1903); at the same time she was said to be "enthusiastically acclaimed by all social classes"(Gimeno, 1900a, p. 554).[32]

26 "excelente pintura de las costumbres napolitanas".

27 "las mujeres descubren con rara penetración los más tenues matices psíquicos".

28 "nadie ha sabido como Matilde Serao revelar el alma femenil".

29 "aman, odian, lloran, porque ella misma supo llorar, odiar y amar".

30 "la gran embriaguez de la mujer feliz que ha sido amada, que lo es y que ama todavía, rodeada de sus hijos, buena madre y amiga generosa".

31 "la inteligencia de Matilde Serao es esencialmente femenina".

32 "Ha dado conferencias en París y en las principales ciudades de Italia, siendo siempre entusiásticamente vitoreada por todas las clases sociales".

## CONCLUSIONS

The commitment to big numbers soon disproved the hypotheses that we had proposed at the very beginning: that Matilde Serao was considered the prototype of the modern woman, that her reputation was like Grazia Deledda's and that it even grew after the latter was awarded the Nobel prize. None of the hypotheses were confirmed, but rather they were modified or rejected. However, we could have validated these hypotheses if we had read only the voices of the (masculine) canon such as Ángel Guerra, or only those of the new (emancipationist) canon consecrated by Carmen de Burgos and Concepción Gimeno de Flaquer. When one changes the scale of representation, the reality one meets with can be very different.

Therefore, it was necessary to accept the fact that Matilde Serao was considered, first, as a novelist and a female writer, and that she was acknowledged as a journalist only to a much lesser extent. Only a few voices underlined the combative power of her word in the newspapers. Secondly, she was seen as Italian, from Naples. Thirdly, she was related to two keywords: "passion" (not only in the references to *Flor de Pasión*) [*Fior di passione*] and 'heart' (and not only because of *Corazón enfermo*) [*Cuore infermo*]. However, when investigating the details of the articles written by individual writers, we found a discourse revolving around other adjectives: "journalist", "realistic", "touching", "Southern". Therefore, a survey from a macro- and micro-perspective was conducted and these different scales yielded analyses that unearthed a different set of narratives, all of which ceased in 1939. After that crucial date, no more references to Matilde Serao can be found in the digitized press in Spanish. The dictatorship manipulated communicative memory with its censorship and taboos so effectively that the cultural memories and, consequently, the cultural practices of many people were destroyed by a minority.

It is time scholars accessed the electronic archives in order to enhance *women writers' historical significance.* Researchers need to draw material from selective prosthetic memories (digital libraries and digital tools) that (re)produce other external memories from the past (the printed press), and to reflect on it. It is high time active citizens transformed passive recollections into active ones, and readers shared a collective, European memory, as the present work in this volume intends to prove.

We personally remember that our own grandmothers read and loved the many editions of *All'erta, sentinella!* and *¡Centinela alerta!*. We owe them the protection of that legacy.

Maria Laura IASCI
Amelia SANZ
Complutense University of Madrid

## MATILDE SERAO'S FICTION TRANSLATED INTO SPANISH

Serao Matilde, 1893, "Salvación" ["Salvazione"], trans. unknown, *El correo de Gerona*, 10 May, p. 2.

Serao Matilde, 1893, "Perdición" ["Perdizione"], trans. unknown, *El correo de Gerona*, 23 May, p. 2.

Serao Matilde, 1893, "Una Florista" ["Una fioraia"], trans. unknown, *El Liberal*, 28 May, p. 1.

Serao Matilde, 1893, "Una Florista" ["Una fioraia"], trans. unknown, *El Liberal de Tenerife: Diario de la mañana*, 28 May, pp. 2-3.

Serao Matilde, 1893, "Salvación" ["Salvazione"], trans. unknown, *El Pueblo: periódico republicano democrático*, 9 July, p. 4.

Serao Matilde, 1893, "Una Florista" ["Una fioraia"], trans. unknown, *El correo de Gerona*, 15 July, pp. 1-2.

Serao Matilde, 1895, "Salvación" ["Salvazione"], trans. unknown, *El Liberal de Tenerife*, 28 February, pp. 2-3.

Serao Matilde, 1899, "Perdición" ["Perdizione"], trans. unknown, *La vida literaria*, 25 March, p. 203.

Serao Matilde, 1900, *"¡Centinela, alerta!", "Terno seco", "Treinta por ciento", "O mi Juanito o la muerte"* ["All'erta, sentinella!", "Terno secco", "Trenta

per cento", "O Giovannino o la morte"], trans. unknown, Madrid, Hispano-Americana (colección *La novela ilustrada*).
Serao Matilde, 1901, *¡Centinela, alerta!* (includes "Terno seco", "Treinta por ciento", and "O mi Juanito o la muerte") ["All'erta, sentinella!", "Terno secco", "Trenta per cento", "O Giovannino o la morte"], trans. unknown, Valencia, Sempere.
Serao Matilde, 1901, "Perdición" ["Perdizione"], trans. unknown, *La Correspondencia de Alicante*, 19 June, pp. 1-2.
Serao Matilde, 1904, "Perdición" ["Perdizione"], trans. unknown, *El Globo. Diario independiente*, 13 September, p. 1.
Serao Matilde, 1907, *Adiós, amor* [*Addio, Amore!*], trans. E. Troisi, Barcelona, Maucci.
Serao Matilde, 1907, *Los amores de la duquesa (corazón enfermo)* [*Cuore infermo*], trans. unknown, Barcelona, Maucci.
Serao Matilde, 1907, *La bailarina* [*La ballerina*], trans. Tomas de C. Duran, Barcelona, Maucci.
Serao Matilde, 1907, *Fantasía* [*Fantasía*], trans. Rafael Ruiz López, Barcelona, Maucci.
Serao Matilde, 1907, *Flor de pasión* [*Fior di passione*], trans. Rámon del Valle Inclán, Barcelona, Maucci.
Serao Matilde, 1909, *¡Centinela, alerta!* [*All'erta, sentinella!*], trans. unknown, Valencia, Sempere.
Serao Matilde, 1909, *El país de la Ilusión. Novela napolitana* [*Il paese di Cuccagna*], trans. by Tomás Orts-Ramos, Barcelona/Buenos Aires, Maucci.
Serao Matilde, 1910, *El país de Jesús* [*Nel paese di Gesù (Ricordi di un viaggio in Palestina)*], trans. Condesa Beretta, Madrid, Francisco Beltrán.
Serao Matilde, 1911, *El castigo* [*Castigo*], trans. A.O.V., Barcelona – Buenos Aires, Maucci.
Serao Matilde, 1917, *¡Centinela, alerta!* [*All'erta, sentinella!*], trans. unknown, Madrid, La novela Ilustrada.
Serao Matilde, 1925, *¡Centinela, alerta!* [*All'erta, sentinella*!], trans. unknown, Madrid, La libertad.
Serao Matilde, 1928, "Cuento sencillo. En la pendiente" ["Trenta per cento"], trans. unknown, *Región,* 1 February, p. 9.
Serao Matilde, 1936, "Dos corazones desgraciados: novela romántica" ["Nebulose"], trans. unknown, *Revista Literaria "Novelas y cuentos"*, pp. 136-159.

# MATILDE SERAO IN SWEDEN

## A Voice of "The New Italy"

In the last decade of the nineteenth century, Matilde Serao was the most translated and the most-read Italian author in Sweden alongside Edmondo De Amicis and Antonio Fogazzaro. More than her male colleagues, Serao was considered a true voice of "the new Italy": a young woman from Naples and the daughter of an Italian patriot,[1] professionally active as a journalist and newspaper editor, connected to the modern Naturalist movement and extensively published by Swedish daily newspapers – all this contributed to make Matilde Serao a prominent literary personality of her time and a public figure known to a broader audience. Later, when she was supplanted by D'Annunzio as the key Italian writer of the day, her journalistic writings on Neapolitan manners and the details of her personal and professional life (the separation from Scarfoglio and, more significantly, her disastrous implication in the Saredo investigation into Neapolitan corruption) would still be widely discussed in the Swedish press.

This chapter examines the reception of Serao's narrative in Sweden, mostly on the basis of contemporary reviews of her work from 1885 to the first years of the twentieth century. Critics reviewed both the original texts published by the Italian writer and the Swedish translations of her work. The corpus of Serao's translations is comprised of six volumes published from 1890 to 1903 in Sweden and Finland, and of over twenty publications that I have retraced in recently digitized Swedish daily newspapers from 1888 to 1897.[2]

Diving into the world of digitized *fin de siècle* newspapers is an exhilarating experience. This world is both distant and familiar,

---

1 Serao was introduced to the Swedish public for the first time by Carl David af Wirsén in 1885 when she was twenty-nine years old.

2 Newspaper publications and volumes overlap to a certain degree as will be shown further. Digitized Swedish newspapers are available at: National Library of Sweden, *Svenska dagstidningar*, http://www.tidningar.kb.se (last accessed 15 December 2020).

provincial, and strangely globalized as journalists refer to news published in German and French media and testify about facts known to us from history books. They are writing for a reader who shares their world views and are often entertaining and polemical. In the history of Scandinavian culture, the 1880s is the decade of "the modern breakthrough":[3] Naturalist poetics start to dominate the literary scene and Strindberg and Ibsen establish themselves as key figures of the new Scandinavian literature. The "woman question" animates discussions on women's roles and rights, at the same time as industrialization and urbanization change the face of Swedish society; the total circulation of Swedish daily newspapers increases tenfold from 1865 to 1900 (Rydén, 2010, p. 420) and around twenty percent of the population emigrates to the New World.

The reception of Serao's fiction takes place in this dynamic but still isolated context. The introducers, translators, and reviewers of Serao appear with initials or write anonymously on the pages of newspapers, but they know each other and are often connected by professional and familial ties. To a modern reader the reviews of Serao's novels may seem very long and detailed, as the critics give lengthy accounts of the plot and are uninhibitedly subjective as they express their own aesthetic preferences or share reminiscences of travels in Southern Italy. Swedish conservatives and liberals, traditionalists and modernists, also take different stances in the reception of this Italian writer in a process that reflects the domestic literary debate and power struggles. The analysis of the Swedish reception of Serao can therefore be divided into four parts. I start with the man who introduced Matilde Serao to the Swedish public, Carl David af Wirsén (1842-1912), a poet, conservative critic and permanent secretary of the Swedish Academy from 1884,[4] who devoted seven lengthy reviews to Serao's works published in Italy. I then examine the extensive publication of Serao's short stories on the pages of Swedish newspapers and the collective volume *From the New Italy: A Collection of Stories* (1890), before moving on to the reviews of Serao's three novels published in Sweden, *Il paese di Cuccagna, Castigo,*

3 This term was coined by the Danish critic Georg Brandes (1842-1927) in 1883.

4 The Swedish Academy was created in 1786 by King Gustaf III with the *Académie francaise* as its model. It consists of eighteen lifetime members and has awarded the Nobel prize in literature since 1901. See on this point Ulla åkerström's chapter in this volume.

and *La ballerina*. The last section of my analysis concerns Serao's image as a public figure in the Swedish press, and in particular her alleged involvement in Neapolitan corruption.

## INTRODUCING SERAO

Carl David af Wirsén's posthumous reputation is mostly connected to the first decade of the Nobel Prize in literature, or rather to the fact that it was not awarded to authors like Zola, Ibsen and Tolstoy, whose candidatures he successfully blocked. A minor romantic poet and a conservative if not reactionary critic with a strong Christian credo, he was also the major introducer of untranslated English, French, German and Italian literature in Sweden through the Academy's newspaper *Post-och Inrikes Tidningar*. Af Wirsén promoted an idealist vision of literature and was a long-time adversary of the more internationally renowned Georg Brandes in the Nordic culture struggles (Rydén, 2010, p. 163). Brandes, who also did his best to deprovincialize Scandinavian literatures by juxtaposing them with their European counterparts, was a strong advocate of French Naturalism. His famous dictum from 1871, "that literature is alive today is shown by the fact that it sets up problems for debate" (cited in Larsen, 2011, p. 21), foregrounded the idea that the critic and the writer should take part in the process of human emancipation and societal progress, something that could not be further removed from the convictions of his Swedish opponent.

In the field of untranslated Italian literature, however, af Wirsén was almost the only reviewer in Sweden, and he covered this field with an unusual sense of benevolence, "as if it were illuminated by the southern sun" (Rydén, 2010, p. 339).[5] Indeed, Serao's "ardent and transparent"[6] style (Wirsén, 1887) evoked for him the beauty of the Gulf of Naples, in particular the road between Sorrento and Castellammare, which he mentioned no less than three times in his articles (Wirsén 1886, 1887, 1890b). Besides Serao, af Wirsén reviewed De Amicis, Carducci,

5 "det var som om den haft söderns sol över sig".
6 "stilens eldfullhet och genomskinlighet".

D'Annunzio and Fogazzaro, whose *Daniele Cortis* he was especially fond of (Rydén, 2010, pp. 340-341).

The first Serao novel that af Wirsén reviewed in September 1885 is *La conquista di Roma*, published the same year in Florence. He introduces the Neapolitan writer as "one of the most gifted coryphaei in Italy's new ultrarealist school" and acknowledges the novel's "indisputable merits", despite the fact that it suffers from an unclear underlying message and protracted descriptions (Wirsén, 1885).[7] From this beginning to the final consecration of Serao in the major national encyclopedia *Nordisk familjebok* [*Nordic Family Book*] in 1917 (*NF*, 1904-1926 (1917), pp. 131-132), Swedish critics emphasize the influence of French Naturalism on her work. In their view, this influence manifests itself in several ways: exhaustive descriptions of everyday life and surroundings, a particular attention to the conditions of working-class people and, especially in *Il paese di Cuccagna*, Serao's affinity with Zola's and Brandes's injunction to "set up problems for debate". Parallel to the critics' disregard for the Italian literary context and their exaggeration of French Naturalist influence runs the essentializing tendency to consider Serao's oeuvre, so to speak, as a direct product of the Neapolitan land and nature itself. The exuberance of southern nature is routinely projected onto Serao's characters and her style of writing. Even reviewers familiar with contemporary Italian literature tend to impose their personal experiences of Italy and Italians as a major frame of reference for interpreting Serao's work.

For af Wirsén, the history of the unconsummated love relationship between Francesco San Giorgio, a young political careerist and "modern atheist and utilitarian", and the "distinguished, good-natured and virtuous" Angelica Vargas (Wirsén, 1885)[8] is an occasion to dwell on the superiority of duty and self-sacrifice to passion. Af Wirsén regrets that Angelica motivates her refusal of Francesco's advances merely through a respect for convention and public opinion ("perché non lo vogliono"), instead of an inner conviction of "compelling duty". This choice of motivation is explained with reference to Serao's "sceptical mind" and her adherence to what doubtless takes place in real life, but it compromises

7 "En bland de mest begåfvade koryféerna i Italiens nya, ultrarealistiska skola [...] obestridliga förtjenster".

8 "moderne ateistens och utilitaristens", "en förnäm, älskvärd och sederen".

"the highest purity" that af Wirsén sees in Angelica's character (*ibid.*).[9] Another reproach concerning lack of clarity addresses the fact that for Serao and San Giorgio, "the conquest of Rome" concerns only the political scene of the new capital, and the plotline could therefore have taken place anywhere in Europe (the same goes for the romantic story), whereas for af Wirsén, the specificity of this city lies in its historical heritage and the "frictions between the worldly and spiritual powers, which were both based in Rome" (*ibid.*).[10] When it comes to Serao's art of description, the reviewer finds the mass scenes of the parliamentary session and the royal ball in the Quirinale "excellent" ("silhouettes of king Umberto and queen Margherita are finely executed"), but the description of San Giorgio's flat and the merchandise at a glove store "is a dry, mechanical enumeration of completely uninteresting objects" (*ibid.*).[11]

The critic, who will later praise Serao's sensuous descriptions of nature, is unable to appreciate the same approach when it comes to manufactured objects and the author's "hypermodern propensity for too-detailed descriptions of all sorts of *accessories*" (*ibid.*).[12] Contrary to the Swedish reviewer, Emilio Cecchi and Natalino Sapegno would later regard Serao's exhaustive descriptions of luxury objects exhibited for sale as "a true homage to aestheticism",[13] constituting a missing link between verismo and D'Annunzio's Decadentism (Cecchi – Sapegno, 1968, p. 374).

Af Wirsén's next two reviews of Serao's earlier novels, *Cuore infermo* (1881) and *Fantasia* (1883) constitute a crescendo of superlatives. In spite of the Neapolitan writer's "adventurous ideas" and "sometimes too luxurious style", the critic concludes that "no modern writer since the days of George Sand has exhibited so much artistry, so much life and so much strength as Matilde Serao in *Cuore infermo*" (Wirsén, 1886).[14] The reviewer performs a typical stereotyping manoeuvre, in claiming that

9 "oafvislig pligt", "skeptiska lynne [...] högsta renhet".

10 "slitningarna mellan den verldsliga och den andliga magten, hvilka begge ega sina målsmän i Rom".

11 "silhuetterna af konung Umberto och af drottning Margherita äro fint utförda", "ett torrt, mekaniskt uppräknande af fullkomligt intresselösa föremål".

12 "hypermoderna benägenhet för mycket utförda beskrifningar af allahanda 'accessoirer'".

13 "un vero omaggio all'estetismo".

14 "äfventyrliga idéer", "stundom alltför luxuösa stil", "vi hos ingen nyare författarinna sedan George Sands dagar funnit så mycken konstnärlighet, så mycket lif och så mycken styrka som i Matilde Seraos *Cuore infermo*".

"the book has the character of Neapolitan nature": "a strong bouquet of heliotrope and jasmine", a style reminiscent of "a volcano that erupts lava streams of passion; a sea of roses that bestows upon us exquisite fragrances as nightingales sing in laurel and magnolia trees" (*ibid.*).[15] It is as if the critic were trying to compete with the writer, before turning back to his usual moralist vocation: "the love of these people has too much of the physical and too little of the spiritual; in the moment of delight, they too easily forget the quiet honour, the calm faithfulness, the powerful, yet often forgotten, but always holy sense of duty that bestows upon life its supreme value" (*ibid.*).[16] However, for af Wirsén, Serao's sensualism and passion "never transgress the frontier of what is offensive and ugly" (*ibid.*)[17] – this will indeed be a topos in the Swedish reception of her work, something that can reconcile conservative critics with Serao's reputation as Naturalist.

In his review of *Fantasia* from 1888, af Wirsén proposes Serao, "a truly poetical nature, a brilliant individual" (Wirsén, 1888),[18] as a role model for Swedish authors:

> [The novel] is characterized by seriousness and moral nobility, at the same time as the style has the beauty that only inspiration and natural taste can bestow. The description of the characters is truthful and rigorous, the oeuvre is so entertaining that the reader cannot stop reading once he has started, and our male and female writers in Sweden have an enormous amount to learn from Matilde Serao when it comes to the art of representation (*ibid.*).[19]

"Nobility", or "noble" (*ädel*) nature, is for af Wirsén both a moral and an aesthetic concept related to purity, and it constitutes the criterion for his critical judgment. For this late romantic and idealist, "a poet's vocation is

15 "boken har i mycket den neapolitanska naturens karakter", "en stark 'bouquet', likasom av heliotrop och jasmin", "ur kratern uppsänder passionens lavaflöden; ett haf af rosor skänker oss döfvande vällukter och näktergalar sjunga bland lager och magnolieträd".

16 "menniskornas kärlek har alldeles för mycket af det fysiska, för lite af det andliga, de hafva för lätt att i stundens fröjd glömma den lugna heder, den stilla trohet, den mägtiga, ofta misskända, men alltid heliga pligtkänsla, hvilka gifva lifvet dess förnämsta värde".

17 "gränslinien till det fula och sårande är icke öfverträdd".

18 "en äkta poetisk natur, en snillrik individualitet".

19 "utmärkt af allvar och moralisk ädelhet, på samma gång som stilen har den fägring, som endast ingifvelse och naturlig smak kunna skänka. Karaktersteckningen har sanning och stränghet, arbetet är så underhållande, att man ej, när man väl börjat läsningen, kan dermed upphöra, och våra författare eller författarinnor i Sverige hafva, hvad sjelfva framställningens konst angår, ofantligt mycket att lära af Matilde Serao".

a priesthood of light; he has the task of revealing a higher world of purity and peace in his oeuvre" (*NF*, 1904-1926 (1921), p. 785).[20] Applying the criterion of nobility to Serao's fiction, af Wirsén concludes that Angelica Vargas' conflict between passion and duty in *La conquista di Roma* could have been depicted more nobly (Wirsén, 1885); the same holds for the portrait of the young girls in "Scuola normale superiore", which is lacking in nobility because of the girls' "epidemic, spasmodic craving for marriage", even if af Wirsén finds the description of the atmosphere before the exam "excellent" (Wirsén, 1887).[21] In the same vein, *Piccole anime* is noble and well written (Wirsén, 1890a). In *Fantasia*, the Swedish academician particularly appreciates the moral message that clearly shows the perils of an exaggerated imagination for the spiritual life of the individual. He concludes that the novel possesses a lasting value because of its "delicate [yet] implacable analysis of the human soul" and suggests that the novel should be translated into Swedish, although a translation should preferably omit "certain unnecessary and quite disturbing descriptions of animal phenomena in Caserta's park" (Wirsén, 1888).[22] The novel will indeed appear in Swedish as *Väninnor* [*(Female) Friends*, 1891], but in neighbouring Finland, where the daily *Nya Pressen* in Helsinki ran it as a serial story from November 1891 to January 1892 and also published it in a separate volume.[23] This anonymous translation probably never made it to Sweden: in contrast with the local editions of Serao, which were advertised hundreds of times in the mass media, there are no traces of this novel on the pages of the Swedish press, and it is also absent from the National Library of Sweden. However, *Fantasia* was published in Sweden thirty years later in serial form in the pages of women's weekly magazine *Idun*, now with the title *Lucia* and translated by Ernst Lundqvist.

---

20 "skaldens kall är ett ljusets prästämbete, han skall i dikten uppenbara en högre värld af renhet och frid".

21 "den epidemiska, den spasmodiska giftaslystnad".

22 "sin fina, obevekliga själsanalys [...] obehöfliga och ganska stötande beskrifningarna på animala företeelser i Casertas park". Here af Wirsén probably objects to Serao's vivid descriptions of swarms of flies and the smell of manure that surround the cows at the agricultural exhibition visited by Lucia Altimare and Andrea Lieti. This scene of two lovers-to-be in such an unromantic environment is clearly reminiscent of Emma Bovary and Rodolphe at the agricultural fair in Rouen in Flaubert's masterpiece. For a more detailed comparison of the two texts, see Kroha, 1987.

23 On Swedish translations of Serao's works published in Finland see Viola Parente-Čapková's chapter in this volume.

The review of *Addio, Amore!* (1890), published the same year by af Wirsén, is less enthusiastic, mainly because of the novel's improbable plot (Wirsén, 1890). However, the critic praises Serao's mass scenes from the San Carlo theatre and the horse race; indeed, "her prose is at its best when she in a sudden *aperçu* provides a glimpse of a landscape or evokes a furtive movement of the soul" (*ibid.*).[24] Similar reflections also appear in his reviews of Serao's three volumes of short stories and sketches, *Il romanzo della fanciulla* (1886), *Piccole anime* (1883b) and *Dal vero* (1879). Even if the problem of plot does not arise in the same way in the short stories, the critic complains about the abundance of descriptions of characters and places, and the absence of a storyline in the texts of this highly esteemed "poetess in prose [...] whose poetical gift has always seemed to us undeniable" (Wirsén, 1887).[25] In "Nella lava", af Wirsén admires images of nature and popular life outside of Naples; in "Telegrafi dello stato" he especially praises Serao's familiarity with the technical aspects of the telegraph office, clearly unaware that the author has spent four years of her life working there. Especially in the first years of Serao's reception in Sweden, critics failed to acknowledge the novelty of this female author's many professional roles – an anonymous reviewer of *Vita e avventure di Riccardo Joanna* (1887) attributed the knowledgeableness of Serao's depiction of the journalistic sphere merely to the fact that she was married to a publicist ("En italiensk tidningsmannaroman", 1889).

The volume *Piccole anime* is for af Wirsén "a good deed" because of Serao's deep sympathy with the children (Wirsén, 1890a).[26] The Swedish academician approvingly quotes the Neapolitan writer's criticism of the impact of modernity and atheism on the children's psyche, echoing today's preoccupations with new types of media: "The modern child reads too many illustrated books and has access to too many newspapers. When his father speaks tranquilly of suicide or his uncle mocks religion, the child is listening" (Wirsén, 1890a).[27] Strangely enough, af Wirsén commented on "Una fioraia" and "Canituccia", unaware of the fact that

---

24 "bäst är hennes prosa, när hon i någon plötslig *aperçu* låter ett landskap framskymta eller någon hemlighetsfull själsrörelse antydas".

25 "en skaldinna på prosa [...] hvars poetiska sinne alltid synts oss oförnekligt".

26 "en god handling".

27 "Det moderna barnet läser för många illustrerade böcker och har till hands för många tidningar. När fadern helt lugnt talar om självmordet eller onkel gör narr af religionen, lyssnar barnet".

these (and two other) stories had already been published in Swedish translation by the conservative daily *Svenska Dagbladet* the previous year. He places "the deeply serious yet artistic sketches 'Perdizione' and 'Gli spostati'"[28] (*ibid.*, p. 3) above the other stories and finishes the review by quoting Luke 17:2, "[i]t were better for him that a millstone were hanged about his neck, and he be cast into the sea, than that he should offend one of these little ones".[29]

The last of af Wirsén's reviews happens to deal with one of Serao's earliest books, *Dal vero* ([1879] 1890),[30] which he treats as a contemporary publication, noting with surprise that it lacks "the almost feverish sensuality" of her first novels (Wirsén, 1891).[31] Besides the usual comments he dwells with amusement on Serao's ironical sketch "Votazione femminile", which mocks the idea of women's suffrage. The conservative af Wirsén shares Serao's position on this issue and hopes that the sketch will never be translated into Swedish: "otherwise the Amazons would show her no mercy and send an expedition to Southern Italy in order to demand satisfaction" (*ibid.*).[32] The sketch was indeed never translated into Swedish, but thirty years after its publication in Italy, the readers of *Svenska Dagbladet* (which in the meantime had turned more liberal) could acquaint themselves with Serao's evolved views on this issue in the article "Matilde Serao on the female question" ("Matilde Serao om kvinnofrågan", 1909). In this reprint of an interview that Serao gave to her German translator Lola Lorme, published in a Viennese newspaper, the author talks about "a beautiful mission to accomplish: to make the woman who is entitled to vote ready for the elections and thereby let her become man's equal",[33] a challenging work for present and future generations (*ibid.*).

After 1891 af Wirsén would not publish any reviews of Serao – he probably saw his tasks accomplished once the Neapolitan writer

28 "de djupt allvarliga, men ock konstnärliga skizzerna 'Perdizione' och 'Gli spostati'".

29 I quote from the *King James Bible*, https://www.kingjamesbibleonline.org/Luke-17-2/ (last accessed 15 December 2020).

30 *Dal vero* was first published 1879 by Perussia & Quadrio in Milan, but af Wirsén refers to an edition from 1890 in his review.

31 "den nästan febrila sensualism".

32 "annars ve Matilde Serao: amazonerna gifva ingen nåd, och de torde utrusta en expedition till Syd-Italien för att tilltvinga sig upprättelse".

33 "en skön uppgift att fylla: den att göra den röstberättigade kvinnan mogen för valet och därigenom gifva henne en möjlighet att bli likställd med mannen".

started to appear in Swedish translation. Another possibility may be that the conservative critic grew disenchanted with Serao after the publication of *Il paese di Cuccagna* (1891) with its clear Naturalist tendencies.

## FIRST SWEDISH TRANSLATIONS

From 1888 to 1897, Swedish daily and weekly newspapers published Serao's texts on at least twenty occasions. The newspapers ranged from conservative to liberal and also exhibited a wide geographical variety, from the capital's major dailies such as *Aftonbladet* and *Svenska Dagbladet* (the latter of which was most active in promoting the Neapolitan writer) to the provincial *Östgöta Correspondenten* and *Kristianstadsbladet.* Some of Serao's stories appeared in serial form: others, like "Canituccia" ["Canituccia"], "Salvazione" ["Räddning"], "Delfina" ["Före brölloppet. En skizz"] and "Novella d'amore" ["Kärlek"], were reprinted several times. The first volume to be discovered by Swedish editors and translators was *Piccole anime* (Serao, 1883b). Starting in 1888, the conservative *Svenska Dagbladet* published half of its ten stories: "Salvazione" ["Räddning"], "Canituccia" ["Canituccia"], "Una fioraia" ["En blomsterflicka"], "Nebulose" ["Nebulosor"] and "Perdizione" ["Dömd"]. From the collection *Fior di passione,* Swedish newspapers selected "Duetto di salone" ["Salongsduett"], "Scena" ["Trohet"], "Novella d'amore" ["Kärlek"], "Delfina" ["Före brölloppet. En skizz"], "La settimana delle novelle (Anniversario)" ["En öfverlöpare"] and "Novella greca" ["Santa Maura. Grekisk novell"]. From *Dal vero* (1879) we find four pieces, "La moglie di un grand'uomo" ["En stor mans hustru"], "Mosaico di fanciulle" (an extract) ["Flicktyper"], "L'idillio di Pulcinella" ["Pulcinellas idyll"] and "Intervento" ["Efter två år"], the latter published in serial form by *Kristianstadsbladet.* "Terno secco" ["Rätta nummer"] appeared in *Stockholms Dagblad* in four parts, which also published "Sogno di una notte d'estate" ["En sommarnattsdröm"] from *Le amanti.* Another longer piece which appeared in serial form was *O Giovannino o la morte* [*Giovannino eller döden*] (1889) in the pages of the liberal *Aftonbladet*, translated by Ernst Lundqvist. It was later published in a volume in Helsinki by *Nya Pressen,* which had been responsible for the Swedish translation of *Fantasia* four years earlier.

With the exception of *O Giovannino o la morte,* all newspaper translations were published anonymously, but we can still attribute them to the pen of Ellen Lundberg-Nyblom (1869-1933) with a high degree of probability. This is due to the fact that three stories, "La settimana delle novelle (Anniversario)" ["En öfverlöpare"], "Novella d'amore" ["Kärlek"] and "Salvazione" ["Räddning"] together with "All'erta, sentinella"[34] were included in an anthology of Italian writers called *Från det nya Italien. En samling berättelser* [*From the New Italy: A Collection of Stories*] (1890), translated by Ellen Nyblom.[35] Besides Serao, this volume included stories by Verga, De Amicis, Giuseppe Giacosa, Contessa Lara (Evelina Cattermole) and Enrico Panzacchi, but the Neapolitan author was evidently considered the most important of these writers: she opened the anthology and accounted for some forty percent of it. This volume was greeted by the Swedish press as an important contribution to the body of Italian literature in Swedish translation; but before turning to the reviews, I will outline some details about Ellen Lundberg-Nyblom (1869-1933) and her parents Carl Rupert Nyblom (1832-1907) and Helena Nyblom (1843-1926), all of whom contributed to the introduction of Serao's work in Sweden.

C.R. Nyblom was active as a scholar, poet and translator; he was appointed as professor in aesthetics, literature and art history at the university of Uppsala in 1867, where he happened to teach both af Wirsén and Strindberg (Rydén, 2010, pp. 155-156). The latter would describe his Uppsala professor as "a banal provincial poet equal to many Stockholm clerks".[36] During his *grand tour* of Europe, Nyblom spent a year in Italy and published his impressions in *Bilder från Italien* [*Images of Italy*] (Nyblom, 1864) under the pen name Carlino; in his memoirs, he would later remember this period as the happiest of his life.[37] An extremely productive translator, mostly from English (Shakespeare, Swift)

34 "Fången på Nisida" or "The prisoner of Nisida" in Swedish translation.
35 She modified her family name to Lundberg-Nyblom after her marriage in 1893.
36 "en banal småstadspoet jämbördig med många Stockholmskontorister".
37 http://www.oversattarlexikon.se/artiklar/Carl_Rupert_Nyblom (last accessed 18 December 2020).

but also of classical poetry, he was elected to the Swedish Academy in 1879. In 1892, Nyblom wrote an enthusiastic preface to the Swedish edition of *Il paese di Cuccagna* [*Luftslott. Napolitansk sedeskildring*], which was translated by his daughter. His wife Helena Nyblom was herself a writer, mostly of short stories, poetry and plays, and she, in turn, composed a preface (Nyblom, 1890) to the collection *From the New Italy.* Their daughter Ellen was just nineteen when she published her first Serao translation in *Svenska Dagbladet*, but by then she had already translated De Amicis' *Cuore* in 1888. She would later follow in the footsteps of her parents as a poet, translator and writer of short stories and travel fiction, most of it concerned with Italy.

It is clear from Helena Nyblom's preface that the Swedish publishers of the anthology had an approach to Italian literature radically different from that of af Wirsén. The authors were selected in order to give a representative picture of the literature of the new Italy, but they also shared a common ambition "to apprehend and study with their artists' eyes the details of nature and real life" (Nyblom, 1890, p. I).[38] This sounds like a Naturalist or verist program, but at the same time there was a balance to be observed in order not to offend public taste, which tended to connect Naturalism to the excesses of Zola and his peers:

> Italians are not afraid to call things by their proper names: yes, they possess a cold-bloodedness when observing cruel and heartrending actions, and in this not many of us Northerners can match them. But they also know how to give the terrible a truly tragic character, a beauty that reconciles us with the dreadful subject matter (*ibid.*).[39]

An anonymous reviewer of the anthology from *Västmanlands Läns Tidning* expressed a similar idea in more direct terms: "The writers belong to the realist school, but still don't allow their portrayal of reality to smell of the gutter and dirt" ("Litteratur", 1890).[40] The reviewer from *Svenska Dagbladet* highlighted the difference between "the explicit, often

38 "med verkliga konstnärsögon uppfatta och studera detaljerna i naturen och det verkliga lifvet".

39 "Italienarna äro icke rädda för att kalla saker vid deras rätta namn: ja, de ega en kallblodighet vid betraktandet af grymma och hjertgripande tilldragelser, hvari icke många af oss nordbor skulle kunna mäta sig med dem. Men så förstå de också att gifva det gräsliga en verkligt tragisk pregel, en skönhet, som försonar oss med det förfärliga i ämnet".

40 "Författarne tillhöra den realistiska skolan, men låta dock ej sina verklighetsskildringar dofta af rännsten och smuts".

sentimental participation of Germanic writers in the characters they portray" and the "dissecting objectivity" of the Italians' descriptions ("Konst och litteratur", 1890b).[41]

Of the six Italian authors included in the anthology, Serao, De Amicis and Verga were mentioned by the reviewers as the best-known outside of Italy ("Konst och litteratur", 1890c). The texts of the Neapolitan author were the most commented on by reviewers. *Göteborgs Aftonblad* praised the "masterly details" (*ibid.*)[42] and dismal atmosphere of "All'erta, sentinella" ["Fången på Nisida"], while "Novella d'amore" ["Kärlek"] was singled out by *Härnösandsposten*: "the manner of her sketching here is beyond the reach of contemporary Scandinavian authors" ("Konst och litteratur", 1890a).[43] The same piece also attracted the most attention in the review by the literary historian and critic Hellen Lindgren (1857-1904) in the liberal *Aftonbladet*. He was a supporter of Naturalism and had published biographies of Zola and Ibsen, but in this case, he was most impressed by the sudden end of the story, in which a married woman sacrifices her love for another man to the sacrosanctity of marriage, but still admits to her husband that she loves another:

> Morality appears here with a ruthless power, as it was sometimes depicted by George Eliot, and even conscience then becomes a kind of passion, a passion for the right action. This way of addressing temptation with an absolute and not a suspensive veto, simply consists in resorting to the language of force in order to eliminate all attachment points for temptation. This seems to be one of the new psychological findings discovered by the female temperament and incorporated into literature (Lindgren, 1890).[44]

The conservative idealist af Wirsén would probably agree with this statement by the progressive admirer of Naturalism Lindgren, even if he would prefer a different kind of phrasing. Despite their different

41 "de germaniska författarnes utpreglade, ofta sentimentala deltagande för de personer de skildra", "dissekrerande objektivitet".

42 "i detaljer mästerlig".

43 "Så, som hon här skizzerat, kan ingen nu lefvande inom de skandinaviska länderna göra det".

44 "Moralen uppträder här med en hänsynslös kraft, som George Eliot någon gång har skildrat, och samvetet blir då ett slags passion äfven det, en passion för det rätta. Detta sätt att möta frestelsen med att sätta emot den ett absolut veto och icke ett blott suspensivt, och som består i att helt enkelt med ett maktspråk afklippa alla frestelsens anknytningspunkter, synes vara en af de psykologiska nyeröfringar, som det kvinliga temperamentet upptäckt och för literaturen förvärfvat".

aesthetic and ideological premises, the two critics seem particularly fascinated with the inner workings of the psychological conflict between passion and duty portrayed by Serao. Unfortunately, in contrast to the permanent secretary of the Swedish Academy, who had an unlimited amount of space at his disposal in the Academy's newspaper, the reviewers of *From the New Italy* had to be brief. The anthology probably got less attention than it deserved, but this would partly improve with the publication of *Il paese di Cuccagna* [*Luftslott. Napolitansk sedeskildring*] in Swedish translation.

## THE SWEDISH RECEPTION OF *IL PAESE DI CUCCAGNA*, *CASTIGO* AND *LA BALLERINA*

The reception of Serao's masterpiece *Il paese di Cuccagna*, and her writings in general, is determined by two key features – the narrative itself and the ambivalence of the contemporary Swedish cultural context towards Italy. On one hand, we find true sympathy for the patriotic revival that led to the unification of the country, and profound admiration for Italian Renaissance culture, and on the other, secular prejudices against Southerners and Catholics, the exotic Other, whose *dolce far niente* is contrasted with the work ethic of the Protestant North. These attitudes could coexist side by side and in the same person, as in the case of Carl Rupert Nyblom himself, who admired Italy and its cultural treasures, and at the same time could be openly racist in his remarks about Southerners, in particular Neapolitans, after his second visit to Italy in 1877.[45] Thirty

45 "Neapolitans are and remain an ugly and shrewd rabble that does not have much in common with the seriousness and dignity of Northern Italians and Romans. […] Refrain, for God's sake, from arranging a journey to Pompeii and Sorrento with Don Pasquale – he will put his 'brother' next to him on the coach-box, where these two satyrs will grin like apes and jabber in a language that probably belonged to the apes, at the same time glancing scornfully at the poor victims in their shaky vehicle" ["Napolitanarne äro och förblifva ett fult och qvickt pack, som icke har mycket gemensamt med allvaret och värdigheten hos norditalienare och romare. […] Akta dig, för allt i verlden, att med Don Pasquale uppgöra ackord om en resa till Pompeji och Sorren to, ty då sätter han sin 'bror' på kuskbocken bredvid sig, der dessa båda satyrer grina som apor och snattra

years after the journey carried out by her father, Ellen Lundberg-Nyblom would address these Scandinavian prejudices against Italians[46] in a straightforward manner in her travel book *Bland italienare. Intryck och upplefvelser* [*Among Italians: Impressions and Experiences,* 1907]. Her main strategy for combating the centuries-old stereotypes consists in restoring the reputation of Italians as hard-working people. The Swedish writer highlights extensively the recent contribution of Italian workers to the construction of roads in the Swiss and Austrian Alps, the hard labour of rice farmers in Northern Italy and the tremendous effort behind the construction of terrace fields in Tuscany and Umbria. Lundberg-Nyblom (1907, pp. 2-4) concludes that Scandinavians have no reason for looking down upon Italians when it comes to their work ethic.

In his preface to *Il paese di Cuccagna* Carl Rupert Nyblom forbears to expose his own negative experiences of Naples and declares without further ado that Matilde Serao is not only "Italy's foremost now living writer, but also one of the most prominent in contemporary literature" (Nyblom, 1892, p. I).[47] The fact that this translation appeared as early as September 1892 probably made it one of the first translations in the world.[48] The Swedish title was *Luftslott*, or "castle(s) in the air"[49] with the addition "a

på ett språk, som troligen varit apornas, under hånfulla sidoblickar på de arma offren ini deras skraltiga åkdon"] (Nyblom, 1883, p. 247).

46 "We, Northerners, have over time developed an opinion, an axiom, that Italians are scoundrels and tricksters, that they murder, plunder and live in idleness and filth. There are still many Scandinavians who imagine that Italians are a horde of swarthy, dirty people, who rest in the shade of pines and grapevines with a bottle of wine and a bowl of steaming macaroni next to them, and then wake up from their *dolce far niente* to commit various misdeeds" ["Hos oss, nordbor, har i tidernas lopp uppstått en sats, som nästan gäller som ett axiom, att italienarne äro skurkar och bedragare, att de mörda och röfva, lefva i lättja och snusk. Det finnes ännu många skandinaver, som föreställa sig, att italienarna bestå af en hord svartmuskiga, smutsiga människor, hvilka i skuggan af pinjer och vinrankor makligt sträcka sig med en fiasco vin eller ett fat med rykande makaroni bredvid sig, och som vakna upp ur sitt *dolce far niente* endast för att begå allehanda illgärningar"] (Lundberg-Nyblom, 1907, pp. 1-2).

47 "Italiens nuvarande förnämsta författarinna, utan en bland de mest framstående inom den samtida litteraturen".

48 In comparison, it may be noted that the French translation, with a preface by Paul Bourget, was published in 1898 (*Au pays de Cocagne. Moeurs Napolitaines*, Paris, Plon) and the English one in 1901 (*The Land of Cockayne*, London, Heinemann). The German translation appeared in 1904 (*Schlaraffenland. Neapolitanischer Sittenroman*, Stuttgart, DVA).

49 Swedish translators of Serao seem to opt for titles that foreground the content of the novels in a straightforward way (Fantasia that would become Väninnor or [Female] friends); this also holds for her short stories. In the case of *Il paese di Cuccagna*, one anonymous reviewer

Neapolitan novel of manners" ["Napolitansk sedeskildring"]. For Nyblom, Serao "was a true daughter of her country [...] intent on representing in vivid pictures the children of the new Italy with their amiable naivety, their exaggerated passion and devotion, but also their flagrant spiritual shortcomings" (*ibid.*).[50] The reviewers were mostly positive, with some exceptions, and elaborated on the peculiarities of the Italian national character as depicted by Serao. The force of the Neapolitans' superstition in its different manifestations ("kabbala", "assistito" Pasqualino de Feo, the tragic story of the Cavalcanti family) made an impression on Swedish critics, as did their recklessness and their childish belief in miracles. To some, the case of the well-to-do middle-class gambler Cesare Fragalà seemed impossible to imagine outside of Italy (Sandberg, 1892). The moral shortcomings of the Neapolitans were associated with the immoral attitude of a state that encourages, or is at least forced to accept, the gambling mania of its citizens for financial reasons ("Literärt", 1892; "Litteratur-revy", 1892). Several critics appreciated Serao's masterly description of mass scenes at the lottery draw and the miracle of San Gennaro ("Literärt", 1892; Nordensvan, 1892; Sandberg, 1892), but also the tragic martyrdom of Bianca Maria ("Litteratur-revy", 1892; Nordensvan, 1892), which may seem too pathetic to today's readers.

The anonymous reviewer of *Nya Dagligt Allehanda* did not share Nyblom's enthusiasm for Serao and *Il paese di Cuccagna* (an "uneven" novel, albeit with some parts possessing literary value) due to "the very drastic description" "of the economic and moral ruin that strikes many (here *all*) victims of gambling" ("Litteratur-revy", 1892).[51] Strangely enough, this is the only review that mentions the quality of Ellen Nyblom's translation ("fully exemplary"),[52] although skeptical about certain Italicisms, like "marchese" (*ibid.*). Analysis of the translation is beyond the scope of this essay, but what may seem surprising to a

commented on the Italian title, stating that it "roughly corresponds to the Germans' Schlaraffenland, the promised land of fantasy" ["motsvarande ungefärligen tyskarnes Schlaraffenland, det drömda förlofvade landet"] ("Literärt", 1892).

50 "en äkta dotter af sitt land [...] har velat i lefvande bilder för sin samtid framställa det nya Italiens barn med deras älskvärda naivitet, deras öfverdrifna lidelsefullhet och patos och äfven deras skriande andliga lyten".

51 "den ekonomiska och moraliska ruin, som drabbar många (här *alla*) spelsjukans offer, är på ett mycket drastiskt sätt beskrifven".

52 "fullt mönstergill".

modern reader is the fact that some "unessential details of descriptions" have been excluded or abridged "for the benefit of the Swedish reader" (Nyblom, 1892, p. II).[53]

Two reviews of Serao's major novel deserve to be mentioned in more detail. The *Aftonbladet* reviewer Georg Nordensvan (1855-1932) started out as a writer and sympathized with the new literary currents of the 1880's but is better known for his work as an art historian (*NF*, 1904-1926 (1913), p. 1279). Although familiar with the new Italian literature, the critic, similarly to C.R. Nyblom, saw Serao as "very representative of the Italian people that she portrayed" with love and courage, but also with accuracy of description (Nordensvan, 1892, p. 5).[54] Out of Serao's novels he placed *Fantasia* above *Il paese di Cuccagna* but pointed out that both are "novels of passions" (*ibid.*).[55] Nordensvan's parallels to Zola concern both Serao's comprehensive descriptions and the organization of the novel: "Similarly to Zola, Matilde Serao has lots of characters at her disposal and lets every one of them come in contact with the novel's focal point, which is the lottery" (*ibid.*).[56] Since the novel aims at depicting a flaw in the national character, the portrayal cannot but be tendentious, according to Nordensvan, but the vivid and colourful rendering of Neapolitan life sustains the reader's interest throughout the whole story (*ibid.*).

Hjalmar Sandberg (1844-1923) reviewed *Il paese di Cuccagna* for *Svenska Dagbladet* where he was editor-in-chief between 1888 and 1891 and to which he later collaborated as a critic of art and literature. As such he was probably responsible for introducing Serao to Swedish readers in the pages of his newspaper, in particular her stories from *Piccole anime*, which he also mentions in his review. Sandberg had a special interest in Italian literature – in 1877 he earned his doctoral degree with a dissertation on Giuseppe Giusti, and he later translated Italian poetry and *Aida*'s libretto (*NF*, 1904-1926 (1916), p. 641). At the beginning of his lengthy review, Sandberg points out that Serao, as well as Antonio Fogazzaro, Giovanni Verga and Luigi Capuana, started out as an author

53 "oväsentliga detaljskildringar", "till fromma för svenske läsare".

54 "i mångt och mycket representativ för det folk, hon tillhör och som hon skildrar".

55 "lidelsens roman".

56 "Liksom Zola rör Matilde Serao sig här med hela massor af figurer och låter dem en hvar på sitt vis komma i beröring med det, som utgör skildringens medelpunkt, och detta är här lotteriet".

of short stories, and goes on to give a detailed background on lottery gambling in Italy (Sandberg, 1892). This subject has also been treated by Giusti in literary form, and in both authors the critic recognizes the gender aspect of gambling: "it is men and not women who draw misfortune upon families" (*ibid.*).[57] Although strictly speaking, Serao's book is concerned with only one aspect of Neapolitan life, it is full of sharply individualized characters, according to Sandberg; furthermore, "the novel's tendency does not manifest itself in direct form [and] the subject is artistically treated in all respects" (*ibid.*).[58]

The second Serao novel, published in Sweden the following year, *Castigo* (*Straff*, 1893), did not impress the local critics. Hellen Lindgren, who had earlier praised the realistic art of the Neapolitan author (Lindgren, 1890), declares without further ado in *Aftonbladet* that *Castigo* "does not belong to the more prominent creations of the Italian writer" (Lindgren, 1893).[59] In spite of the author's usual sensitivity and colourfulness, the reviewer finds the novel lacking in development and moderation, and sees only "a constant fortissimo and repetition of the same motive [...] a continuous intensification, where every sentence is a crescendo with stronger and more violent adjectives" (*ibid.*).[60] As such, the novel is more of a product of the writer's imagination, which for this critic constitutes a clear disadvantage. For Lindgren, the reason behind this "blunder" by the "undisputedly gifted"[61] Neapolitan author lies in the necessity to produce as many novels as possible in order to satisfy the demands of the market (*ibid.*). This line of reasoning is also prominent in the second (anonymous) review in *Nya Dagligt Allehanda*, where it is noted that Serao's book appeared in a new novel series, which, according to the reviewer, was aimed at "offering considerable quantities at a cheap price" while still maintaining "a good quality of output" ("Romanöfversättningar", 1893).[62] As such, the novel should satisfy the demands of "female novel-devourers" since it deals with "love, infidelity, jealousy, revenge",

57 "är det männen, icke qvinnorna, som draga olycka öfver familjen".

58 "Bokens tendens framträder ingenstädes direkt. Ämnet är i detta som i andra hänseenden fullt konstnärligt beherskadt".

59 "hör icke till den italienska författarinnans mera framstående alster".

60 "ett ständigt fortissimo och ett upprepande af samma motiv [...] denna eviga stegring, där hvarje sats är ett crescendo med allt starkare och våldsammare adjektiv".

61 "detta missgrepp af en författarinna med Matilde Seraos obestridda talang".

62 "bjuda ansenliga qvantiteter för billigt pris", "varan äfven qvalitativt måtte blifva god".

"is full of strong passions and dismal, heartrending portrayals" and is "exciting, entertaining, 352 pages long and costs 2.25 crowns" (*ibid.*).[63] The translation was done by the young Ellen Wester (1873-1930) under the pseudonym of E. Weer. The previous year, she had been responsible for the Swedish version of De Amicis *Amore e ginnastica* [*Gymnastik och kärlek*], and she would later become an important translator, mostly from Slavic languages (Skuncke – Wester, n.d.).[64]

The last of Serao's novels to be introduced to Swedish readers, in 1903, was *La ballerina* [*Dansösen*] (1899), translated by Ernst Lundquist (1851-1938), who had previously been responsible for the publication of *O Giovannino o la morte* [*Giovannino eller döden*] by *Aftonbladet*. It is significant that his name appears in full in both cases – Lundquist was one of Sweden's best-known translators and his signature was considered "a guarantee of quality" (Håkanson – Rehn, n.d.).[65] Thematically, this novel may be seen as a return to the more humble characters of Neapolitan society that had populated Serao's earlier fiction, after her excursion to the world of the affluent in *Castigo* and other novels. Fredrik Vetterlund (1865-1960), a literary critic and a promoter of idealist romanticism alongside af Wirsén, reviewed this short novel for *Aftonbladet*, praising Serao's ability to create vivid portraits of her characters. He mentions Zola's strong influence on Serao's descriptive art, while noting that the surprising development of the plot could hardly be considered in line with the approach of the French master (Vetterlund, 1903). The critic concludes that Serao succeeds in attaining the truly touching without being sentimental and underlines the usually good quality of Lundquist's translation (*ibid.*).

The following years saw a diminished interest in Serao's fiction in Sweden, with a minor revival in the 1920s when the women's weekly magazine *Idun* published *Fantasia* and a few of her stories in new translations. It is difficult to speculate about the reasons for this decline – the publication of Serao's short stories in the Swedish mass media all but ceased after 1897. However, interest in Serao's public persona

63 "romanslukerskan", "om kärlek, otrohet, svartsjuka, hämnd, den är fyld af starka lidelser, dystra, gripande skildringar, den är spännande, underhållande, 352 sidor stark och kostar 2 kr. 25 öre".

64 http://www.oversattarlexikon.se/artiklar/Ellen_Wester (last accessed 21 December 2020).

65 "ansågs borga för kvalitet", http://www.oversattarlexikon.se/artiklar/Ernst_Lundquist (last accessed 21 December 2020).

remained constant for another couple of years and culminated in the accusations of corruption in the wake of senator Saredo's investigation.

## MATILDE SERAO AS A PUBLIC FIGURE

In 1893, both *Svenska Dagbladet* and *Stockholms Dagblad* reported on the "literary lawsuit" surrounding Matilde Serao's rights to the column "Api, mosconi e vespe" after she left *Il Corriere di Napoli* and started *Il Mattino* with Scarfoglio ("Litterär process", 1893a, 1893b). In the first years of the new century, the news of Serao's separation from her husband, the subsequent trial concerning their financial undertakings and the publication of Scarfoglio's love letters to the actress Lydia Gautier all made it to the pages of the major Swedish newspapers *Svenska Dagbladet* and *Dagens Nyheter.* Another kind of reporting of a more cheerful nature treated Serao's journalistic activities and her articles for *Il Mattino,* in which she answered readers' questions. These articles, published in *Göteborgs Aftonblad*, gave an insight into Neapolitan manners and traditions and concerned family life, how to get engaged, the size of a dowry, suitable wedding gifts and so on ("Dag för dag", 1899; "Ur en romanförfattarinnans breflåda", 1900).

In the autumn of 1901, major Swedish newspapers reported extensively on Serao's implication in senator Saredo's corruption investigation. The Italian government appointed Giuseppe Saredo (1832-1902) head of a commission to curb corruption and political malpractice in Naples' municipal and provincial administration. His investigation lead to the resignation of the city's mayor and exposed the extensive involvement of high-ranking officials and dignitaries in illicit activities, indicated as *alta camorra.*[66] If the first article in *Svenska Dagbladet*, entitled "Corruption in Naples" ("Korruptionen i Neapel", 1901a), expressed astonishment that the prominent author figured in Saredo's report, the articles of *Dagens Nyheter* were entitled plainly "Matilde Serao and the camorra" on three occasions ("Camorran och Mathilde Serao", 1901; "Mathilde Serao och

66 See Sinisi, 2017, http://www.treccani.it/enciclopedia/giuseppe-saredo_%28Dizionario-Biografico%29/ (last accessed 20 December 2020).

camorran", 1901a, 1901b). Several other newspapers reported about the accusations that Serao had accepted money in return for positions in the public administration of Naples. Scarfoglio's and Serao's combative replies to Saredo's accusations were published by Swedish media and became news in their own right. Swedish journalists commented with some amusement on the eloquent replies of the famous couple partly because of completely different rhetorical traditions – where Italians prefer hyperbole, Swedes opt for understatement. Matilde Serao's letter in her defence, published in Germany by *Berliner Tagesblatt*, was reprinted in full both by *Svenska Dagbladet* ("Korruptionen i Neapel", 1901b) and *Dagens Nyheter* (in different translations), the latter describing it as an interesting "document humain" ("Mathilde Serao och camorran", 1901a). In December 1901 a long virulent comment on Serao's defence was published by *Svenska Dagbladet* in "Bref från Italien" ["A Letter from Italy"] by the pseudonymous A.A., which I unfortunately have not been able to decipher. The author gives a historic background to corruption in Southern Italy before delivering a ferocious attack on the Neapolitan writer:

> Who feels sympathy for her bombastic reply: 'how dare they defame and smear me, a woman, a mother, a writer, without giving me the right to defend myself' etc. etc. The whole world knows that she is *not* what a spouse and mother should be, and the time has come to unmask the way she pursues journalism. – Ah, it is enough to see her, this vulgar type, enough to hear her voice, her laugh, to judge her character. [...] If these words came from someone else than Matilde Serao, perhaps they could have persuaded the reader that an innocent has been condemned, but now they are not convincing. It is sad that a writer of such indisputable talent as Matilde Serao could sink so low ("Bref från Italien", 1901, p. 7).[67]

For this anonymous author, Serao, as a professional journalist and editor, does not correspond to traditional gender models, and the same goes for

67 "Hvem känner väl deltagande för hennes uppstyltade: 'Mig, en kvinna, mig, en familjemoder, mig en författarinna, vågar man smäda och smutskasta, utan att gifva mig rätt till försvar', etc. etc. Hela världen vet att hon är allt hvad en maka och moder icke bör vara, och att tiden är inne att afslöja det sätt, på hvilket hon bedrifver journalism. – Ah, det är nog att se henne, denna vulgära typ, nog att höra hennes röst, hennes skratt, för att bedöma karaktären. [...] Om dessa ord kommit från en annan än Matilde Serao, hade de kanske kunnat öfvertyga om att en oskyldig blifvit dömd, men nu förmå de det ej. Sorgligt är, att en författarinna, med den obestridliga talang Matilde Serao besitter, kunnat sjunka så djupt".

her external appearance.[68] By the standards of the time,[69] women should content themselves with a subordinate position in the public space, and the transgression of gender stereotypes easily resulted in accusations of immorality and unnaturalness or falseness. Apart from the gendered aspect of this clearly misogynistic critique directed against Serao, the text contains the common element of exoticism regarding the Italian national character. The author notes that "Italy is a land of great contrasts" with regard to the landscape and wonders if it is "strange that the national character exhibits the same contradictions?" (*ibid.*).[70] Such coexistence of contradictions would then explain the fact that a talented writer can be guilty of corruption. So even if the ferocity of this attack on Serao is quite surprising, it is probable that quite a few commentators in Sweden saw Serao as guilty of the accusations levelled against her – the fact that a report by a senior government official could have been manipulated in some way would have been difficult to imagine for many Swedes.

In March 1903 *Aftonbladet, Dagens Nyheter* and *Svenska Dagbladet* reported that a tribunal in Naples acquitted Serao on all charges, and the court decision was greeted with lively ovations. It is hard to say whether all the bad publicity connected with the Saredo investigation influenced Serao's reception in Sweden in any profound way, but the fact that *La ballerina* was published in Swedish translation *after* the acquittal in May 1903 does not seem accidental in this context.

In the Swedish encyclopedia *Nordisk familjebok,* Matilde Serao was afforded an article of twenty-six lines (*NF*, 1904-1926 (1917), pp. 131-132). It was probably authored by Georg Nordensvan, who was responsible for

68 Ten years later, Swedish correspondent John Hertz would make sarcastic remarks about the body of "Italy's most distinguished female journalist", stereotyping her as distinctively Southern when they found themselves next to each other during the commemorative ceremony of Italy's unification: "The temperamental Neapolitan writer, whose voluminous proportions and air of authority represent a *matrona* type of dimensions unusual in Northern latitudes, commented loudly and uninhibitedly on both the speakers and the audience" ("Italiens förnämsta kvinnliga journalist", "Den temperamentfulla neapolitanska romanförfattarinnan, som med sin volym och pondus representerar en matronatyp af på nordligare breddgrader sällsynta dimensioner, kommenterade lika högljudt som ogeneradt omväxlande talarna och publiken" (Hertz, 1911).

69 For recent scholarship on gender roles in the public sphere during this period, see Mitchell – Sanson, 2013.

70 "Italien är de stora motsatsernas land. [...] Är det underligt om landets folkkaraktär bjuder på samma motsatser?".

many Italian biographies and who joined the editorial committee of the encyclopedia two years later. The article gives a detailed enumeration of Serao's journalistic activities and books up to *L'anima semplice: Suor Giovanna della Croce* (1901). It states that Serao's narrative art, influenced by French Naturalism, is "vivid and natural; polemical tendencies against the shortcomings of society are rarely missing, but they do not overshadow the actual material being observed" (*NF*, 1904-1926 (1917), p. 131).[71] Gunhild Bergh, in her *Modern italiensk litteratur* (1930), which until the present day remains the only history of post-Risorgimento literature in Swedish, treats Serao along with other Verists in the first chapter dedicated to the "Regionalist novel" ["Regionalistisk roman"]. She there repeats the well-known opinions of Benedetto Croce, who regarded Serao as a great observer of environments she was familiar with and as less skilled at constructing consistent novelistic plots (Bergh, 1930, pp. 23-26). What may seem most remarkable today is the fact that the Neapolitan author is granted three pages, while her Verist colleagues Capuana and De Roberto get only two pages each.

## CONCLUSIONS

The reception of Matilde Serao's works in late nineteenth-century Sweden may seem to be the result of different fortunate and adverse circumstances, of the contributions of individual cultural mediators, of global literary trends and of specific editorial decisions. The conservative critic and permanent secretary of the Swedish Academy C.D. af Wirsén made an important contribution by introducing Serao's original work to the Swedish public in his seven articles. In spite of his scepticism about this Neapolitan author's "ultrarealistic" tendencies, af Wirsén helped to establish Serao's reputation as an important Italian writer with a unique colourful style, as a master of description and as an insightful painter of human passions. The diffusion of Serao's narratives in Sweden was facilitated by the fact that she was an author of short stories at a time

71 "liffull och naturlig, polemiska tendenser mot samhälleliga brister saknas sällan, men få icke öfverväldiga det faktiska iakttagelsematerialet".

when newspapers frequently published new fiction on their pages, sometimes in serial form. The family of the academy member C.R. Nyblom had an important role in promoting Serao's work in Sweden, authoring prefaces to her volumes and – in the case of Ellen Nyblom – translating her works into Swedish. Contrary to af Wirsén's orientation, they chose to promote Serao as a representative of the new Italy's realist school and concentrated on her verist narrative, especially *Il paese di Cuccagna*. Serao's moderate Verism, her accurate portrayal of the common people and of the psychological workings of passions, garnered admiration from Swedish critics. The Neapolitan writer was often described as a true daughter of her country by critics, but behind this labelling lies a certain essentializing tendency to regard Serao's work as a product of Neapolitan society and southern nature rather than to interpret it in a contemporary Italian literary context. In the wake of the critical success of the anthology *From the New Italy* (1890) and *Il paese di Cuccagna* in 1892, Swedish editors published *Castigo*, one of Serao's less successful novels, in 1893. This choice turned out to be a disappointment, and it would take ten years before another Serao novel, *La ballerina* [*Dansösen*], appeared in Swedish translation. With the benefit of hindsight, we can conclude that things could have worked out differently – the Swedish 1890's could have been a perfect time for the Neapolitan author's fiction, which was permeated with sensuality, fantasy, romance and beauty. In Sweden as in many other European countries, the Naturalist and socially-oriented narrative of the 1880s was succeeded by the more aesthetically sensitive literature of the 1890s, and this is also corroborated by the enthusiastic reception of D'Annunzio. Unfortunately, the Swedish translation of *Fantasia*, which was carried out in Finland, never made it to Sweden (the domestic translation was carried out only in 1921-1922), and after *Castigo*'s lack of success editors were unwilling to translate another of Serao's passionate novels. Swedish translations of Serao's texts, which were not examined in this essay, may constitute an interesting field for further research. In particular, it would be intriguing to see what parts of *Il paese di Cuccagna* were omitted in the translation, and also to compare different translations of the same short stories carried out during this period and later over the course of the twentieth century. In spite of the declining amount of Swedish translations after 1900, Serao continued to be a well-known public figure and kept appearing on the pages of

Swedish newspapers, especially in connection with the scandal caused by the Saredo corruption investigation. The author who often depicted and criticized the shortcomings of the national Italian character was now attributed similar moral flaws and became a victim of old ethnic prejudices and gender stereotypes. Serao was eventually cleared of all charges, and her enduring popularity in Sweden is testified to by her presence in encyclopedias, and even more significantly by the fact that she was nominated for the Nobel prize at the beginning of the 1920s.

Igor TCHEHOFF
Uppsala University

## MATILDE SERAO'S FICTION TRANSLATED INTO SWEDISH

Serao Matilde, 1890, *Från det nya Italien. En samling berättelser* [*From the New Italy: A Collection of Stories*; it contains Serao's "La settimana delle novelle (Anniversario)"/"En *öfverlöpare*", "Novella d'amore"/"Kärlek", "Salvazione"/ "Räddning", "All'erta, sentinella" / "Fången på Nisida"], trans. Ellen Lundberg-Nyblom, Stockholm, Fahlcrantz.

Serao Matilde, 1891, *Väninnor* [*Fantasia*], trans. unkown, Helsinki, Nya Pressensföljetongsbibliotek.

Serao Matilde, 1892, *Luftslott. Napolitansk sedeskildring* [*Il paese di Cuccagna*], trans. Ellen Lundberg-Nyblom, Stockholm, H. Geber.

Serao Matilde, 1893, *Straff: roman* [*Castigo*], trans. E. Weer [pseud. of Ellen Wester], Stockholm, Hökerberg.

Serao Matilde, 1895, *Giovannino eller döden* [*O Giovannino o la morte*], trans. Ernst Lundquist, Helsinki, NyPressens följetongsbibliotek.

Serao Matilde, 1903, *Dansösen* [*La ballerina*], trans. Ernst Lundquist, Stockholm, Ljus.

# REFERENCES[1]

## ARCHIVAL SOURCES

Unpublished and uncatalogued material from the Archive of the Swedish Academy.

## PRINTED SOURCES

"Actualidad extranjera", 1903, "Actualidad extranjera: Matilde Serao", *Heraldo Alavés: Diario independiente de la tarde*, 3, 19 November, p. 1.

Alas "Clarín" Leopoldo, 1898, "Palique", *El Heraldo de Madrid*, IX, 13 February, p. 1.

Alexandrova Nadezhda, 2012, *Robini, kukli ichelovetsi. Predstavi za zhenite v periodikata na Vazrazhdaneto i v prozata na Lyuben Karavelov* [*Slaves, Dolls, Individuals: Representations of Women in Nineteenth-Century Bulgarian Periodicals, and in Ljuben Karavelov's Fiction*], Sofia, Sonm.

Amoia Alba, 1996, *20$^{th}$-Century Italian Women Writers: The Feminine Experience*, Carbondale – Edwardsville, Southern Illinois University Press.

Añaza Ramiro de, 1912, "El feminismo en la música", *La prensa: diario republicano*, I, 1 June, p. 1.

Andersin Hanna, 1892, "Etelä-Euroopan nykyisen kaunokirjallisuuden alalta. Italialaista nykykirjallisuutta. Italialaista romanikirjallisuutta" ["On Contemporary Literature from Southern Europe. Contemporary Italian Literature. Italian Novel"], *Valvoja*, 11, 1 November 1892, pp. 550-567.

Andreev Ivan, 1851, *Kratka geografia matematicheska, fizicheska i politicheska* [*A*

1 As specified in the Introduction, bibliographical details of Serao's works of fiction in translation are given at the end of the relevant chapters.

*Brief Mathematical, Physical and Political Geography*], Bucharest, Kopainogova knigopechatnitza.

Annenskaya Alexandra *et al.* (eds), 1908, *O detskih knigah: Kritiko-bibliograficheskij ukazatel' knig, vyshedshih do 1 janvarja 1907 g., rekomenduemyh dlja chtenija detjam v vozraste ot 7 do 16 let* [*Children's Book: Critical Bibliographical Index of Books Published before January 1, 1907, Recommended for Reading for Children Aged between 7 and 16*], Moscow, Trud.

Araujo Gómez Fernando, 1900, "Matilde Serao", *La España moderna*, December, pp. 174-178.

"Art, Fashion, and Gossip", 1887, "Art, Fashion, and Gossip in London", *Irish Times*, 5 November, p. 7.

Asor Rosa Alberto, 2009, *Storia europea della letteratura*, vol. 1, *Le origini e il Rinascimento*, Turin, Einaudi.

Assmann Jan – John Czaplicka, 1995, "Collective Memory and Cultural Identity", *New German Critique*, 65, pp. 125-133.

Assmann Aleida, 2010, "Canon and Archive", *A Companion to Cultural Memory Studies*, ed. Astrid Erll – Ansgar Nünning, Berlin, De Gruyter, pp. 97-107.

Badalić Tanja, 2014, *Reception of European Women Writers in Slovenian MulticulturalTerritory of the 19th Century until the End of the First World War*, Ph.D. diss., University of Nova Gorica, http://www.ung.si/~library/doktorati/interkulturni/32Badalic.pdf.

Balestracci Fiammetta, 2006, "L'editoria come transfer culturale. Autori e libri italiani nel sistema editoriale tedesco 1880-1945", *Italiani in Germania tra Ottocento e Novecento. Spostamenti, rapporti, immagini, influenze*, ed. Gustavo Corni – Christof Dipper, Bologna, Il Mulino, pp. 393-413.

Banti Anna, 1965, *Matilde Serao*, Turin, UTET.

Bauman Zygmunt, 1996, "From Pilgrim to Tourist, or a Short History of Identity", *Questions of Cultural Identity*, ed. Stuart Hall – Paul Du Gay, London, Sage Publications, pp. 18-36.

Bauman Zygmunt, 1997, "Tourists and Vagabonds: Heroes and Victims of Postmodernity", *Postmodernity and its Discontents*, Cambridge, Polity, pp. 83-94.

Ben-Arieh Yehoshua, 1979, *The Rediscovery of the Holy Land in the Nineteenth Century*, Detroit, Wayne State University Press.

Benjamin Walter, 2008, "Paris, the Capital of the Nineteenth Century", *The Work of Art in the Ages of its Technological Reproducibility and Other Writings in Media*, ed. Michael Jennings – Brigit Doherty – Thomas Levin, Cambridge, MA, Harvard University Press, pp. 96-115.

Berger Henning, 1908, "Franska teater" ["French Theatre"], *Nya Pressen*, 16, 18 January, p. 3.

Bergh Gunhild, 1930, *Modern italiensk litteratur* [*Modern Italian Literature*], Stockholm, Naturoch kultur.

Berman Antoine, 2000, "Translation and the Trials of the Foreign", *The Translation Studies Reader*, ed. Lawrence Venuti, London – New York, Routledge, pp. 240-253.

Blanck W. de, 1910, "Modesto homenaje a un gran modesto. George Hérelle, príncipe de los traductores", *Diana: revista ilustrada,* II, 40, 10 June, pp. 7-8.

Bordonada Angela Ena (ed.), 2013, *La otra Edad de Plata: temas, géneros y creadores (1898-1936),* Madrid, Editorial Complutense.

Borgese Giuseppe Antonio, 1910, "San Gennaro secondo Matilde Serao", *La Vita e il Libro,* 3 vols, Turin, Bocca, vol. 1, pp. 375-386.

Bourget Paul, 1892, *La Terre promise,* Paris, Alphonse Lemerre.

Bourget Paul, 1895, *The Land of Promise,* New York, F. Tennyson Neely Publisher.

Bracco Roberto, 1941, "La più vera Matilde Serao (Dopo la sua morte)", *Nell'arte e nella vita,* Lanciano, Carabba, pp. 101-109.

"Bref från Italien", 1901, "Bref från Italien. Apropos Neapelskandalerna" ["A Letter from Italy: Apropos of the Scandals in Naples"], *Svenska Dagbladet,* 16 December, pp. 7-8.

Brendon Piers, 1991, *Thomas Cook: 150 Years of Popular Tourism,* London, Secker and Warburg.

Brilli Attilio, 2009, *Il viaggio in Oriente,* Bologna, Il Mulino.

Britannica, The Editors of Encyclopaedia, 2021, "William Heinemann", *Encyclopedia Britannica,* https://www.britannica.com/biography/William-Heinemann.

Broomans Petra, 2009, "Introduction: Women as Transmitters of Ideas", *From Darwin to Weil: Women as Transmitters of Ideas,* ed. Petra Broomans, Groningen, Barkhuis, pp. 1-20.

Burgos Carmen de, 1905, "Misión educadora de la mujer en el periodismo", *Unión Ibero-americana,* 19, 31 December, pp. 85-86.

Butler Judith, 1997, *Excitable Speech: A Politics of the Performative,* London – New York, Routledge.

Buzzi Giancarlo, 1981, *Invito alla lettura di Matilde Serao,* Milan, Mursia.

"Camorran och Mathilde Serao", 1901, "Camorran och Mathilde Serao. Ett pikant svaromål" ["The Camorra and Mathilde Serao. A Piquant Answer"], *Dagens Nyheter,* 29 November, p. 2.

Castro Cristóbal de, 1904, "Las mujeres del día", *Los Lunes del Imparcial,* 38, 22 October, p. 3.

Cavaglion Alberto, 2016, *Verso la Terra Promessa: scrittori italiani a Gerusalemme da Matilde Serao a Pier Paolo Pasolini,* Rome, Carocci.

Cazzato Luigi Carmine, 2017, "Fractured Mediterranean and Imperial Difference: Mediterraneanism, Meridionism, and John Ruskin", *Journal of Mediterranean Studies*, 26, 1, pp. 69-78.

Cecchi Emilio – Sapegno Natalino, 1965-1969, *Storia della letteratura italiana*, 9 vols, Milan, Garzanti.

Coaloa Roberto, 2016, "Il Nobel perso per due inchieste", *Libero*, 12 August, p. 21.

Cohen-Hattab Kobi – Yossi Katz, 2001, "The Attraction of Palestine: Tourism in the Years 1850-1948", *Journal of Historical Geographic*, 27, 2, pp. 166-177.

Colussi Davide, 2009, "Lettere di Leo Spitzer a Benedetto Croce e a Elena Croce", *Annali dell'Istituto Italiano per gli Studi Storici*, 24, pp. 403-478.

Colussi Davide, 2010, "Spitzer e Croce", *Leo Spitzer. Lo stile e il metodo. Atti del XXXVI Convegno Interuniversitario (Bressanone-Innsbruck, 10-13 July 2008)*, ed. Paccagnella – Gregori, Padua, Esedra, pp. 65-83.

"Cómo ha nacido", 1900, "Cómo ha nacido la novela italiana", *La España moderna*, 12, 134, 1 February, pp. 165-168.

Comte Auguste, 1905, "Recuerdos de un diplomático", *La Época*, 22 February, p. 4.

"Congreso feminista", 1908, "Congreso feminista", *Nuestro tiempo*, 8, 5 May, pp. 261-262.

Contini Gianfranco, 1985, "Giustificazione", *Leo Spitzer, Saggi di critica stilistica*, Florence, Sansoni, pp. 7-12.

Contini Maria Teresa (ed.), 1978, *Gli italiani nella fotografia di Mario Nunes Vais*, Catalogo, Florence, Centro D.

Croce Benedetto, 1903, "Note sulla letteratura italiana nella seconda metà del secolo XIX.V. Matilde Serao", *La Critica*, 1, pp. 321-351.

Croce Benedetto, 1919, *Pagine sulla guerra, raccolte da G. Castellano*, Naples, Ricciardi.

Croce Benedetto, 1928, *Scritti vari. Pagine sulla guerra, seconda edizione con aggiunte*, III, Rome – Bari, Laterza.

Croce Benedetto, 1929, "Matilde Serao," *La letteratura della Nuova Italia. Saggi critici*, 6 vols, Rome – Bari, Laterza, vol. 3, pp. 33-72.

"Dag för dag", 1899, "Dag för dag" ["Day by Day"], *Göteborgs Aftonblad*, 2 June, p. 3.

Danchev Ivan, 1911, "Matilda Serao" ["Matilde Serao"], *Mir*, 22 September, p. 3.

D'Annunzio Gabriele, [1891] 1988, *Giovanni Episcopo. Prose di romanzi*, 2 vols, Milan, Mondadori, vol. I, pp. 337-394.

Daskalova Krassimira, 2012, *Zheni, pol i modernizatsia v Balgaria, 1878-1944* [*Women, Gender, and Modernization in Bulgaria, 1878-1944*], Sofia, Universitetsko izdatelstvo "Sv. Kliment Ohridski".

Davey Richard, 1905, "Translator's Note", Matilde Serao, *In the Country of Jesus*, trans. Richard Davey, London, Heinemann, pp. XIII-XIV.

De Brémont Anna, 1911, *Oscar Wilde and his Mother: A Memoir*, London, Everett & Co.

De Caprio Caterina, 2000, "Matilde Serao fra i bauli di Thomas Cook", *Inaffidabili e pellegrini. Viaggiatori italiani tra Ottocento e Novecento*, Naples, Libreria Dante & Descarted, pp. 107-124.

Deledda Grazia, 1913, *Syankata na minaloto* [*Shadows of the Past*], Sofia, D. Yurukova.

De Liso Daniela, 2019, "Matilde Serao, la 'letterata viaggiante'. Storie di vita e di viaggi tra Napoli e il mondo sul finire dell'Ottocento", *Annali della Fondazione Verga*, 12, pp. 179-196.

Della Badia Stefania, 2011, "Inviati speciali e letterati viaggianti," *Il Mattino: 1892-1917*, Naples, Loffredo Editore, pp. 143-164.

De Montera Pierre – Tosi Guy, 1972, *D'Annunzio – Montesquiou – Matilde Serao*, Rome, Edizioni di storia e letteratura.

Di Bitonto Benedetto Francesco, 2009, "Nel Paese di Gesù. Ricordi di un viaggio in Palestina. Teologia della sostituzione di uno scritto napoletano di fine Ottocento", *La Rassegna Mensile d'Israele*, 75, 1-2, pp. 125-142.

"Diversiones públicas", 1915, "Diversiones públicas", *La Época*, 11 May, p. 4.

Dornis Jean, 1907, *Le Roman italien contemporain*, Paris, Ollendorff.

E.G., 1892, "Literaturbref VI. Öfversikt" ["On Literature VI. Overview"], *Nya Pressen*, 303, 6 November, p. 2.

Ekonen Kirsti, 2012, "Slaavilainen kirjasto, ystävyyden ele vai venäläistämisen väline?" ["Slavonic Library – A Gesture of Friendship or a Tool for Russification?"], *Idäntutkimus*, 3, pp. 3-11, http://www.helsinki.fi/idantutkimus/arkisto/2012_3/it_3_2012_ekonen.pdf.

"El aventurero italiano", 1918, "El aventurero italiano: Luca Cortese", *El Liberal*, XL, 7 May, p. 3.

"El país de Jesús", 1910, "El país de Jesús por Matilde Serao", *El Labaro: diario independiente,* XIV, 23 April, p. 2.

Engman, Max, 2009, *Pitkät jäähyväiset. Suomi Ruotsin ja Venäjän välissä vuoden 1809 jälkeen* [*The Long Goodbye: Finland between Sweden and Russia after 1809*], Helsinki, WSOY.

"En italiensk tidningsmannaroman", 1889, "En italiensk tidningsmannaroman" ["An Italian Newspaperman Novel"], *Svenska Dagbladet*, 6 May, p. 2.

"Escritora vengativa", 1905, "Escritora vengativa", *El Castellano,* III, 985, 7 November, p. 1.

Espmark Kjell, 2001, *Litteraturpriset. Hundra år med Nobels uppdrag* [*The Prize in Literature. Hundred Years of Nobel's Assignment*], Stockholm, Norstedts.

Even-Zohar Itamar (ed.), 1990, *Polysystem Studies*, special issue of *Poetics Today: International Journal for Theory and Analysis of Literature and Communication*, 11, 1.
Fanning Ursula, 1994, "Matilde Serao (1856-1927)", *Italian Women Writers: A Bio-Bibliographical Sourcebook*, ed. Russell Rinaldina, Westport, Greenwood Press, pp. 386-394.
Fanning Ursula, 2002, *Gender Meets Genre: Woman as Subject in the Fictional Universe of Matilde Serao*, Dublin, Irish Academic Press.
Fanning Ursula, 2006, "Aspetti inaspettati dell'amicizia femminile nel lavoro di Matilde Serao", *Matilde Serao. Le opere e i giorni*, ed. Angelo R. Pupino, Naples, Liguori, pp. 125-137.
Fanning Ursula, 2007, "From Domestic to Dramatic: Matilde Serao's Use of the Gothic", *The Italian Gothic and Fantastic: Encounters and Rewritings of Narrative Traditions,* ed. Francesca Billiani – Gigliola Sulis, Madison – Teaneck, Fairleigh Dickinson University Press, pp. 119-138.
Fanning Ursula, 2013, "Maternal Prescriptions and Descriptions in Post-Unification Italy", *Women and Gender in Post-Unification Italy: Between Private and Public Spheres*, ed. Katharine Mitchell – Helena Sanson, Oxford, Peter Lang, pp. 13-37.
Ferrandiz José, 1910, "El país de Jesús", *El País*, XXIV, 8, 19 April, p. 1.
Ferroni Giulio, 1991, *La storia della letteratura italiana. Dall'Ottocento al Novecento*, Turin, Einaudi.
Ferroni Giulio, 2002, *Storia e testi della letteratura italiana*, Milan, Mondadori.
Fitzsimons Eleanor, 2015, "Entering *The Woman's World*: Oscar Wilde as Editor of a Woman's Magazine", *The Victorian Web*, https://victorianweb.org/.
Fogazzaro Antonio – Starbuch Ellen, 2000, *Carteggio (1885-1910)*, ed. Luciano Morbiato, Vicenza, Accademia Olimpica.
Fogu Claudio, 2020, *The Fishing Net and the Spider Web: Mediterranean Imaginaries and the Making of Italians*, Cham, Springer International Publishing/Palgrave Macmillan.
F.M., 1927, "Matilde Serao", *La Revista blanca*, 6, 126, 1 September, p. 12.
Frice Vladimir, 1911, "Dve ital'janskie romanistki" ["Two Italian Novelists"], *Novy Zhurnal Dlya Vseh*, 35, pp. 95-102.
Fuks E.V., 1907, "Matilde Serao. Iz lichnyh vospominanij" ["Matilde Serao. From Personal Memories"], *Zhensky Vestnik*, 4, pp. 117-119.
Genette Gérard, 1976, *Figures I*, Paris, Seuil.
G.H.T., 1907, "Kvinnan i tidningsvärlden" ["Woman in the World of the Press"], *Nya Pressen*110, 25 April, p. 4.
Gimeno de Flaquer Concepción, 1899, "Gemma Ferruggia", *El Álbum ibero-americano*, 24, 30 June, pp. 278-280.

Gimeno de Flaquer Concepción, 1900a, "Mujeres del siglo XX", *El Álbum ibero-americano*, 28, 30 July, pp. 554-556.

Gimeno de Flaquer Concepción, 1900b, "Mujeres del siglo XIX" *El Álbum ibero-americano*, 47, 22 December, pp. 554-556.

Gimeno de Flaquer Concepción, 1902, "Novelistas contemporáneas. Matilde Serao", *El Álbum ibero-americano*, 30 May, pp. 280-281.

Gimeno de Flaquer Concepción, 1908, "Crónica femenina y feminista", *El Álbum ibero-americano*, 14 June, p. 2.

Gisolfi Anthony, 1968, *The Essential Matilde Serao*, New York, Las Americas Pub. Co.

Gladstone William, 1879, *Gleanings of Past Years, 1843-1878*, London, J. Murray.

Goethe Johann Wolfgang von, [1816-1817] 2008, *Italienische Reise [Italian Journey]*, Grünwald, Stiebner Verlag.

Gosse Edmund (ed.), 1890, *Fantasy: A Novel*, trans. Henry Harland – Paul Sylvester, London, William Heinemann.

Green Stephanie Summer 1997, "Oscar Wilde's *The Woman's World*", *Victorian Periodicals Review*, 30, 2, pp. 102-120.

Guerra Ángel, 1903, "Grazia Deledda", *La Época*, 29 January, pp. 1-2.

Guerra Ángel, 1904, "La poesía actual en Italia", *La Ilustración española y americana*, 48, 28, 30 July, pp. 51-55.

Guerra Ángel, 1905a, "Emilia Pardo Bazán", *El Globo. Diario independiente*, XXI, 16 February, p. 1.

Guerra Ángel, 1905b, "Un novelista. Victor Catalá", *La Epoca*, 16 December, p. 3.

Guerra Ángel, 1911, "Las grandes escritoras modernas", *La ilustración artística*, 14 August, p. 527.

Guerra Ángel, 1927a, "Matilde Serao", *El Orzán*, X, 20 August, p. 1.

Guerra Ángel, 1927b, "La nueva novela de Matilde Serao", *La Esfera*, 9 July, p. 30.

Håkanson Nils – Rehn Mats, n. d., "Ernst Lundquist", *Svenskt översättarlexikon* [*Swedish Translator Lexicon*], http://www.oversattarlexikon.se/artiklar/Ernst_Lundquist.

Hermans Theo, 1999, *Translation in Systems: Descriptive and System-Oriented Approaches Explained*, Amsterdam, St. Jerome Publishing.

Hertz John, 1911, "Rom i 50-årsjubileets tecken" ["Rome in the Sign of the 50th Jubilee"], *Dagens Nyheter*, 2 April, p. 5.

Hirn Marja *et al.*, 2010, *Esitys Helsingin yliopiston kirjaston kokoelmapoliittiseksi ohjelmaksi* [*Proposition for a Political Programme of the Helsinki University Library Collection*], http://hdl.handle.net/10138/171788.

Iasci Laura – Sanz Amelia, 2018, "Matilde Serao in the Spanish Digitized

Newspapers: A Collection of References", *E-Prints-UCM*, http://eprints.ucm.es/45974/.

Ilieva Boyka, 2012, *Italia v kulturata na Balgarskoto vazrazhdane. Prevodi i literaturni Vliania* [*Italy in the Culture of the Bulgarian Revival: Translations and Literary Influences*], Blagoevgrad, Universitetsko izdatelstvo "Neofit Rilski".

"In the Country of Jesus", 1905, "In the Country of Jesus", *London Evening Standard*, 1 December, p. 6.

"In the Country of Jesus", 1906, "In the Country of Jesus [review]", *The Independent*, 60, 24 May, p. 1226.

Isomaa Saija, 2012, "Kirjallisuus ja moraaliset emootiot. Tendenssikirjallisuuden 1800-lukulainen lajitausta" ["Literature and Moral Emotions: The Poetics of the Nineteenth-Century Nordic *Tendensroman*"], *Kirjallisuudentutkimuksen aikakauslehti AVAIN*, 3, pp. 5-19.

James Henry, 1901, "Matilde Serao", *North American Review*, 172, pp. 367-380.

James Henry, 1914, *Notes on Novelists*, London, J.M. Dent & Sons.

James Henry, 1920, *Letters*, 2 vols, New York, Scribner, vol. 1, pp. 268-271.

J.D., 1917, "Matilde Serao", *La Moda elegante. Periódico especial de señoras y señoritas, indispensable en toda casa de familia*, 76, 40, 30 October, pp. 184-185.

Jeuland-Meynaud Maryse, 1973, *La Ville de Naples après l'annexion, 1860-1915*, Aix-Marseille, Éditions de l'Université de Provence.

Jockers Matthew L., 2013, *Macroanalysis: Digital Methods and Literary History*, Urbana – Chicago – Springfield, University of Illinois Press.

Jokinen Ulla, 1986, "Italian kaunokirjallisuuden kääntäminen suomeksi" ["Translation of Italian Fiction into Finnish"], *Rapporti culturali tra Italia e Finlandia. Atti del convegno, Turku/Åbo 26-27 settembre 1986*, ed. Lauri Lindgren, Turku – Åbo, Henrik Gabriel Porthan Instituutti/Institutet, pp. 155-167.

*Kansan Lehti*, 1908, Publicity of Serao's novel, *Kansan Lehti*, 168, 25 July p. 2.

Karttunen Liisi, 1927, "Kirjallisuus ja taide: Matilde Serao" ["Literature and Art: Matilde Serao"], *Helsingin Sanomat*, 207, 4 August, p. 5.

King James Bible, https://www.kingjamesbibleonline.org/Luke-17-2/

Kivistö Sari – Riikonen H. K., 2007, "Käännöstoiminta työväenliikkeen piirissä" ["Translation Activity in the Workers' Movement"], *Suomennoskirjallisuuden historia II, [History of Literary Translation into Finnish II]*, Helsinki, Suomalaisen Kirjallisuuden Seura, pp. 349-356.

Klinge Matti, 1990, *Let Us Be Finns: Essays on History*, trans. Martha Gaber Abrahamsen Mary Lomas – Mirja Lavanne – David Morris, Helsinki, Otava.

Knapas Rainer, 2012, *The Helsinki University Library – The National Library in Finland: 1640-2010*, Helsinki, Suomalaisen Kirjallisuuden Seura.

Konstantinova Zdravka, 2012, "'Zhenski svyat' – parvoto ni sledosvobozhdensko periodichno izdanie za zheni" ["Women's World" – The First Bulgarian Women's Periodical after the Liberation], *Medii i obshtestveni komunikatsii*, 12, http://www.media-journal.info/?p=item&aid=183.

"Konst och litteratur", 1890a, "Konst och litteratur" ["Art and Literature"], *Härnösandsposten*, 21 November, p. 3.

"Konst och litteratur," 1890b, "Konst och litteratur" ["Art and Literature"], *Svenska Dagbladet*, 27 November, p. 3.

"Konst och litteratur", 1890c, "Konst och litteratur" ["Art and Literature"], *Göteborgs Aftonblad*, 13 December, p. 3.

"Korruptionen i Neapel", 1901a, "Korruptionen i Neapel" ["Corruption in Naples"], *Svenska Dagbladet*, 29 October, p. 1.

"Korruptionen i Neapel", 1901b, "Korruptionen i Neapel. Ett bref från Matilde Serao", ["Corruption in Naples. A Letter from Matilde Serao"], *Svenska Dagbladet*, 27 December, p. 7.

Koskenniemi Veikko Antero, 1913, Review of *Vartia, pidä varasi!* [*All'erta, sentinella!*], *Kirjastolehti*, 10, 1 December, p. 173.

Kradetskaya Susanna, 2013, "Women's Herald (1904-1917): The Editing Experience of the Feminist Journal in Russia", *Woman in Russian Society*, 1, pp. 72-81.

Kroha Lucienne, 1987, "Matilde Serao's Fantasia: An Author in Search of a Character", *The Italianist*, 7, pp. 45-62.

"La condesa", 1921, "La condesa de Pardo Bazán", *La correspondencia de España: diario universal de noticias*, LXXIV, 12 May, p. 5.

"La poetisa del dolor", 1903, "La poetisa del dolor", *La España moderna*, 15, 1 December, pp. 151-172.

Lappalainen Päivi, 2007, "The Politics of Naturalism: Women and Fiction in the 1880s", *Women's Voices: Female Authors and Feminist Criticism in the Finnish Literary Tradition*, ed. Päivi Lappalainen – Lea Rojola, Helsinki, Finnish Literature Society, pp. 35-52.

Larsen Svend Erik, 2011, "Georg Brandes: The Telescope of Comparative Literature", *The Routledge Companion to World Literature*, ed. Theo D'haen – David Damrosch – Djelal Kadir, London – New York, Routledge.

Leclerc Herreros Margarita, 1928, "La mujer, ¿es superior al hombre?", *La voz de Menorca: diario republicano*, XXIII, 17 December, p. 1.

Lefevere André, 1992, *Translation, Rewriting and the Manipulation of Literary Fame,* London, Routledge.

"Libros populares", 1901a, "Libros populares ¡Centinela alerta!", *La Unión republicana*, 6, October, p. 2.

"Libros populares", 1901b, "Libros populares ¡Centinela alerta!", *El País,* XV, 18 October, p. 3.

Lilius Pirkko, 2003, "Suomennoshistorian pohjoismainen perintö" ["The Nordic Heritage of the History of Translating into Finnish"], *Nerontuotteita maailmalta. Näkökulmia suomennosten historiaan* [*Products of Genius from the World: Perspectives on the History of Translating into Finnish*], ed. Pirkko Lilius – Heta Makkonen-Craig, Helsinki, Helsingin yliopiston käännöstieteellisiä julkaisuja 4, MonAKO, Helsingin yliopisto, pp. 28-46.

Lindgren Hellen, 1890, "Från alla håll. En studie i bokmarknaden" ["From Everywhere. A Study of the Book Market"], *Aftonbladet*, 6 December, p. 5.

Lindgren Hellen, 1893, "Konst och litteratur" ["Art and Literature"], *Aftonbladet*, 4 December, p. 3.

"Literärt", 1892, "Literärt" ["On Literature"], *Stockholms Dagblad*, 2 October, p. 3.

"Litteratur", 1890, "Litteratur" ["Literature"], *Västmanlands Läns Tidning*, 18 December, p. 3.

"Literatura", 1900, "Literatura. Matilde Serao", *La España moderna*, 12, 144, 1 December, pp. 171-175.

"Litteratur-revy", 1892, "Litteratur-revy" ["A Literary Review"], *Nya Dagligt Allehanda*, 22 October, p. 3.

"Litterär process", 1893a, "Litterär process" ["A Literary Lawsuit"], *Svenska Dagbladet*, 15 April, p. 4.

"Litterär process", 1893b, "Litterär process" ["A Literary Lawsuit"], *Stockholms Dagblad*, 16 April, p. 5.

Lundberg-Nyblom Ellen, 1907, *Bland italienare. Intryck och upplefvelser* [*Among Italians. Impressions and Experiences*], Stockholm, Wahlström & Widstrand.

Lo Gatto Ettore, 1971, *Russi in Italia*, Rome, Editori riuniti.

Luhmann Niklas, 2000, *Art as a Social System*, Stanford, Stanford University Press.

L. W-r., 1909, "Pienoiskuvia elämästä" ["Miniatures from Life"]. *Raataja* 18 – 19, 25 November, pp. 268-269.

Mäkinen Ilkka, 2009, "Kirjasto fennomaanien kansansivistysohjelmassa" ["Library in the Fennomans' Programme of Educating the People"], *Suomen yleisten kirjastojen historia* [*History of the Public Libraries in Finland*], Helsinki, BTJ Kustannus, pp. 151-213.

Mandal Anthony – Southam Brian (eds), 2007, *The Reception of Jane Austen in Europe,* London, Bloomsbury Publishing.

Mannerheim library A-Ö, 2016, Online catalogue, Mannerheim Museo, https://view.publitas.com/mannerheim-museo/mannerheim-library-a-o/page/1.

Martin-Gistucci Marie Gracieuse, 1973, *L'Oeuvre romanesque de Matilde Serao*, Grenoble, Presses Universitaires.

"Mathilde Serao och camorran", 1901a, "Mathilde Serao och camorran. Ett nytt svar" ["Matilde Serao and the Camorra. A New Answer"], *Dagens Nyheter*, 21 December, p. 2.

"Mathilde Serao och camorran", 1901b, "Mathilde Serao och camorran" ["Matilde Serao and the Camorra"], *Dagens Nyheter*, 27 December, p. 1.

"Matilde Serao om kvinnofrågan", 1909, "Matilde Serao om kvinnofrågan" ["Matilde Serao on the Female Question"], *Svenska Dagbladet*, 21 September, p. 9.

"Matilde Serao", 1905, "Matilde Serao", *The Leeds and Yorkshire Mercury*, 1 December, p. 2.

"Matilde Serao", 1906, "Matilde Serao", *Manchester Courier*, 10 January, p. 10.

"Matilde Serao", 1910, "Matilde Serao", *Helsingin Kaiku*, 22, p. 33.

Melis Rossana, 2009, "Tra filologia e opera d'arte: il Manuale della letteratura italiana di Francesco Torraca (1886-1887; 1910)", *Il canone letterario nella scuola dell'Ottocento*, ed. Renzo Cremante – Simonetta Santucci, Bologna, Clueb, pp. 279-329.

Melis Rossana, 2010, "Dal saggio su Matilde Serao del 1912 a quello sui Malavoglia del 1956", *Leo Spitzer. Lo stile e il metodo. Atti del XXXVI Convegno Interuniversitario* (Bressanone-Innsbruck, 10-13 July 2008), ed. Paccagnella – Gregori, Padua, Esedra, pp. 497-517.

Melis Rossana, 2011, "Matilde Serao: una voce per le donne nel 'Capitan Fracassa'", *Scrittrici/Giornaliste. Giornaliste/Scrittrici. (Atti del Convegno 'Scritture di donne fra letteratura e giornalismo', Bari, 29 novembre-1° dicembre 2007*, 4 vols), ed. Adriana Chemello – Vanna Zaccaro, Bari, Università degli Studi Aldo Moro, vol. 3, pp. 151-169.

"Menudencias", 1903, "Menudencias", *El radical*, II, 22 November, p. 2.

Mitchell Katharine, 2022, *Gender, Writing, Spectatorships: Evenings at the Theatre, Opera, and Silent Screen in Late Nineteenth-Century Italy and Beyond*, London, Routledge.

Mitchell Katharine, 2014, *Italian Women Writers: Gender and Everyday Life in Fiction and Journalism, 1870-1910*, Toronto, University of Toronto Press.

Mitchell Katharine – Sanson Helena (eds), 2013, *Women and Gender in Post-Unification Italy: Between Private and Public Spheres*, Oxford – Bern, Peter Lang.

Moe Nelson, 2002, *The View from Vesuvius: Italian Culture and the Southern Question*, Berkeley, University of California Press.

Monterrey Margarita-María de, 1903, "Matilde Serao", *Helios*, 1, 1 July, pp. 492-496.

Monticone Alberto, 1971, *La Germania e la neutralità italiana 1914-1915*, Bologna, Il Mulino.

Moretti Franco, 2013, *Distant Reading*, London, Verso.

Muiluvuori Jukka, 2016, "Koskelainen, Yrjö", *Kansallisbiografia-verkkojulkaisu* [Online Publication of the Finnish National Biography], *Studia*

*Biographica*, 4, Helsinki, Suomalaisen Kirjallisuuden Seura, http://urn.fi/urn:nbn:fi:sks-kbg-001625.

Muret Maurice, 1906, *La Littérature italienne d'aujord'hui*, Paris, Perrin.

Nadson Semyon, 1887, *Literaturnye ocherki (1883-1886) S.ya. Nadsona* [*Critical Essays by S.ya. Nadson (1883-1886)*], St Petersburg, Skorokhodov.

National Library of Sweden, *Svenska dagstidningar*, http://www.tidningar.kb.se.

Nazarska Zhorzheta, 2003, *Universitetskoto obrazovanie i balgarskite zheni 1879-1944* [*The University Education and Bulgarian Women 1879-1944*], Sofia, IMIR.

Neera (Anna Radius Zuccari), 1893, *Voci della notte*, Naples, Luigi Pierro.

Nediani Tommaso, 1899, "A proposito di un libro di Matilde Serao", *Cultura sociale, politica, letteraria* 2, 24, 16 December, pp. 382-383.

Negri Ada, 1896, "Liricheski stihotvorenia ot Ada Negri" ["Lyrical Poems by Ada Negri"], *Den*, 8, pp. 704-706.

*NF*, 1904-1926, *Nordisk familjebok* [*Nordic Family Book*], 38 vols, Stockholm, Nordisk familjeboks förlags AB.

Niemi Juhani, 2007, "Antologioiden kulta-aika" ["The Golden Age of Anthologies"], *Suomennoskirjallisuuden historia I.* [*History of Literature Translated into Finnish I*], ed. H.K. Riikonen – Urpo Kovala – Pekka Kujamäki – Outi Paloposki, Helsinki, Suomalaisen Kirjallisuuden Seura, pp. 371-376.

Nordensvan Georg, 1892, "Konst och litteratur" ["Art and Literature"], *Aftonbladet*, 8 October, pp. 5-6.

Nyblom Carl Rupert, 1864, *Bilder från Italien. Tecknade af Carlino* [*Images of Italy. Drawn by Carlino*], Uppsala, W. Schultz.

Nyblom Carl Rupert, 1883, *Ett* år *i Södern. Bilder från Italien tecknade af Carl Rupert Nyblom* [*A Year in the South. Images of Italy by Carl Rupert Nyblom*], Uppsala, W. Schultz.

Nyblom Carl Rupert, 1892, "Förord" ["Preface"], Matilde Serao, *Luftslott. Napolitansk sedeskildring* [*Il paese di Cuccagna*], trans. Ellen Lundberg-Nyblom, Stockholm, H. Geber, pp. I-II.

Nyblom Helena, 1890, "Förord" ["Preface"], Matilde Serao *et al.*, *Från det nya Italien. En samling berättelser* [*From the New Italy. A Collection of Stories*], trans. Ellen Lundberg-Nyblom, Stockholm, Fahlcrantz, pp. I-II.

Obenzinger Hilton, 2009, "Americans in the Holy Land, Israel and Palestine", *The Cambridge Companion to American Travel Writing*, ed. Alfred Bendixen – Judith Hamera, Cambridge, Cambridge University Press, pp. 145-164.

O'Farrell Mary Ann, 2006, "Missing Jane Austen: Henry James Considers the Old Maid", *The Henry James Review*, 27, 1, pp. 1-9.

"Ojeada", 1904, "Ojeada sobre la Italia intelectual", *La España moderna*, July, pp. 190-194.

Ojetti Ugo, 1895, *Alla scoperta dei letterati,* Milan, Dumolard.
Ojetti Ugo, 1899, *Alla scoperta dei letterati,* Milan, Fratelli Bocca.
Ojetti Ugo, 1896-1897, "Dneshnata italianska literatura" ["Present Day Italian Literature"], *Iskra*, 4-5, pp. 715-718.
Oliva Gianni, 2016, "Matilde Serao: il coraggio di esserci e dirlo. Un ritratto della scrittrice autorevole voce dell'Italia unita", *Il Corriere del Ticino*, 30 July, p. 25.
Paccagnella Ivano – Gregori Elisa (eds), 2010, *Leo Spitzer. Lo stile e il metodo. Atti del XXXVI Convegno Interuniversitario* (Bressanone-Innsbruck, 10-13 July 2008), Padua, Esedra.
Palermo, Antonio, 1972, *Da Mastriani a Viviani*, Naples, Liguori.
Pancrazi Pietro, 1944, "Introduzione", Matilde Serao, *Opere*, ed. Pietro Pancrazi, 2 vols, Milan, Garzanti, vol. 1, pp. VII-XXX.
Palosuo Veikko Juhana, 1991, *La dottoressa Liisi Karttunen Roomassa 1907-1944,* Helsinki, Palosuo.
Papini Giovanni, 1904, "Pis'mo iz Italii" ["A Letter from Italy"], *Vesy*, 1, pp. 19-28.
Parente-Čapková Viola – Lappalainen Päivi, 2017, "Transnational Reception: NordicWomen Writers in *Fin de Siècle* Finland", *NORA – Nordic Journal of Feminist and Gender Research*, 25, 4 (special issue: *Gender in Literary Exchange*, ed. Anka Ryall – Anne-Birgitte Rønning), pp. 263-278.
Partzsch Henriette, 2014, "The Complex Routes of Travelling Texts: Fredrika Bremer's Reception in Nineteenth-Century Spain and the Transnational Dimension of Literary History", *Comparative Critical Studies*, 11, 2-3, pp. 281-293.
Petkov Botyu, 1868, *Kratka vseobshta geografia* [*A Brief Universal Geography*], Plovdiv, Pechatnitzata na D. Manchev.
Piazza, Isotta, 2012, "Dal pellegrinaggio al romanzo: la declinazione Cattolica della scrittura di viaggio nel secondo Ottocento", *Viaggiare con i libri. Saggi su editori e viaggi nell'Ottocento*, ed. Gianfranco Tortorelli, Bologna, Edizioni Pendragon, pp. 309-328.
"Pienoiskuvia elämästä", 1909, "Pienoiskuvia elämästä" ["Miniatures from Life"], *Kaiku*, 118, 13 October, p. 9.
Plarr Victor, 1899, "Richard Davey", *Men and Women of the Time: A Dictionary of Contemporaries*, London, George Routledge and Sons, p. 272.
Pupino Angelo Raffaele, 1978, "Matilde Serao in Francia", *Nuovi Argomenti*, 57 (January-March), pp. 233-248.
Pupino Angelo Raffaele, 2004, *Notizie del Reame*, Naples, Liguori.
"¿Qué libros se leen?", 1903, "¿Qué libros se leen en Italia?", *La Lectura*, 15 May, p. 297.

Radulov Sava, 1843, *Stihiyni urotsi zemleopisania* [*Elementary Lessons in Geography*], Smyrna, Tipografia A. Damyanova.

Razzano Pier Luigi, 2016, "L'affresco di donna Matilde che non piaceva al fascismo. L'illusione della Grande Guerra", *La Repubblica*, 9 April, p. 19.

Renzi Lorenzo, 1976, "Presentazione", *Leo Spitzer, Lettere di prigionieri di guerra italiani (1915-1918)*, Turin, Boringhieri, pp. VII-XXXIII.

Revel Jacques (ed.), 1996, *Jeux d'échelles. La micro-analyse à l'expérience*, Paris, Gallimard.

Richards Christine, 1999, "The Critical Point of View: Henry James on Matilde Serao", *The Italianist*, 19, 1, pp. 86-105.

Ricorda Ricciarda, 2011, *Viaggiatrici italiane tra Settecento e Ottocento*, Bari, Palomar.

Rizzi Andrea, 2016, *Le relazioni Italo-Finlandesi nella documentazione del Ministero degli Affari Esteri italiano e nel "Memoriale" di Attilio Tamaro (1929-1935)*, Ph.D. diss., University of Turku, https://www.utupub.fi/bitstream/handle/10024/122992/diss2016Rizzi.pdf?sequence=2%09&isAllowed=y".

Romani Gabriella, 2007, "Matilde Serao (1856-1927)", *Encyclopedia of Italian Literary Studies 2, N-Z*, ed. Marrone Gaetana – Puppa Paolo – Somigli Luca, New York – London, Routledge, pp. 1733-1736.

Romani Gabriella, 2013, *Postal Culture: Reading and Writing Letters in Post-Unification Italy*, Toronto – Buffalo – London, University of Toronto Press.

"Romanöfversättningar", 1893, "Romanöfversättningar" ["Novels in Translation"], *Nya Dagligt Allehanda*, 27 December, p. 6.

Romero Dolores (ed.), 2014, *Los márgenes de la modernidad: temas y creadores raros y olvidados en la otra Edad de Plata*, Sevilla, Punto Rojo.

Rossi Riikka 2007, *Le Naturalisme finlandais – une conception entropique du quotidien,* Helsinki, Finnish Literature Society.

Russ Joanna, 1983, *How to Suppress Women's Writing*, Austin, University of Texas Press.

Rydén Per, 2010, *Den framgångsrike förloraren: en värderingsbiografi över Carl David af Wirsén* [*The Successful Loser. An Evaluative Biography of Carl David af Wirsén*], Stockholm, Carlsson.

Saarenheimo Kerttu, 2000, "V. A. Koskenniemi e l'Italia", *Settentrione. Rivista di studi italo-finlandesi*, n. s., 12, pp. 55-75.

Said Edward, [1978] 1991, *Orientalism: Western Conceptions of the Orient*, London, Penguin.

Said Edward, 1982, "Opponents, Audiences, Constituencies and Community", *Critical Inquiry*, 9, 1, pp. 1-26.

Sainio Venla, 2001, "Andersin, Hanna", *Kansallisbiografia-verkkojulkaisu* [Online publication of the Finnish National Biography], *Studia Biographica,* Helsinki, Suomalaisen Kirjallisuuden Seura, http://urn.fi/urn:nbn:fi:sks-kbg-008548.

Saint-Amour Paul, 2019, "The Medial Humanities: Toward a Manifesto for Meso-Analysis", *M/m*, vol. 3, Cycle 4, 1 Febr. 2019, https://modernismmodernity.org/forums/posts/medial-humanities-toward-manifesto-meso-analysis.

Salsini Laura, 1999, *Gendered Genres: Female Experiences and Narrative Patterns in the Works of Matilde Serao*, London – Madison, Fairleigh Dickinson UP.

Sambuco, Patrizia, 2015, *Italian Women Writers 1800-2000*, Madison – Teaneck, Farleigh Dickinson University Press.

Sandberg Hjalmar, 1892, "Litteratur" ["Literature"], *Svenska Dagbladet*, 3 November, p. 3.

Sarcina Angela, 1995, *La signora del Mattino, con antologia dei Mosconi di Matilde Serao*, Naples, Edizioni la Conchiglia.

Scappaticci Tommaso, 1995, *Introduzione a Serao*, Rome – Bari, Laterza.

Schleiermacher Friedrich, 2003, Extracts from "über die verschiedenen Methoden des Übersetzens" ["On the Different Methods of Translation"], *Translation/History/Culture: A Sourcebook*, ed. Andre Lefevre, New York – London, Routledge, pp. 141-166.

Schneider Jane, 1998, *Italy's Southern Question: Orientalism in One Country*, Oxford, Berg.

Schwartz Cecilia, 2020, "From Nuoro to Nobel: The Impact of Multiple Mediatorship on Grazia Deledda's Movement within the Literary Semi-Periphery", *Topics and Concepts in Literary Translation*, ed. Roberto A. Valdeón, London – New York, Routledge, pp. 68-84.

Scriboni Mirella, 1996, "Il viaggio al femminile nell'Ottocento: la principessa di Belgioioso, Anna Nizzoli e Carla Serena", *Annali d'Italianistica*, 14, pp. 304-325.

"Serao", 1902, "Serao", *La Correspondencia de España: diario universal de noticias*, LIII, 12 March, p. 3.

Serao Matilde, 1879, *Dal vero*, Milan, Perussia & Quadrio.

Serao Matilde, 1881, *Cuore infermo: racconto*, Turin, F. Casanova.

Serao Matilde, 1883a, *Fantasia: romanzo*, Turin, Casanova.

Serao Matilde, 1883b, *Piccole anime*, Rome, A. Sommaruga.

Serao Matilde, 1884a, *Il ventre di Napoli*, Milan, Treves.

Serao Matilde, 1884b, *La virtù di Checchina*, Catania, Giannotta.

Serao Matilde, 1885, "V Zhenskoy shkole" ["Scuola normale femminile"], trans. A.V., Russkaya *Mysl*, 7, pp. 161-193.

Serao Matilde, 1886, *Il romanzo della fanciulla*, Milan, Treves.

Serao, Matilde, 1887, *Vita e avventure di Riccardo Joanna*, Milan, G. Galli.

Serao Matilde, 1888, *Fior di passione: novelle*, Milan, G. Galli.

Serao Matilde, 1889, *All'erta sentinella! Terno Secco. Trenta per cento. O Giovannino o la morte. Racconti napoletani*, Milan, Treves.

Serao Matilde, [1879] 1890, *Dal vero*, Milan, G. Galli.
Serao Matilde, 1891, *Il paese di Cuccagna: romanzo napoletano*, Milan, Treves.
Serao Matilde, 1893, *Castigo*, Turin, F. Casanova.
Serao Matilde, 1898, *Nel paese di Gesù (Ricordi di un viaggio in Palestina)*, Naples, Tocco.
Serao Matilde, 1899, *La ballerina*, Catania, N. Giannotta.
Serao Matilde, 1901a, *L'anima semplice: Suor Giovanna della Croce. Romanzo*, Milan, Fratelli Treves.
Serao Matilde, 1901b, *Ljubov' ubijcy* [*All'erta, sentinella!*], Moscow, Posrednik.
Serao Matilde, 1905, *In the Country of Jesus*, trans. Richard Davey, London, Heinemann.
Serao Matilde, 1906a, *Dopo il perdono*, Rome, Nuova Antologia.
Serao Matilde, 1906b, *Sognando*, Catania, Giannotta.
Serao Matilde, 1908, *Naples: les legendes et la réalité* [*Il ventre di Napoli*], Paris, Félix Juven.
Serao Matilde, 1909, *Evviva la vita: romanzo*, Rome, Nuova Antologia.
Serao Matilde, 1912, *Evviva la guerra! (primavera italica)*, Naples, F. Perrella & C.
Serao Matilde, 1913, *Erzählungen, Skizzen und Sagen* [*Stories, Sketches and Legends*], with notes and glossary by Pia Di Mayo-Gelati, Heidelberg, Groos.
Serao Matilde, 1926, *Mors tua...romanzo in tre giornate*, Milan, Treves.
Serao Matilde, [1881] 1988, *Cuore infermo*, pref. Sandra Petrignani, Rome, Lucarini.
Serao Matilde, [1900] 1989, *Saper vivere: norme di buona creanza*, Florence, Passigli.
Serao Matilde, 1991, *The Conquest of Rome* [*La conquista di Roma*], trans. Ann Caesar, London, Pickering and Chatto.
Serao Matilde, [1894] 1992, "I cavalieri dello Spirito", Antonio Fogazzaro, *Sonatine Bizzarre. Scritti dispersi*, Rome, Ripostes, pp. 53-59.
Serao Matilde, 1994a, "Toukokuu ja San Gennaron ihme" ["Maggio e il miracolo di San Gennaro"], trans. Jukka Nyman, *Settentrione. Rivista di studi italo-finlandesi*, n.s., 6, pp. 169-184.
Serao Matilde, 1994b, *Flor de pasión* ["Fior di passione"], trans. Ramon del Valle Inclán, Madrid, Lipari ediciones.
Serao Matilde, 2006b, "Checchina's Virtue" ["La virtù di Checchina"], *Writing to Delight: Italian Short Stories by Nineteenth-Century Women Writers*, trans. Tom Kelso, ed. Antonia Arslan – Gabriella Romani, Toronto, University of Toronto Press, pp. 375-386.
Serao Matilde, [1926] 2016, *Mors tua...romanzo in tre giornate*, Rome, Studio Garamond.
"Severed Hand", 1925, "Matilde Serao's the Severed Hand", *Daily Mail*, 18 September, p. 8.

Sforza Raffaella, 1994, "Matilde Serao: una scrittrice per una città", *Settentrione. Rivista di studi italo-finlandesi. Nuova serie,* 6, pp. 167-169.

Shaffer Elinor – Brown Catherine (eds), 2016, *The Reception of George Eliot in Europe*, London – Oxford, Bloomsbury Publishing.

Singer Armand, 1976, *Paul Bourget*, Boston, Twayne Publishers.

Sinisi Lorenzo, 2017, "Giuseppe Saredo", *Dizionario Biografico degli Italiani*, http://www.treccani.it/enciclopedia/giuseppe-saredo_%28Dizionario-Biografico%29/

Skuncke Marie-Christine – Wester Ellen, n. d., *Svensk* översattarleksikon [*Swedish Translator Lexicon*], ed. Lars Kleberg, http://www.oversattarlexikon.se/artiklar/Ellen_Wester.

Soiza Reilly Juan José, 1907, "Tres ilustres escritoras de Italia", *Caras y caretas* (Buenos Aires), X, 472, 19 October, p. 7.

Sollini Giuseppe, 1907, "La donna nell'Italia meridionale", *Vita femminile italiana*, 1, 9, pp. 1011-1017.

Soriano Rodrigo, 1902, "S.M. La enagua", *La Justicia: semanario republicano*, III, 17, 24 April, p. 2.

Spackman Barbara, 2017, *Accidental Orientalists: Modern Italian Travelers in Ottoman Lands*, Liverpool, Liverpool University Press.

Spitzer Leo, 1914, "Matilde Serao (Eine Charakteristik)" ["Matilde Serao (A Character Study)"], *Germanisch-Romanische Monatsschrift*, 6, pp. 573-584.

Spitzer Leo, 1920, *Die Umschreibungen des Begriffes 'Hunger' im Italienischen* [*Connotations of the Term Hunger in Italian*] Halle, Niemeyer.

Spitzer Leo, 1921, *Italienische Kriegsgefangenenbriefe* [*Italian War Prisoners' Letters*], Bonn, Hanstein.

Spitzer Leo, 1922, *Italienische Umgangssprache* [*Conversational Italian*] Bonn, Schroeder.

Spitzer Leo, 1960, "Sviluppo di un metodo", *Cultura Neolatina*, XX, pp. 109-128.

Spitzer Leo, 2007, *Lingua italiana del dialogo*, ed. Claudia Caffi – Cesare Segre, trans. of Spitzer (1922), Milan, Il Saggiatore.

Strada Vittorio (ed.), 1995, *I russi e l'Italia*, Milan, Scheiwiller.

Suolahti Elina, n. d., "Letteratura italiana tradotta in finnico", Unpublished manuscript (courtesy of the author).

Suomela-Härmä Elina, 2007, "Italian kirjallisuus" ["Italian Literature"], *Suomennoskirjallisuuden historia II.* [*History* of *Literary Translation into Finnish*], Helsinki, Suomalaisen Kirjallisuuden Seura, pp. 119-132.

Sutherland John, 2009, "Richard Davey", *The Longman Companion to Victorian Fiction*, Harlow, Longman, p. 217.

Svensén Bo, 2001a, *Nobelpriset i litteratur. Nomineringar och utlåtanden 1901-1950. Del 1: 1901-1920* [*The Nobel Prize inf Literature. Nominations and Assessments. Part 1: 1901-1920*], Stockholm, Svenska Akademien and Norstedts.

Svensén Bo, 2001b, *Nobelpriset in litteratur. Nomineringar och utlåtanden 1901-1950. Del 2: 1921-1950* [*The Nobel Prize in Literature. Nominations and Assessments. Part 2: 1921-1950*], Stockholm, Svenska Akademien and Norstedts.

Sylvester Paul, 1889, "Matilde Serao", *The Woman's World*, 3 vols, London, Cassels, vol. 2, pp. 552-557.

"Tanssijatar", 1910, "Tanssijatar" ["The Dancer"], *Suomalainen*, 21 October, pp. 11-12.

Terán Luis de, 1902a, "Fogazzaro", *La Lectura*, May, pp. 507-508.

Terán Luis de, 1902b, "Matilde Serao", *La Lectura*, September, pp. 497-499.

Tiozzo Enrico, 2009, La letteratura italiana e il premio Nobel. Storia, critica e documenti, Florence, Olschki.

Tiozzo Enrico, 2013, *Il Nobel svelato. Segreti, errori e verdetti del premio per la letteratura*, Turin, Nino Aragno Editore.

Tolstoy Leo, 1937, "Pisma k V.G. Chertkovu" ["Correspondence with V.G. Chertkov"], ed. M.V. Muratov, *Oeuvres complètes*, 1928-1958, 90 vols, Moscow, Khudozhestvennaya literatura, vol. 87, pp. 66-67.

Torraca Francesco, 1910, *Manuale della letteratura italiana. Appendice al volume III*, Florence, Sansoni.

Trevisan Alessandra, 2019, *"Vogliatemi bene": lettere di Matilde Serao a Gabriele D'Annunzio*, Venice, Università Ca' Foscari.

"Una matinée", 1925, "Una matinée de la compañía francesa para señoritas", *La Época*, 4 May, p. 2.

"Ur en romanförfattarinnans breflåda", 1900, "Ur en romanförfattarinnans breflåda" ["From the Mailbox of a Novel Writer"], *Göteborgs Aftonblad*, 12 May, p. 4.

Vacheva Albena, 2014, *V periferiyata na kanona. Balgarskite pisatelki prez parvata polovina na XX vek* [*On the Periphery of the Canon: Bulgarian Women Writers in the First Half of the Twentieth Century*], Sofia, Prosveta.

V.A.K. [Veikko Antero Koskenniemi], 1908, "Kertomakirjallisuutta. Matilde Serao: *Tanssijatar*" ["Narrative Prose. Matilde Serao: *Tanssijatar/ La Ballerina*"], *Aika* 7, pp. 272-274.

Valle Ellen, 2007, "The Reception of Jane Austen in Finland", *The Reception of Jane Austen in Europe,* ed. Anthony Mandal – Brian Southam, Oxford, Bloomsbury Publishing, pp. 169-187.

Valmont Blanca, 1907, "Crónica por Blanca Valmont", *La* Última *moda,* XX, 8 December, p. 2.

Vannucci Marcello, 1957, *Mario Nunes Vais gentiluomo fotografo*, Florence, Bonechi.

Vazov Ivan, 1979, *Sabrani sachinenia* [*Collected Works*], 22 vols., Sofia, Balgarski pisatel, vol. 22.

Vermeer Hans, 1996, *A Skopos Theory of Translation (Some Arguments for and against)*, Heidelberg, TEXTconTEXT.

Venuti Lawrence, 2000, "Genealogy of Translation Theory: Jerome", *The Translation Studies Reader*, ed. Lawrence Venuti, London, Routledge, pp. 483-502.

Vetterlund Fredrik, 1903, "Konst och litteratur. Öfversättningslitteratur II" ["Art and Literature. Literature in Translation II"], *Aftonbladet*, 26 September, p. 6.

Viitanen Frans Oskar, 1908a, [Preface – untitled], Serao Matilde, *Tanssijatar: pieni elämäntarina,* Tampere, Kossi Kaatra, pp. 3-4.

Viitanen Frans Oskar, 1908b, [Preface – untitled], Serao Matilde, *Korkokeinottelua,* Tampere, Osuuskunta Wäinämöinen, pp. 3-4.

Vtt, 1909, "Kirjoja" ["Books"], *Tampereen Sanomat*, 252, 30 October, p. 3.

Wandruszka Maria Luisa, 2010, "L'Esprit des femmes nella stilistica spitzeriana", *Leo Spitzer. Lo stile e il metodo. Atti del XXXVI Convegno Interuniversitario* (Bressanone-Innsbruck, 10-13 July 2008), ed. Paccagnella – Gregori, Padua, Esedra, pp.153-162.

Wellek René, 1991, *A History of Modern Criticism 1750-1950: German, Russian, and Eastern European Criticism, 1900-1950*, 8 vols, New Haven, Yale University Press, vol. 7.

Wessman Sari, 2001, *Analisi di alcuni tipi di sintagmi aggettivali nel Ventre di Napoli di Matilde Serao.* Pro gradu (unpublished MA Thesis), Helsinki, Helsingin yliopisto.

Wharton Edith, 1934, *A Backward Glance*, New York, D. Appleton-Century Company.

Wirsén Carl David af, 1885, "Litteratur" ["Literature"], *Post- och Inrikes Tidningar*, 12 September, p. 3.

Wirsén Carl David af, 1886, "Italiensk litteratur" ["Italian Literature"], *Post- och Inrikes Tidningar*, 16 July, p. 3.

Wirsén Carl David af, 1887, "Litteratur" ["Literature"], *Post- och Inrikes Tidningar*, 31 October, p. 3.

Wirsén Carl David af, 1888, "Italiensk litteratur" ["Italian Literature"], *Post- och Inrikes Tidningar*, 10 March, p. 3.

Wirsén Carl David af, 1890a, "Litteratur" ["Literature"], *Post- och Inrikes Tidningar*, 24 May, p. 3.

Wirsén Carl David af, 1890b, "Litteratur" ["Literature"], *Post- och Inrikes Tidningar*, 12 July, p. 3.

Wirsén Carl David af, 1891, "Litteratur" ["Literature"], *Post- och Inrikes Tidningar*, 27 June, p. 3.

Wood Sharon, 1995, *Italian Women's Writing 1860-1994*, London – Atlantic Highlands, Athlone.

Y.K. [Koskelainen Yrjö], 1908, "Kertomuksia ja kuvauksia. Matilde Serao.

*Tanssijatar – Korkokeinottelua*" ["Stories and Depictions. Matilde Serao. *La ballerina – Trenta percento*"], *Valvoja*, 9, pp. 564-566.
Z., 1902, "Desgarrada. Caïel. Lisboa", *La Época*, 28 September, p. 1.
Zanini-Cordi Irene, 2008, *Donne sciolte. Abbandono ed identità femminile nella letteratura italiana*, Ravenna, Longo.
Zamacois Eduardo, 1929, "Lo que le gusta al público", *Nuevo mundo*, 36, 18 January, p. 3.
Zeda (Francisco Fernández Villegas), 1900, "La poesía en el teatro", *La Época*, 804, 1 January, p. 1.
Zeda (Francisco Fernández Villegas), 1903, "Novedades literarias", *Las Provincias. Diario de Valencia*, 8 March, p. 1
Zeda (Francisco Fernández Villegas), 1904, "Lecturas de la semana 'La busca' novela, por Pío Baroja", *La Época,* 20 February, p. 1.

# INDEX OF NAMES

# ABSTRACTS

Gabriella ROMANI, Ursula FANNING and Katharine MITCHELL, "Introduction"

The Introduction outlines the manner in which the volume came into being, explaining how the editors and contributors wish to explore Serao and the reception of her work outside of Italy and in a predominantly European context. This new perspective allows for a consideration of the circulation, translation and transnational consumption of Serao's writings, while also considering the cultural assumptions of her mediators.

L'introduction revient sur la genèse de l'ouvrage et explique la volonté des éditeurs et des auteurs d'étudier l'œuvre de Serao et sa réception en dehors de l'Italie, dans un contexte majoritairement européen. Cette nouvelle perspective permet d'examiner la circulation, la traduction et la consommation des écrits de Serao dans divers pays, tout en tenant compte des impensés culturels de ses médiateurs.

Ulla ÅKERSTRÖM, "Matilde Serao and her 'Lost Nobel Prize'"

Matilde Serao was first brought to the attention of the Swedish Academy as a candidate for the Nobel Prize in Literature in 1922. The essay discusses the persistent assumption whereby Serao's novel *Mors tua* (1926) was the reason she "lost" the Nobel Prize to Grazia Deledda in 1927. Based on analysis of nomination letters and written reports in the Academy's archive in Stockholm, the article also disputes the claims that Mussolini had something to do with Serao's possible Nobel Prize.

C'est en 1922 que le nom de Matilde Serao a été avancé pour la première fois à l'Académie suédoise au titre de candidate au prix Nobel de littérature. Cet essai évoque l'hypothèse persistante selon laquelle le roman de Serao *Mors tua* (1926) lui a valu de « perdre » le prix Nobel au profit de Grazia Deledda en 1927. En se basant sur l'analyse des lettres de nomination et des rapports écrits présents dans les archives de l'Académie à Stockholm, cet article conteste également que Mussolini est impliqué dans la candidature au prix Nobel de Serao.

Nadezhda ALEXANDROVA and Boyka ILIEVA, "The Reception of Matilde Serao in Bulgaria, 1890s-1920s"

Matilde Serao was the first Italian woman writer to be translated into Bulgarian. The essay explores her literary presence, reception and cultural influence in Bulgaria (1880-1918). It aims to identify the original titles of Serao's printed works, often changed drastically, and the identities of her translators, often disguised under pseudonyms. It includes a discussion of the quantitative data of her reception and of the most common thematic choices for her Bulgarian translations.

Matilde Serao a été la première femme écrivaine italienne à être traduite en bulgare. Cet essai se penche sur sa présence littéraire, la réception de son œuvre et son influence culturelle en Bulgarie (1880-1918). Il vise à identifier les titres originaux des œuvres imprimées de Serao, qui ont souvent été radicalement modifiés, ainsi que l'identité de ses traducteurs, souvent cachée derrière des pseudonymes. L'article étudie des données quantitatives sur la réception de ses œuvres et sur les choix thématiques les plus courants pour ses traductions bulgares.

Maria BELOVA, "The Circulation and Critical Reception of Matilde Serao's Writings in Russia"

Matilde Serao's works were published extensively in Russia between the mid-1880s and the first decade of the twentieth century. After exploring the translations of her works in Russia and their reception in journals and newspapers of the time, the chapter focuses on the multiple editions of *All'erta, sentinella!* that circulated under different titles. The second part of the chapter explores Serao's reception in Russian literary circles through the analysis of the critic Vladimir Frice's views.

Les œuvres de Matilde Serao ont été largement publiées en Russie entre le milieu des années 1880 et la première décennie du XX^e siècle. Après avoir étudié les traductions de ses œuvres en Russie et leur réception dans les revues et journaux de l'époque, ce chapitre s'intéresse aux multiples éditions d'*All'erta, sentinella !* qui circulaient sous différents titres. La seconde partie du chapitre étudie la réception de Serao dans les cercles littéraires russes à travers l'analyse des textes du critique Vladimir Frice.

Ursula FANNING, "Re-Reading Serao through Anglocentric Eyes"

This essay discusses some critical evaluations of Matilde Serao's writings from her own time, focussing mainly on the English-language context (American, English and Irish) in which her work was received and analysed. Important factors in considering her reception in these contexts are gender-related issues and her Neapolitan-ness, Southernness and/or Italian-ness. These factors are often as revealing of her critics and the views of their societies as they are of the author and her work.

Cet essai étudie plusieurs recensions critiques des œuvres de Matilde Serao, publiées à son époque, en se concentrant principalement sur le contexte anglophone (américain, anglais et irlandais) dans lequel son travail a été reçu et analysé. L'étude de la réception de ses écrits dans ces contextes tient compte de facteurs importants, notamment les problématiques liées au genre et le caractère napolitain, méridional et/ou italien de Serao. Ces facteurs en disent souvent autant sur les critiques de Serao et des points de vue de leurs sociétés que sur l'autrice et son œuvre.

Rossana MELIS and Maria-Luisa WANDRUSZKA, "Vienna December 1912: Leo Spitzer on Matilde Serao"

Matilde Serao's novels were widely translated in German-speaking countries starting from the end of the nineteenth century. In 1912, Leo Spitzer devoted his inaugural lecture at the University of Vienna entirely to Serao's oeuvre, underlining the idiosyncrasies between her life choices and her work, and noting the remarkable art she had produced. Published in a periodical in 1914, Spitzer sent the lecture to Benedetto Croce as a token of his friendship and his interest toward Italian culture.

Les romans de Matilde Serao ont été largement traduits dans les pays germanophones à partir de la fin du XIX<sup>e</sup> siècle. En 1912, Leo Spitzer consacre à l'œuvre de Serao l'intégralité de sa leçon inaugurale à l'université de Vienne, soulignant en quoi l'autrice se distingue dans ses choix de vie et son travail, et louant l'œuvre remarquable qu'elle a produite. Publiée dans un périodique en 1914, cette leçon est envoyée par Spitzer à Benedetto Croce en signe de son amitié et de son intérêt pour la culture italienne.

Viola PARENTE-ČAPKOVÁ, "Matilde Serao in Finland"

The chapter discusses the Finnish reception of Matilde Serao at the turn of the twentieth century, by employing a *meso-analysis* that combines *distant reading* of larger online datasets with *close reading* of the texts. It explores Serao's multilingual reception in Finland's library collections, the translations of her works into the two official languages of Finland, Finnish and Swedish, and her reception in the contemporary press in terms of reviews, articles, advertisements and obituaries.

Le chapitre traite de la réception finlandaise de l'œuvre de Matilde Serao au tournant du XX$^{e}$ siècle, au moyen d'une *méso-analyse* qui combine la *lecture distanciée* (distant reading) de grands ensembles de données en ligne et une *lecture attentive* (close reading) des textes. Il explore la réception multilingue de Serao dans les collections des bibliothèques finlandaises, les traductions de ses œuvres dans les deux langues officielles de la Finlande, le finnois et le suédois, et sa réception dans la presse contemporaine en termes de critiques, d'articles, de publicités et de nécrologies.

Gabriella ROMANI, "Matilde Serao in the Holy Land"

In 1893 Matilde Serao travelled to Jerusalem and wrote articles about her journey in a newspaper series, later collected in the volume *Nel paese di Gesù* (1898), and translated into English in 1905. This chapter analyses the production and subsequent English translation of Serao's travelogue, traditionally neglected by critics, arguing that it marks a crucial moment in her career at a time when she was seeking renewal in her artistic inspirations and affirmation domestically and abroad.

En 1893, Matilde Serao se rend à Jérusalem et écrit des articles sur son voyage dans une série de journaux, rassemblés plus tard dans le volume *Nel paese di Gesù* (1898) et traduits en anglais en 1905. Ce chapitre analyse la genèse du récit de voyage de Serao, ainsi que sa traduction anglaise ultérieure. Ce texte historiquement négligé par les critiques marque un moment crucial dans sa carrière à un moment où elle cherchait à renouveler ses inspirations artistiques et à s'affirmer dans son pays et à l'étranger.

Maria Laura IASCI AND Amelia SANZ, "Matilde Serao in the Spanish Press at the Turn of the Century"

A significant number of Serao's translations was published in Spain in the early twentieth century. This chapter focuses on the reactions to her translations in the Spanish press, drawing on the resources offered by the Virtual Newspaper Libraries of the Hemeroteca Digital and the Virtual Library of Spanish Newspapers, which include 800 references to Serao. At the beginning of Franco's dictatorship references to Matilde Serao can no longer be found in the digitized Spanish press.

De nombreuses traductions de Serao ont été publiées en Espagne au début du XXe siècle. Ce chapitre *étudie* les réactions de la presse espagnole *à ses traductions, en s'appuyant sur* les ressources offertes par les bibliothèques virtuelles de journaux de l'Hemeroteca Digital et la Bibliothèque virtuelle des journaux espagnols, qui comprennent 800 références à Serao. Au début de la dictature de Franco, on ne trouve plus aucune référence à Matilde Serao dans la presse espagnole numérisée.

Igor TCHEHOFF, "Matilde Serao in Sweden. A Voice of the 'New Italy'"

This chapter explores the reception of Matilde Serao's works in Swedish newspapers from 1885 to the first years of the twentieth century. Before the translation of her masterpiece *Il paese di Cuccagna* (1891) as early as 1892, Serao was already known in Sweden thanks to the critic C.D. af Wirsén, who promoted her as a major contemporary author. Equally important were the anonymous translations of Serao's short stories published between 1888 and 1897, here attributed to Ellen Lundberg-Nyblom.

Ce chapitre traite de la réception des œuvres de Matilde Serao dans les journaux suédois, de 1885 aux premières années du XXe siècle. Avant la traduction de son chef-d'œuvre *Il paese di Cuccagna* (1891) dès 1892, Serao était déjà connue en Suède grâce au critique C.D. af Wirsén, qui l'a présentée comme une autrice contemporaine de premier plan. Les traductions anonymes des nouvelles de Serao, publiées entre 1888 et 1897 et attribuées ici à Ellen Lundberg-Nyblom, ont joué un rôle tout aussi important.

# TABLE OF FIGURES

# TABLE OF CONTENTS

IMPRIM'VERT®

Achevé d'imprimer par Corlet,
Condé-en-Normandie (Calvados),
en Juillet 2022
N° d'impression : 176821 - dépôt légal : Juillet 2022
Imprimé en France